Relational Presentation

A Visually Interactive Approach

Condensed Edition

Robert A. Lane

Chantal Bossé

A Production of Aspire Communications

About the Author

Robert resides in sunny Tucson, Arizona, USA. He is an internationally recognized lecturer, trainer and author, specializing in digital media techniques for interactive communication and teaching.

Robert completed a B.S. in Physics at the University of Arizona and currently is pursuing a M.S. in Educational Technology. His fascination with optical physics and the brain's processing of visual information led naturally to formation of the *Relational Presentation* methodologies featured in this book. The following pages distill approximately eight years of his work, along with the inspirations of many like-minded colleagues.

Aspire Communications

Aspire's mission is to provide training, consultation and support to a wide variety of individuals and institutions implementing Relational Presentation methods. Team members include trainers, researchers, executives, presentation professionals, graphic designers, media specialists and software developers. Aspire offers workshops and seminars, both onsite and online (live or self-paced), to augment your learning experience. Attendees tap into an active community of skilled relational presenters, to share resources and ideas. The final chapter of this book discusses these and other ways of expanding and improving your learning experience. You may also wish to visit the Aspire Web site for more current information.

About the Author

About the Author

Chantal lives with her family in an idyllic country environment near Montreal, Quebec, Canada. She is a talented instructional designer, trainer and presentation specialist. Chantal has been working diligently for several years to help improve the effectiveness of interactive presentation. Those efforts and insights, in addition to benefitting her loyal customers, are now available to you as well, interwoven throughout the pages of this book.

Chantal completed a B.S. in Biochemistry at the University of Sherbrooke and has worked as a telecommunications specialist and instructional designer in coursework development. She joined the Aspire Communications team as an independent consultant in 2005 and provides valuable services and support to relational presenters. We are grateful for her help.

CHABOS, Inc.

In addition to work with us, Chantal manages her own company called CHABOS, to help presenters maximize the creativity and effectiveness of their presentations and training materials. We send development projects her way when assistance is needed with presentation network planning, construction and design. For more information on CHABOS services, visit their Web site at:

www.chabos.ca

Executive Editor: Judy McCabe
Technology Project Manager: Bethany Snow
Marketing Manager: Steve Hards
Project Manager: Chantal Bossé

For more information about Aspire's online or onsite workshops, contact us at:

Aspire Communications
902 N. 4th Avenue
Tucson, AZ, 85705
USA
Phone: 520-629-0282
Fax: 520-629-9573
E-mail: support@aspirecommunications.com
Web: http://www.aspirecommunications.com

Aspire also offers a full range of consultation, customized training and support options.

Library of Congress Control Number: 2007904507
Publisher: BookSurge, LLC
North Charleston, South Carolina

Condensed Edition: ISBN(13): 978-0-9794156-1-6
ISBN(10): 0-9794156-1-6

Contents

Contents

Contents

Contents

Contents

Contents

Contents

Contents

What You Will Need

Although this book covers PowerPoint design skills in minute detail, it assumes you already know the basics, such as creating slide shows, adding slides, adding text to slides, and presenting in Slide Show mode. If you are new to PowerPoint, or wish to fine tune knowledge of basic operations, reading a standard PowerPoint training book first might be a good idea—or consult PowerPoint's help files. Relational Presentation methods focus heavily on understanding the potential uses of AutoShapes, pictures, hyperlinks, and Custom Shows. These topics tend to be glossed over, or not covered at all, in normal presentation classes. They are nevertheless essential to visually interactive communication and are explored at length in this book.

You also will need all of your existing slide shows and other presentation-related materials. This book is intended to be thoroughly hands on. The main idea is to turn your own presentation content into a highly organized, interlinked network of slide shows where any piece of content is available quickly, on demand. It is important that you begin applying the concepts learned to your own materials right away. Don't wait! Each chapter provides useful perspectives and techniques that can be incorporated into your presentation activities immediately.

Finally, be prepared to provide lots of careful thought and creativity, as you decide how your presentation content will be transformed into a powerful new communication model.

Note to the Reader

To a large extent, your mastery of concepts contained in this book will relate to your willingness to temporarily set aside everything you currently know about PowerPoint, and then rebuild those concepts. Relational Presentation is founded upon the use of PowerPoint because of its ease of application and well-designed functionality. But lessons in this course have implications far beyond PowerPoint itself. The real mark of success with these concepts is learning to include rich digital media into normal communications so that you can spontaneously customize a message to anyone, anywhere—quickly, fluidly, and effectively. In other words, what you are learning here is a new language, a visual language. PowerPoint just happens to be the best foundation at the moment for nurturing the new vocabulary.

Some of you are presenters only and have other people designing your materials for you. Some of you are those designers. Probably a majority are both. Regardless of category, all readers will benefit by reading every section of this book. Designers must endeavor to understand the world of presenters, and vice versa. One of the most important lessons you can learn from the following pages is that live, digital communication is a complex system of presenter, audience, content, equipment, and environment. Designers who build networks without fully understanding the limitations and opportunities their presenters face probably will produce poor-quality results. In the same vein, a presenter who likes to fiddle with presentation materials and make last minute changes to materials someone else has created should beware. If that person does so in a Relational Presentation context, without first taking the time to understand network functionality, he or she can easily wreak havoc on the process.

Presenters must help their designers understand the full depth of content needed and guide, if not lead, the organizational activities involved in planning stages. That is to say, your busy schedule cannot preclude you from taking the time to give designers a detailed glimpse inside your brain and, therefore, be somewhat involved with the nuts and bolts. Likewise, designers are encouraged to imagine themselves on stage, mentally fielding questions or making navigation decisions. Does your design logic make sense? Can you find content easily? If you can't, probably the presenter won't be able to either.

In summary, regardless of your actual role, try to understand perspectives of both designer and presenter. Also consider these strategies for improving your learning performance:

- Monitor your thoughts. If you find yourself saying, "This won't work in our context," or "I'll never get the hang of this," actively set those thoughts aside for the moment and press forward. You never know when a particular technique might come in very handy six months from now. And you CAN do this. The most common reason people fail to implement Relational Presentation methods is that they convince themselves the old way is good enough. It isn't!
- Realize that in many ways, Relational Presentation is an art. Designing and presenting this way takes time to learn and master. Give yourself that time.

"I'm embarrassed to admit I didn't even know PowerPoint had hyperlinks or supported alternative forms of presentation. I've always just put my slides in a line like everyone else, I guess. Boy, this is a different way of looking at things."

Workshop Attendee

Chapter 1

Where We've Been and Where We're Heading

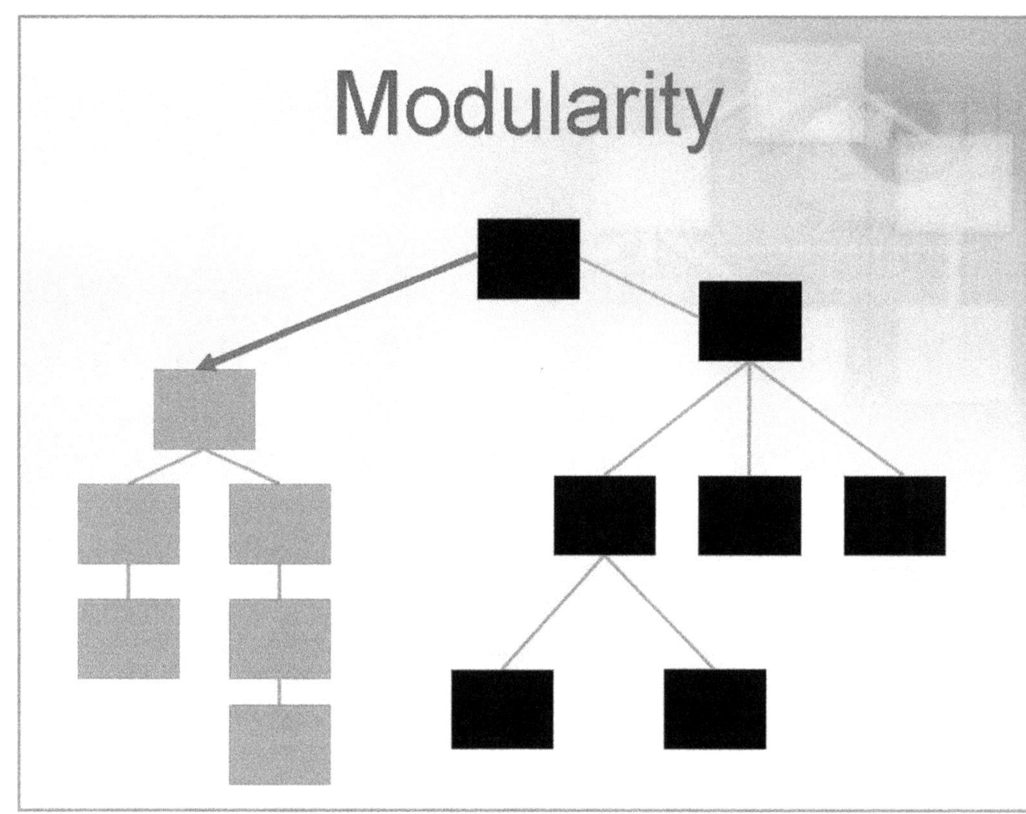
Modularity

1.1 Digital Presentation's Journey

When Microsoft purchased PowerPoint in 1987, few imagined how profoundly the software would eventually shape and dominate public speaking. In fact, many speakers resisted the transition at first, clinging to their Genigraphics art, their transparencies, their 35-millimeter slides, or simply speaking without visual support at all. Even so, the move toward digital presentation eventually proved irresistible. With a mouse and keyboard, any beginning presenter or designer could now crank out their own visual displays in a couple of hours, without being dependent upon graphic designers. In a sense, PowerPoint came to represent *freedom from the man*, a feeling of self-accomplishment that "I did this myself and it looks better than your old transparencies." Amateur designers took control of content production, while still tapping into what was then considered sophisticated and trendy *display-by-computer*.

Enthusiasm among presenters grew as more and more came to see the value of computer-enhanced display, but soon problems in paradise surfaced. In the mid-1990s debate erupted over PowerPoint's growing influence and what many perceived as its detrimental impacts, debate that continues to this day. Academics and presentation professionals lamented the application's pushy style—the fact that it locks presenters into defined paths and dictates what can be presented and discussed. They fretted also about its trivialization of complex subjects through the use of simplistic graphics and bullet points.

Presentation geeks and pointy-heads weren't the only ones unhappy. Audience members began seeing themselves as victims of low-quality, boring (perhaps *cheap* and *throwaway* are better words) performances. Presenters unwittingly crammed half-a-book's worth of text onto a few slides, read the slides during performances, and justified the abysmal results by saying, "Well, I need to have all that text and detail on my slides because I print them as handouts." Grumbles and snickers around water coolers resulted in the "death by PowerPoint" and "death by bullet points" mantras that crisscrossed the country.

Presenters, quite innocently, were being lulled into a trap created by PowerPoint's simple design and corresponding ease of use. When first opening the software, a new user saw a white background with text boxes. Lo and behold, all he or she had to do was type some text, add a few more slides, add more text, and *voila!* a presentation was born. This combination of text-based presentation, along with rigid, sequential delivery (first slide to last in a single slide show) came to form what is now known as the *standard presentation model*. This model, even today, utterly dominates digital communication around the world. It also is an almost 100 percent guarantee of sleep-inducing monotony.

Clearly there was a problem but no obvious solutions surfaced at the time. So PowerPoint designers gave the software more bells and whistles, adding ever fancier animations, graphically attractive templates, sound effects, and methods for inserting rich media. Presenters responded accordingly. They dumped mountains of text onto pretty backgrounds, in equally linear and restrictive slide shows, with bullet points spinning to the sound of screeching tires.

Audiences (to no one's surprise) soon reached a boiling point and insurrections began. Many outspoken individuals began openly declaring their disgust for the software's existence, and some management forbade its use. PowerPoint presentations came to be seen as a necessary evil of sorts. Sadly, one of the most useful, influential, easy to use, and stunningly powerful software applications ever created (in our opinion) sat humiliated, limping along with few users grasping its true value and potential.

1.2 The Need for Change

Some years back, we reached our own boiling point with the standard presentation model and wondered if there was a better way. Could digital delivery be more flexible, conversational and responsive to an audience? How could we make our performances more immediately relevant, graphically attractive and entertaining? Was there a way of building PowerPoint content that could span multiple audiences, in different contexts, so we wouldn't have to continually cannibalize and rebuild slide shows for every performance?

What started as a fledgling quest eventually evolved into a full-fledged mission, a passion that now has touched thousands of presenters and designers just like you. Our hope is to help you, and consequently us, change the accepted presentation model—and in that sense perhaps we will change the way the world communicates. Momentum has been building in that direction for some time now and only continues to grow.

The references to *we* in this book refer to the authors and an extended team of individuals working alongside to develop visually interactive techniques. Our opinions are a collage of personal experiences and theories, along with those of many other speakers who have received training over the years. Unfortunately, no formal research yet exists to either confirm or refute the many perspectives offered in this book. Such studies hopefully will begin in the near future and will help solidify best practices. For now, we recommend simply giving the collective wisdom featured here a try, in your situation, and see how it works. You are on the cutting edge of digital communication's progressive course and are helping create a new presentation paradigm. That new paradigm, the new model, is called *Relational Presentation.*

1.3 What You Will See and Do From Here

Most of the graphics in this book are screenshots of actual slides used in Aspire's Relational Presentation training.

The examples pictured complement the topics being discussed and serve as a model for your own slide designs. They follow design principles and concepts we highly recommend and give visual guidance as to how we use PowerPoint during training sessions.

Becoming a relational presenter and/or designer is an open-ended adventure in that there are very few absolute *do this* and *don't do that* requirements. This book provides a wealth of suggestions (sometimes strong recommendations) but, for the most part, how you proceed depends a great deal upon your own personality, likes and dislikes, subject matter focus, needs, and so forth. The next two chapters do, however, give you a sense of what you are getting yourself into: We preview major concepts and principles behind the Relational Presentation paradigm. You may find some of these ideas common sense. Others may seem a bit foreign perhaps. Either way, we trust you will be sufficiently challenged and entertained.

"Since I've been using Relational Presentation methods, my invitations to lecture have increased so much that I am unable to accept them all."

Catherine Watson Genna, BS, IBCLC
http://lactspeak.com/speakers/Catherine-Watson Genna/

Chapter 2

What Is Relational Presentation?

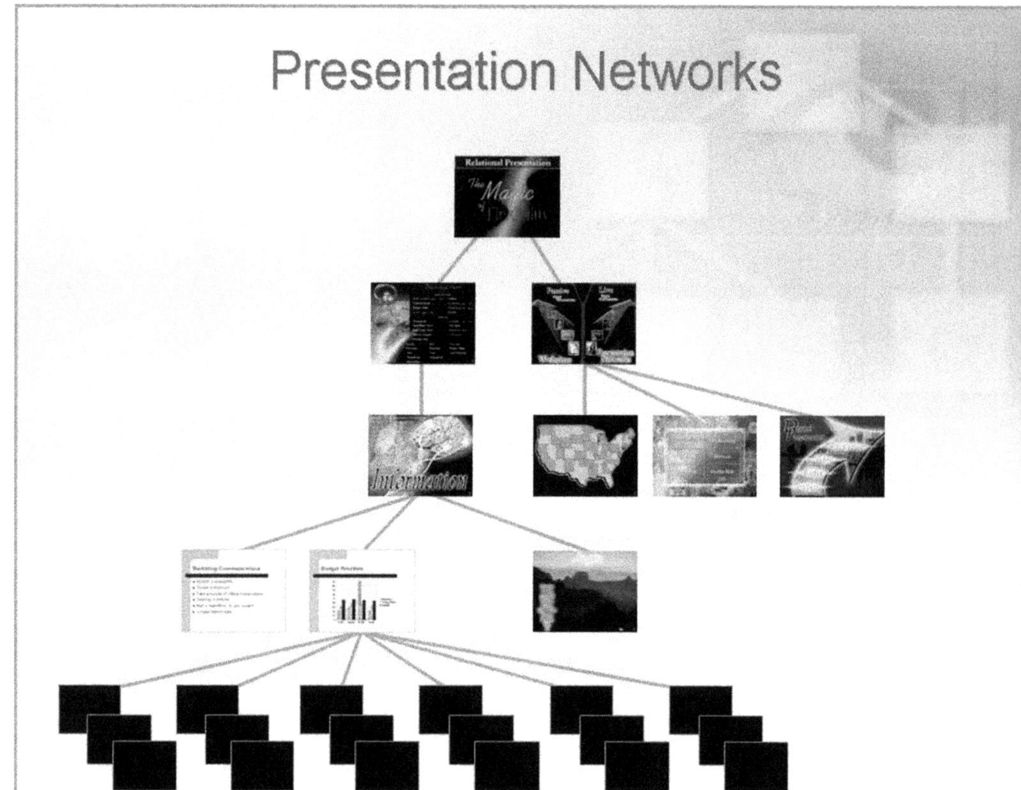
Presentation Networks
Relational Presentation
Information

2.1 About Relational Presentation

Throughout this book, we explore a style of digital communication known as *Relational Presentation*, and a question often arises about what the name actually means. The name has two equally important implications.

In one sense, the term *relational* refers to the importance of a speaker establishing a relationship with the audience. Relational Presentation methods tailor visual and verbal messages to the needs and interests of viewers on the spot. They provide *informational customer service*, so to speak. In more ways than one this process involves listening to the audience, relating to their situation, and then dynamically making adjustments during the delivery process. A relational approach is very different from belting out a canned, rigid spiel that proceeds regardless of circumstances. It involves recognizing and playing off of the connection to recipients. You influence them; they influence you. In a very real sense, the message evolves along the way according to input received.

The word *relational* also implies a similarity to the operational logic of a relational database. In fact, the functionality behind Relational Presentation closely resembles aspects of database design. Individual pieces of a message relate to all the other pieces, typically in hierarchical structures via links. Instead of having multiple copies of a slide spread across several presentations, a particular slide exists in one location only, and then is referenced as needed, anywhere, anytime.

2.2 Why Does It Matter?

Why are relationships between presenter and audience, or between pieces of content, important? To a relational presenter these relationships are everything. They enable conversational interaction. Interaction, in turn, enhances the speaker's role. Whether selling, teaching, training, or simply presenting information, well-done dynamic delivery almost invariably improves effectiveness, not to mention expanding viewer perception of expertise. Quite frankly, it's also a fun and compelling way of approaching live presentation. Stale topics take on the life of a café conversation. Having full versatility to express yourself freely while on stage, both verbally and visually, is almost addicting at times. For the moment, you'll just have to take our word that such is true. Soon enough, you may be saying the same thing.

2.3 What Inspired These Ideas?

The methodologies taught on succeeding pages are unique in a presentation context and to the best of our knowledge can be found nowhere else. At the same time, they really are nothing new. Similar logic and processes have guided other forms of media use for decades. We simply are applying these valuable techniques to speaking contexts, perhaps on a scale never before proposed. The inspiration for doing so came from two important observations.

First, we noticed many speakers, whose styles were dynamic and eloquent BEFORE using PowerPoint, seemed to become robotic and less natural once introduced to the software. Long, linear slide shows with preordained slide-to-slide advancement were wreaking havoc on otherwise conversational delivery styles. Basically, the presentation medium was breaking the relationship between sender and receiver, with detrimental consequences.

Second, we noticed the standard slide show model was outright inefficient and ineffective. Sometimes we would build elaborate, time-consuming, superduper shows that in our opinion were the greatest technological achievements known to mankind at the time. Even so, every audience was different. For each performance our masterpieces had to be torn apart and reassembled. Eventually, pieces of old presentations were spread all over the place, with various versions of slides duplicated across multiple shows. The whole process was a mess. We desperately needed a content management system. Our "aha" moment came upon realizing "Hey, we never use the exact same slide shows for different audiences, but we sure do use components of those same materials over and over again." For instance, certain introductory materials were universal, regardless of who the audience happened to be. This simple realization completely changed our organizational strategies.

2.4 The Theory Behind Visual Interactivity

About the same time, we began adding high-quality visual information to our presentation materials. At first, the goal was simply for slides to look good. Later, we explored using images to supplement or replace monotonous textual components and communicate a visual message, even if no actual words were said. Back then, we didn't have a clue why any of this was important. It just seemed like the right thing to do. There was, perhaps, an intrinsic sense that words alone, whether printed or spoken, are not enough.

In this process, one of the main goals became connecting what is said verbally with supporting visual elements that reinforce those words. If we *said* it, we tried to *show* it at the same time. Years later, it became apparent this dual mode of communicating ideas takes advantage of a basic process in our brain known in cognitive psychology as *Dual Coding*.

Figure 2.1

Dual Coding Theory asserts our brains process verbal and visual information differently and store the results in different areas. Thus, if we give people information in verbal form only, they will process and encode that information in the brain's verbal channels. Visual information, similarly, is encoded in the visual channels. The theory further suggests that presenting the same information both verbally and visually at the same time results in the material being encoded twice, potentially producing stronger recall and understanding of the topics.

Relational Presentation capitalizes on this process in several ways. By displaying meaningful visual information simultaneously with supporting verbal detail, messages are in fact dual coded. To accomplish this feat, the presenter often navigates to slides on demand, showing visual detail that relates to ongoing verbal exchanges. What this looks like in practice is someone might ask a question and you then find yourself saying, "Let me show you something that may help answer your question," while in the process of navigating to needed content.

2.5 A Shift in Thinking

Dual coding can occur, of course, during standard linear presentations. But often the right visual you need is not on the current slide, or on the next slide, or even on another slide somewhere in the current show. Therefore, a true dual channel approach involves flexible delivery, where any slide in any show is always available. Flexible delivery, in turn, involves a substantial shift in thinking about what it means to *give a presentation*. Being able to customize visual display to the needs of the moment is enormously powerful; it also requires setting aside many established habits PowerPoint users tend to embrace.

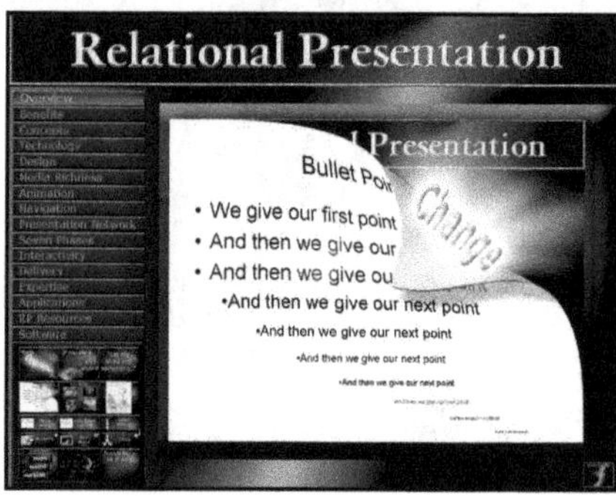

Figure 2.2

Making that shift in thinking is absolutely essential to your success while implementing these ideas. Therefore, we will approach the transition from numerous angles so that you will be well prepared. Sometimes the change is subtle, and other times it involves a complete flip of expectations.

For example, learners often approach Relational Presentation methods from the perspective of "Wow. I'm going to learn some really cool PowerPoint techniques that will jazz up my slide shows and blow my audiences away." Technically this will be true; you certainly will learn many fancy, showy methods that turn the traditional PowerPoint paradigm upside down. Even so, you may be very surprised at the results of your work.

Ironically, most—if not all—of those fancy techniques will have an effect opposite expected. Rather than drawing more attention to your technical prowess, they will cause PowerPoint's presence to be LESS noticeable. The software will fade into the background where it belongs, to provide a support role for the presenter. You want this to happen. Remember that you, your content, your message, and your connection to the audience are the true foci, not the technology. What all of the sophisticated methods you learn in this book do, if used properly, is focus more attention back onto you.

Think of it this way: In a relational context, slides become a natural part of ongoing interactions and exploration; they no longer especially stick out, interfere, or dictate what must be said and when it should be said. PowerPoint becomes a tool that enables what we call *Visual Dialogue*, adding flexible use of visual elements to your normal verbal framework.

The pitfall some presenters fall into at this point is thinking, "Yeah, yeah. I can see the advantage of synchronous visual and verbal presentation. What's the big deal? I'll be able to do this in my sleep." Relational Presentation methods ARE relatively simple and straightforward, all in all. Most people grasp the basic ideas quickly and begin applying them right away. Still, if the process was that easy and obvious, a lot more people would be presenting this way—but they are not. In reality, the changes necessary are more involved than first meets the eye. Becoming a polished relational speaker requires a period of adjustment and a healthy portion of open-mindedness and experimentation.

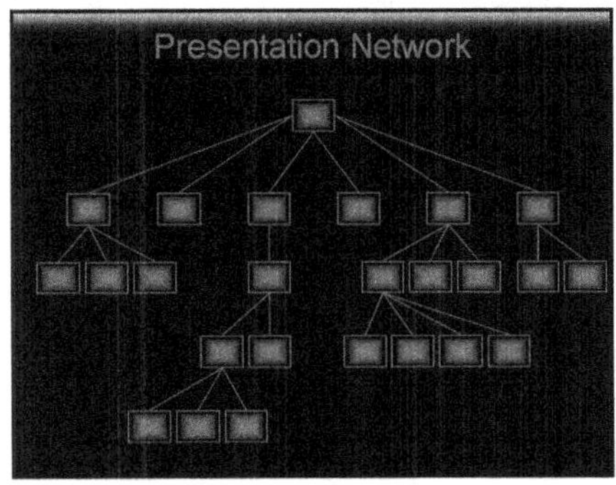

Figure 2.3

Imagine trying to take all of your knowledge and expertise, everything in your brain that represents who you are and what you know, and digitizing that information. Such a collection could represent thousands upon thousands of slides. Now, contemplate locating one of those slides, right now, to illustrate a thought that just occurred to you while talking with an audience member. How do you do that? How do you basically show your thoughts as they occur, just as you would spontaneously think of words to say?

These questions can be scary to people initially contemplating a visually interactive approach. They illustrate the complexity behind Relational Presentation's simple exterior. "What if I'm up front and can't remember where I put a slide?" That's a legitimate concern. The good news is that superior design can dramatically reduce content's organizational complexity, so that presenters CAN spontaneously display specific visuals—easily.

Such content management strategies are possible by analyzing all your content and organizing this material into hierarchically arranged modules. These modules are then tied together via hyperlinks. The result is called a *Presentation Network* and has a structure closely resembling a Web site with interlinked Web pages. The steps used to form a Presentation Network's organizational logic are collectively called *Information Architecture* and are little more complicated than separating apples from oranges. Pieces of related information are grouped together in small clusters, which are then grouped under broader clusters, and then broader clusters still, and so on. Eventually, the result is a hierarchal *road map* of sorts, outlining the categories that form the network's branches and subbranches.

Figure 2.4 Courtesy Fry's Food and Drug

How does using a Presentation Network help you? Think of a grocery store as an example. Perhaps you decide to buy a single green apple. In which direction do you walk after first entering the front door? You certainly don't head toward dairy, cosmetics or canned goods. You walk toward the produce section. That single decision effectively eliminates most other products in the store because those products at the moment are irrelevant. Upon reaching produce, you ignore the tomatoes, cucumbers, and onions to focus on the apples section. Finally, you select a green apple from the varieties available.

In this example the store is equivalent to a Presentation Network. To find desired content, you must work your way down from the broadest possible starting point, in this case *the entire store*. In a Presentation Network, the starting point is called a *Main Switchboard*. By moving through progressively specific levels you soon reach the desired goal, which may be either a slide show or a specific slide within a show.

Let's take the analogy a step further. Pretend you create a Presentation Network that actually contains a picture of every individual product in the grocery store. Perhaps there are 10,000 products total. Using the hierarchical logic just described, locating the one apple picture out of 10,000 choices is very easy. Starting with the highest point (the Main Switchboard representing the entire store) the desired slide is only three clicks away.

Click 1 takes you to a section containing produce-related pictures. If there are 100 produce categories (apples being one of them), this single click just eliminated 9,900 other product categories, or 99 percent.

Click One

Figure 2.5 Courtesy Fry's Food and Drug

Click 2 selects the apples category, meaning that of the remaining 100 categories, we eliminated another 99 categories, or another 99 percent.

Click Two

Figure 2.6 Courtesy Fry's Food and Drug

Click 3 specifically selects the green apple picture from the several varieties of apples available in the one remaining produce category. Locating one picture out of 10,000 choices was that fast and easy.

Click Three

Figure 2.7 Courtesy Fry's Food and Drug

2.6 The Significance of Visual Clues

In a live context, flexible delivery enables immediate customization of visual subject matter, a process we refer to as *Visual Interactivity*. A visually interactive presenter may, for example, choose to show more or less detail about a particular topic, depending on the time available and audience interest or need. A skilled relational presenter takes this concept a step further and becomes *Visually Fluent*. Visually fluent speakers are able to navigate within a network so gracefully that they give little conscious thought to the process. Spontaneously selecting content at this stage is equivalent to driving a car through town. Decisions are being made constantly and dynamically, but mostly at a subconscious level out of habit.

Figure 2.8

Visual Fluency does not happen by accident. Obviously, a presenter must know his or her content, be a reasonably good public speaker, and rehearse delivery. One additional element must be in place as well: Slide design should incorporate what are known as *Visual Clues*, features that either directly or indirectly aid a presenter in some way. Such aids might take the form of helping him or her find active links on a slide, know where to look for content in the network, or know what content will appear once a link is clicked.

We analyze Visual Clues extensively later on in this book. For now, think of them as similar to road signs that direct a speaker and guide use of the network. Slides in a relational context almost always have a dual purpose. At one level, they communicate a message to viewers (content). On another level, and simultaneously, they communicate messages to the presenter, simplifying his or her role and smoothing out the delivery process.

Relying on Visual Clues is especially important when navigation on slides is invisible (a common tactic with advanced Relational Presentation design). On the slide pictured in Figure 2.8, suppose we want to change the apple color from red to yellow to green, without the audience knowing how. Making slides identical, except for apple color, creates an illusion of the apple changing color when moving between slides. In other words, the background remains the same and only the apple changes, giving the impression we are still on the same slide and somehow changed only the apple color.

To accomplish the effect, we add invisible AutoShapes loaded with hyperlinks to the slides, allowing random access of any slide from any other slide. By doing so, we are able to click the hyperlinks and appear to change the apple's color at will, in any desired order.

However, in this case we chose to make the hyperlinks for accessing the other slides invisible. So how does the presenter know where they are? How does she know where to click? That's where a Visual Clue becomes essential. We decided to place the invisible shapes (links) on top of the different sections of the basket in the background. Therefore, clicking the first basket section appears to change the apple color to red. Clicking the second section changes it to yellow, and the third section changes it to green.

What is really going on? The basket sections serve as visual guides for where to find the invisible AutoShapes. The AutoShapes contain a hyperlink to respective slides. Clicking a link takes the user to that slide, thus completing the effect. Without the initial Visual Clues, the presenter would not know where to find the links in the first place. Viewers, of course, have no idea any of this process is happening, and, if you think about it, there is no reason they should know.

2.7 Becoming a Systems Thinker

In addition to the Dual Coding Theory mentioned earlier, the Relational Presentation model is based upon a fundamental characteristic of the world around us—the fact that everything is connected to, and exerts influence on, everything else around it. Our speaking performances do not occur in a vacuum. They are a complex interplay of many variables, all interacting with and changing each other. Consequently, relational presenters must consider implications of Systems Theory.

If you are an experienced presenter, you probably are well aware of how unpredictable speaking environments can be. Myriad variables can, and

Figure 2.9

often do, influence the flow of events, positively or negatively. Having the flexibility to adjust to these variables as they occur can mean the difference between an inadequate and a successful event.

We find many presentation professionals, teachers, and especially sales executives, are fond of insisting that a speaker must do his or her homework and know the audience being addressed. That's fine. We agree, but what if your homework is misinformed or unexpected events skew your carefully laid plans? Do you then give up the PowerPoint side of your message and abandon those meticulously planned slides? Many speakers do when their linear slide shows no longer match the reality of the situation.

Relational presenters are not so constrained. Certainly good planning and organization are a must, yet we will never be able to predict everything. Often we can't see into the future with much accuracy at all. Many aspects of the system around us are out of our control. Preparing for the unexpected and building in contingency options, therefore, is the best way to approach any live delivery. If you can't adjust the other variables, you better be able to adjust your message.

Books could be filled with stories of events that did not proceed as expected in our case. Once when we were conducting back-to-back, all-day trainings, we witnessed an interesting phenomenon. Multiple members of the first group on the first day were struggling to stay awake—in the morning sessions no less! Our training materials are quite engaging normally, and such a situation had never occurred before. Initially we were concerned and at a loss for what to do, considering a day and a half of intense training remained for this group. Apparently, certain vibrations and background noises in the room, an overly warm room temperature, the training facilities' dim lights (for best viewing of presentation materials in this case), Monday morning melancholy, and so forth were causing the problem.

We couldn't fix all those variables and didn't even have time to analyze what they were at the time. Instead, we made adjustments from our side, with content and timing modifications.

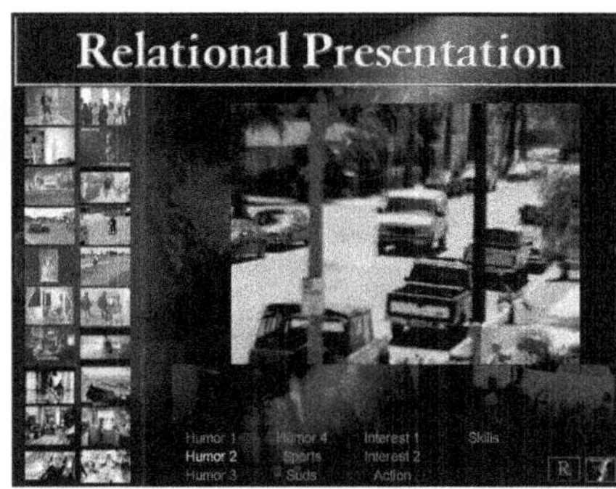

Figure 2.10

Here's how we spontaneously and successfully maneuvered in reaction to these surprise circumstances: The Aspire network contains an entire section dedicated to video, where approximately 200 clips wait for on-demand access. On the screen shot here (Figure 2.10) video plays in the upper right portion of the slide, while a strip of thumbnail-based links appears on the left and text-based links for other movie categories appear at the bottom. This arrangement allows us to easily flip between and start any video, in any category, as needed.

Normally during training sessions we play a couple of these clips after each break, to liven up the atmosphere and refresh participants. Most of our choices are humorous because laughter sends a rush of blood to the brain and provides a very good start to upcoming periods of concentration. As it turns out, laughter also enlivens the drowsy. So guess what we did on this particular day. We played nearly three times as many clips as usual. They are only 30 to 90 seconds long, so weaving them throughout the agenda was not a problem. The clips had the same effect as TV commercials, giving people a break between short periods of concentration.

Interestingly, in afternoon sessions and on the following day, the drowsiness factor did not reappear and fewer clips were needed. To our surprise, the second group two days later had an unusually high intensity of concentration. For that group we substantially reduced the normal number of clips shown. In this case, the standard amount of diversionary entertainment seemed to be a distraction and, therefore, was removed.

We share this story to illustrate that *one-size-fits-all* presentation strategies simply do not work well in the real world. You are not in full control of the environment, no matter how carefully you plan or research ideal outcomes. Adjustment through the use of agile visual presentation strategies is essential to quality performance. Otherwise, you miss opportunities.

2.8 Guiding Principles

Some people seem to adopt a relational approach with ease while others struggle. It's our hope you will be in the first group, and toward the end of this book we share strategies for improving your likelihood of being so. To that end, there are four principles you should ponder right from the beginning. These principles summarize the changes in attitude and perspective you will need and form a kind of litmus test for your success. If they already resonate with your values and beliefs, you are set. Otherwise, progress may be somewhat of an uphill climb.

> **Principle 1: Minimize *throwaway* content, slide shows that are assembled quickly for a particular audience and then never used again. Begin developing high-quality, reusable content that is applicable across multiple audiences and contexts.**

Figure 2.11

This principle encourages thinking of presentation materials in much the same way as you would high-quality Web pages. Quality Web sites are designed to be relatively permanent and meaningful to a wide array of viewers, yet still communicate core messages. In the same way, slides in your network can convey universal and reusable messages. For example, slides might show pictures of company products. Such slides have multiple possible uses in different contexts, for sales, training, informational meetings, and so forth. They are multi-use pieces of content that need not be restricted to a single performance on a particular date. In fact, you might wish to place these slides in a permanent and categorically arranged location so they can be accessed as needed, perhaps by several presenters. Doing so significantly reduces the amount of remodeling and rebuilding needed across events.

Principle 1 sometimes proves challenging to beginners for the following reason: Creating recyclable content implies analyzing existing slides to decide which components are universal. Many presenters *fly by the seats of their pants* when creating content and have never taken time or effort to plan and coordinate their overall message strategy. Likewise, most companies and institutions have not made such an effort and, to our amazement, often do not see the necessity of doing so. As a result, speakers typically do not have a clear sense of what those core, reusable slides should be. Moving away from a throwaway-slide mentality requires careful thought and analysis.

Principle 2: Everywhere possible, change text-based content into a display of rich media (pictures, graphics, video, animations, diagrams, graphs). Become a truly visual communicator.

Figure 2.12

This process involves what we call *thinking visually,* determining how you can use visual information to SAY what otherwise might be relegated to words alone. For example, if you are a trial attorney before a jury, pictures of an accident scene (or pictures of example accident scenes) from different angles and distances would likely help viewers better understand your arguments than would a bullet-point list or a purely verbal (non-PowerPoint) presentation. Keep in mind that a vast amount of human communication does not take verbal form. Your slides do not always need to be verbal either.

Replacing text with media is critical for several reasons. Consider how much we rely on visual information to make sense of the world around us. Visually meaningful and stimulating displays in PowerPoint can say far more than words alone ever will. In fact, some research suggests that text on a slide (or computer screen) may be treated by the brain as verbal rather than visual information, meaning text-based slides perhaps provide very little visual stimulation at all.

Another reason for using rich media is a phenomenon we call *Entertainment Expectancy*. Do you know one reason why audiences seem bored halfway through a typical presentation? Look at what they are watching on television, in movie theatres, on quality Web sites, and while playing video games. Do we see many bullet points in these forms of media? No. Other media are becoming ever more graphically rich and visually detailed. Presenters cannot take this fact lightly. Like it or not, your slide shows are competing to some extent with these other formats. If your displays are not at least remotely similar in quality to what people are seeing all around, every day, what is there in your performance to interest the viewer? And if there isn't anything visually interesting, why are you using PowerPoint at all?

Principle 2 likewise is a struggle for some. "I'm not a graphic designer. I don't know how to edit video. I don't have time. I don't have enough resources to pay for this kind of content," and a thousand other excuses are put forward. Maybe all of the above are true. Still, the Entertainment Expectancy is there and it's not going away any time soon. Digital communicators ignore it to their peril.

Think back to earlier comments about the Relational Presentation model requiring a shift in thinking. Part of this shift is realizing and accepting that effective speakers in the next decade will augment their skill sets and become media-based presenters. That may mean enhancing your abilities in graphic design, audio editing, video editing, and animation. If unable or unwilling to pursue these skills, you need people around you who have them. Approach this process as you would learn a foreign language—meticulously and seriously. Adding visual language to your vocabulary will only enhance effectiveness. In the not so distant future, learning media creation skills will be equivalent to learning how to type or write. Take the time. Make it a priority.

> **Principle 3: Add flexibility to your delivery by abandoning the *single-slide-show-per-performance* model. Instead, create a network of interlinked, hierarchically arranged content that allows fast selection of relevant information as needed.**

As mentioned previously, such an arrangement of content is formally called a *Presentation Network*. Overall, a Presentation Network's structure resembles that of a Web site, yet is purely PowerPoint-based. A presenter frequently uses various styles of hyperlink-based navigation, called *Navigation Elements*, to move around between different sections of the network, rather than always advancing from slide to slide in a linear show. During this process he or she MUST ALWAYS be able to find slides relevant to ongoing topics or interaction—quickly, easily, and gracefully.

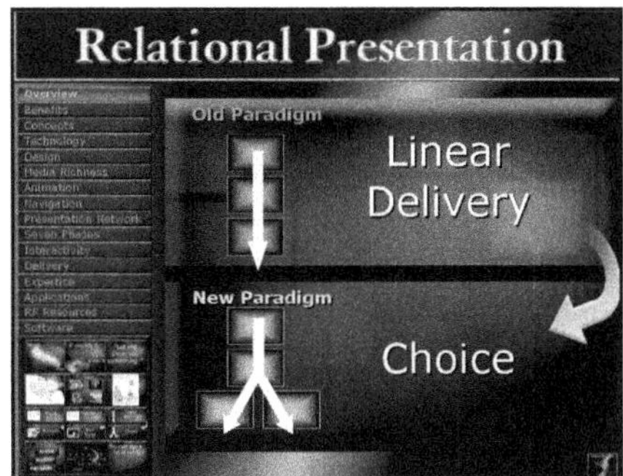

Figure 2.13

Armed with a Presentation Network, you probably will employ different strategies than would a typical speaker/designer. Instead of building long, single shows for each new performance, most slides needed already will exist as part of the permanent network. In most cases only a handful of new slides are created for any given audience and those slides, thereafter, become part of the permanent network. One never knows. Any of those slides may be needed again someday, if for no other reason than to refer to their original use.

As with the former two principles, Principle 3 goes against the grain of normal experience and may seem hard to accept at first. Our habits frequently lock us into thinking of a *presentation* as nothing more than a single slide show that contains all the needed slides. The idea of dividing a message into smaller pieces, and maybe even separate slide shows, feels strange at first.

What experienced relational presenters know, and you may have to take on faith at the moment, is that having *choice of content* while in front of an audience actually produces far greater security and confidence. By following suggestions in this course, your peace of mind probably will improve considerably. A well-designed network makes interactive, spontaneous digital delivery even easier than using linear slide shows—or not using PowerPoint at all. Give it a try and see.

Principle 4: Regardless of how much you may view your role as presenter to be that of *information giver*, the informational side of your performance is one of the least important reasons for being in front of people. Rather, your primary roles are to connect with viewers, entertain them, and bring your topics to life in a simple way viewers can relate to and understand. When using Relational Presentation techniques, your role changes from being a *lecturer* to that of *conversationalist* and *entertainer*. Your ultimate goal is to sell viewers on the fact that your message is worth their attention.

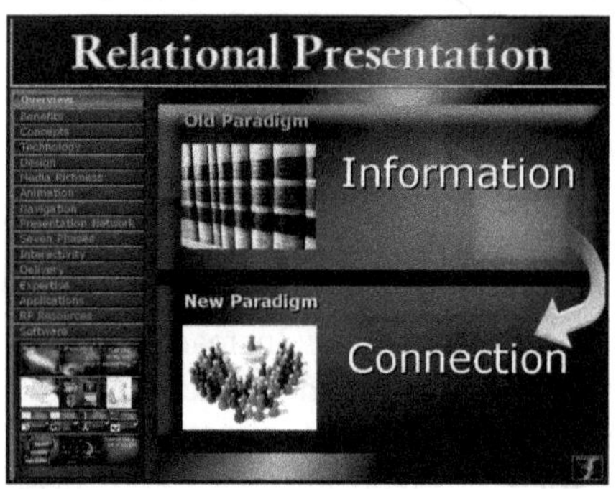

Figure 2.14

This principle is the most controversial of all and the most difficult to believe. It is a major break from the old paradigm. The majority of presentation designers seem to feel compelled to pack as much detail as possible onto slides, as though viewers will actually walk away remembering all that detail. They won't. They won't even remember a tiny fraction of it. The more information a slide contains, the less specific details are retained.

Principle 4 advises speakers to greatly simplify the amount of information on any given slide and leave the detail to handouts, books, Web sites, CD ROMs, and other resources. We place only one major idea per slide and fill in detail verbally. Instead of delivering an encyclopedia worth of information in a short period of time, the focus is more on the quality of time spent connecting with the interests and needs of viewers. Simple topics that summarize complexity and entice people to explore more deeply are more effective than volumes of facts.

In a sense, this principle asserts the speaker is there to put a human face on data, concepts, requests, or procedures. In doing so, regardless of how you look at it, he or she is essentially an entertainer. Successful relational presenters build a relationship with the audience and use that connection to convince viewers the topic at hand is worthy of both their attention and further exploration. Without that attention, we have nothing. Personality reigns supreme over excessive content appearing on slides. Ultimately, people remember the connection to you much more than they do the specifics of your bullet points.

2.9 Additional Thoughts

About now there may be a sense of "Hmm. Relational Presentation sounds like a lot of work and change compared with the way I normally do things." True, there is some extra work involved and modifications will be necessary. Consider, however, the value of that effort. Capturing and holding people's attention is immensely valuable and worth it. The presenter has direct access to hearts and minds, more so perhaps than is possible with any other form of media. What is that worth in terms of time investment? A lot! Imagine if we were to say, "Well I don't know if Web sites are worth it, or intranets, or brochures, or books." Those forms of outreach ARE valuable and so is creating, and skillfully delivering, relational messages.

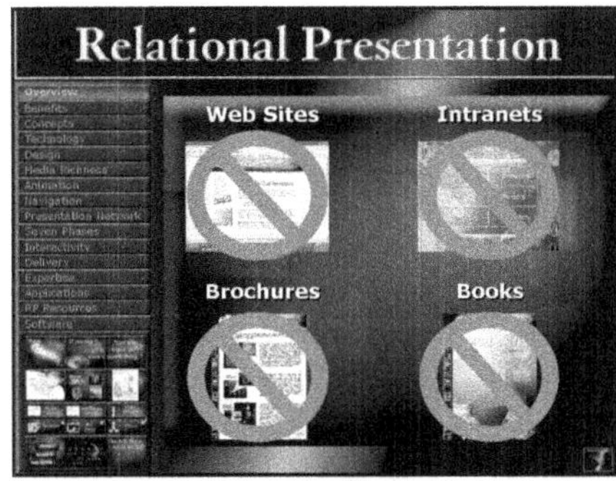

Figure 2.15

"I have only just begun to apply the most basic techniques taught in this workshop, and already am seeing their positive impact and receiving affirmative feedback from my audiences."

Rev. Will Nelken
Trinity Community Church
San Rafael, California
www.tccsr.org

Chapter 3

How Does This Approach Help Me?

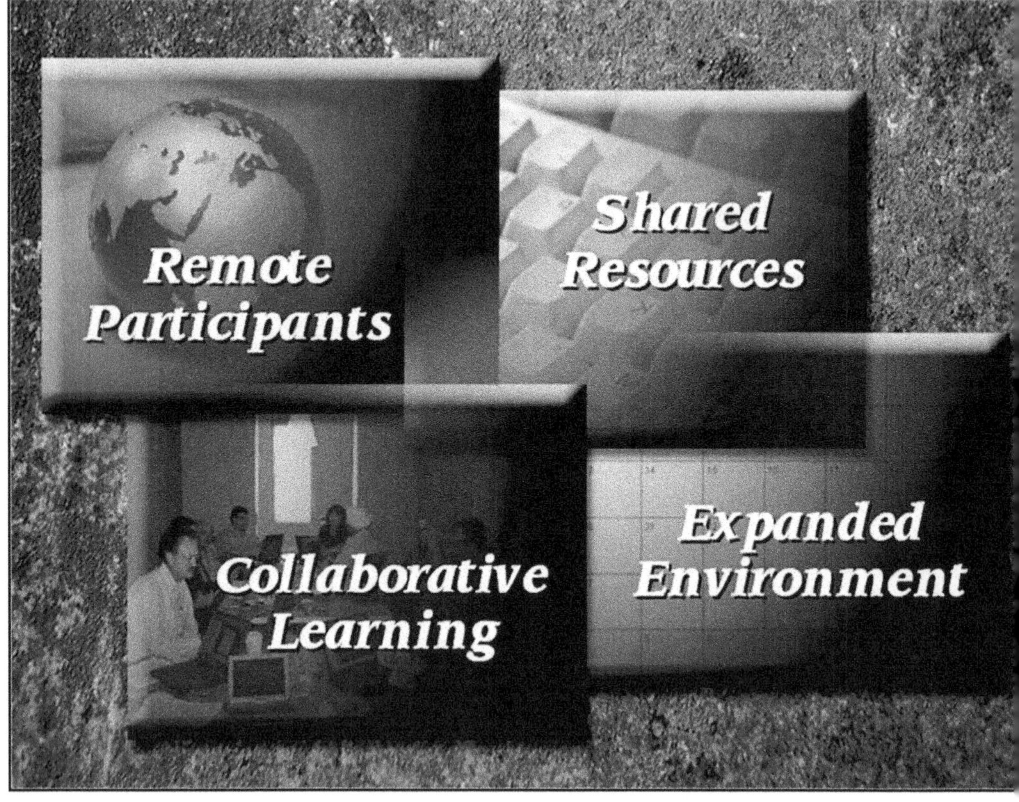
Remote
Participants
Shared
Resources
Collaborative
Learning
Expanded
Environment

3.1 Benefits Introduction

If the Relational Presentation model requires a substantial shift in thinking, you may be wondering, "What's in it for me? Why should I go through the extra work of learning and applying these ideas?"

There are quite a few reasons, actually. Most of them probably apply directly to your situation in one way or another. This chapter analyzes real-world speaking environments to determine how visually interactive techniques can apply and what benefits are available to enhance your talks.

As part of the analysis, we'll track the experiences of Bill, a hypothetical speaker who uses standard presentation methods. Bill has not yet read this book and is assumed to know little about dynamic, interactive display of visual media. He is an executive and an expert in his field but just as well could be an engineer, a teacher, a lawyer, a pastor, or a representative of any other profession. Bill finds himself facing a collage of awkward scenarios that by sheer coincidence happen to correspond almost identically with our experiences and with stories we've heard.

You may recognize some of your own world in his predicaments and in other cases described in this chapter. We try to cover a broad spectrum of speaking environments, but if we miss yours don't worry. The concepts here are quite universal. Suggestions or strategies offered within sales or teaching contexts might work equally well for keynote speeches and small group collaborations. Use your imagination to stretch these examples into your own realm of experience.

3.2 Customization

Today is show time and the moment has arrived for Bill to approach the podium with his single 65-slide linear show. It contains mostly bullet points, with a graph here or there and perhaps a few small pictures. He feels a little trickle of sweat forming on his forehead because there is a lot of information to cover. Questions arise about what information is where, on which slide ... or is it there at all? Bill suddenly thinks about one of the previous presenter's comments and realizes, "It sure would make more sense now for me to start with *that slide from my other show* and *show that set of data,*" neither of which he originally anticipated needing. But, of course, it's too late to change the presentation now. For the

Figure 3.1

rest of his talk, Bill, like millions of other speakers every day, will be locked in a set sequence of content, without the freedom to customize or adjust his visual display to the circumstances.

Digital presentation doesn't have to be so rigid. Some obvious benefits of navigation-based delivery include being able to spontaneously skip slides and add unplanned material, or otherwise customize messages. If Bill were using a relational approach, he might have slides from past presentations available on demand or anticipate needing certain categories of slides during contingencies.

In cases where time is running out, he might skip less important slides along the way (such as extra tables, graphs, or examples) and the audience would never know the difference. Ideally, Bill should never again need to rush through content in a panic to reach the conclusion section.

With this kind of flexibility, he has the option of addressing random questions on the spot, verbally and visually. If he happens to be on slide 20 and the content needed to answer the question is on slide 50, not a problem. Even if the desired slide is in another slide show entirely, he can quickly navigate to that material, answer the question, and instantly return to the former slide.

The beauty of having an interlinked, randomly accessible collection of slides (a Presentation Network) is that any topic can be added, subtracted, or modified as desired. Then what used to be called a *presentation* begins to look a lot more like a *conversation,* where the flow of information matches perceived needs. Such modifications may be the direct result of interactions with the audience, or simply presenter choice.

Some speakers are uncomfortable at first with the notion of conversational presentation. They see themselves as lecturers, givers of information, one-way conduits of wisdom. But human interactions don't work that way. A speaker is not a machine transferring information to other machines. To be an effective digital communicator, we must conform delivery to the realities of the environment and perceived knowledge base of viewers. The LECTURER mentality is a past attitude that is gradually disappearing as interactive, media-based communication becomes more pervasive. The new paradigm values responsiveness and tailored solutions.

3.3 Hidden and Subtle Features

Optical illusions and hidden features available through Relational Presentation methods might further enhance Bill's customization activities. Supplemental information on slides can be hidden until needed, or displayed only if needed. Likewise, invisible navigation can hide the fact that he has multiple parallel presentation tracks at his disposal. For instance, he might reach a point in his presentation where he normally gives an example. Unknown to the audience is that there are three hidden tracks (versions) of that example from which Bill can choose: a short, medium length, and long version. Depending on how much time is left in the performance, he can choose any of the three options or ignore the example altogether. Viewers won't even know a choice was possible or made.

He might set up animations to display additional detail or highlight sections of a slide, all on demand of course. A single slide can be tailored differently to various audiences, depending on what might be relevant to them. An architect might adopt this approach when assisting with a historic remodeling project. One day he presents to the planning commission, the next day to a neighborhood association, and the next day to construction workers. Each group will desire different levels of detail and will approach issues from different angles. Even so, many of the same slides can be useful across all groups, in varying degrees. In this case, setting up a slide with levels of depth might mean having a general schematic that also can display engineering specs, historic guidelines, or artistic details when appropriate.

Perhaps you are selling cosmetics from your home. One customer will show interest in one product whereas another will not. If shows have hidden detail available, you can focus on products that stir interest and gloss over the rest. In this way you are tailoring the topics to the viewers' needs and desires.

Figure 3.2

The slide shown as Figure 3.2 may look innocent enough. It sits at the very top of the Aspire network. To an unsuspecting onlooker, it is nothing more than a slide containing graphics and text. In reality, this single slide controls our entire network. It contains five hidden vertical menus that can be animated into view at any time, in any order, and transports our trainers and presenters to any of more than 14,000 other slides.

3.4 Categorical Selection

One of the most potent advantages of network-based presentation is having immediate access to categories of content that are grouped by similarity. In many cases, arranging slides by category rather than in linear shows greatly simplifies and accelerates the process of finding a specific slide when needed. For example, we have all of our video clips located within a *video category*. When looking for a particular clip, we don't worry about remembering whether it's on slide 38 in show 562 or elsewhere. As strange as it may sound, all of our nearly 200 video clips exist in a single slide show and that show is available from every other show. So there is NEVER a question of where to find a clip. All clips are available on demand from a single location.

Most of our content categories are grouped within an enveloping category called a *Resources Section*. How this area of a network is arranged varies considerably from presenter to presenter, but a Resources Section typically holds broad, generic categories such as those pictured in Figure 3.3—pictures, video, audio, Web links, and so forth.

In most networks, every single slide contains a direct link to the Resources Section. Thus a presenter is never more than a click away from this potentially massive reservoir of supporting material. A French teacher might have an audio section filled with recordings of different people (who speak with different accents or dialects) saying phrases. She can then spontaneously expose students to alternative ways of hearing the same phrases. A church worship leader might have numerous categories of song lyrics ready for display upon request from worshipers.

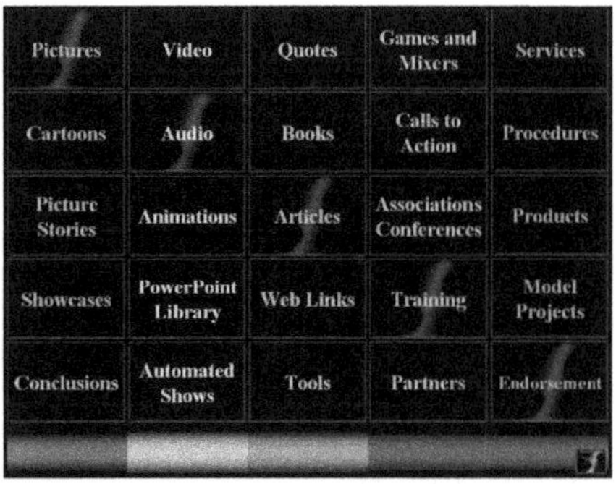

Figure 3.3

Some speakers take advantage of a similar strategy for conclusion slides by creating a separate *Conclusions Section* they can jump to at any time and gracefully end a performance when time is running out. This section might feature multiple ways of concluding, according to presenter preference on a given day. A salesperson uses such a section to great advantage as a way of closing the deal at any time. In Aspire's case, we chose to not use a clearly defined Conclusions Section because our entire network is always available for review in real time.

3.5 The Presenter's Aid

Checking back with Bill, we see he does indeed spend quite a bit of time facing the screen, or looking down at his computer monitor to read his slide content. He presumably needs the slide text as a kind of cheat sheet to help him remember what to say. Unfortunately, handling PowerPoint this way results in prolonged broken eye contact with the audience and is a sure formula for viewer disengagement. Digital content in this case not only provides little visual stimulation, it creates a tangible barrier between giver and receiver. As audience participants, we expect more of a direct connection with the speaker whether we consciously realize it or not.

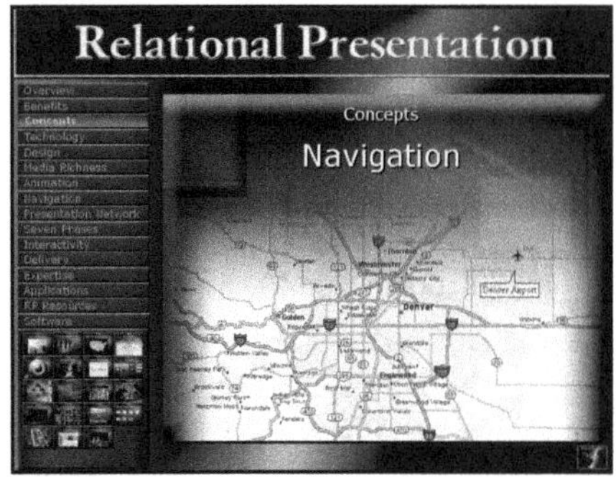

Figure 3.4

In all fairness, though, it is reasonable for Bill to want a cheat sheet in some form. Trying to remember meticulous detail on 65 slides, along with how those slides are ordered, is silly and unnecessary. In fact, we strongly suspect that being forced to recall all of this information and sequencing (a result of using purely linear slide shows) is a major contributor to people's fear of public speaking. It's like the terror of having to memorize your lines in the kindergarten play and wondering if you will forget something important when the spotlight hits. Such rigidity is unnatural and there is a better way.

First of all, we noted earlier that Bill is an expert in his field. Sit him down with a cup of coffee or a glass of wine in a restaurant and he probably would talk nonstop for days about all he knows and does. The question then is how can we capture this relaxed, conversational fluidity and transfer it into a speaking environment? The answer, ironically, is to take away textual detail on slides and replace it with small Visual Clues. Again, we discuss Visual Clues in more detail later but their importance here cannot be overstated.

What will help Bill the most is using these cues to continually *prime the pump* of his knowledge, thereby encouraging him to converse about what he already intrinsically knows well, rather than lecture from memory. That is, his cheat sheet from now on will not be paragraphs of bullet points or even a separate printed notes page. Visual elements on slides will come to his aid instead. As mentioned previously, in Relational Presentations slides serve two purposes: On one level they provide content to the audience as one would expect. On another level they serve as constant views into the future—road maps, if you will, for the speaker. Even something as simple as a text-based menu at the bottom of slides gives clues about what slides are coming up, or are available, and helps a speaker recall topics and think ahead.

Speakers who master visually interactive presentation constantly use their slides as visual aids, subtly and with little thought staying oriented within their message. While navigating to a needed slide or slide show, for example, Bill could take note of the other menu options available and say to himself, "Oh yeah. That's what I need to talk about next, but for the sake of time I better skip that other topic." Or he might notice slides he sometimes uses to tell a story and think, "Based on the looks of confusion I'm getting, maybe I should take a couple of minutes to show those story slides." All of this decision-making is ongoing during the performance.

Here's a concrete example: Pretend you are an Aspire trainer and are delivering a half-day seminar on Relational Presentation techniques at a conference. You will need access to approximately 500 training slides (many of which are displayed in this book). Probably only a fraction of those slides will be used. Nevertheless, all must be available, and you need to know where they are and what they say.

This task is far more complex than Bill's speech, and yet can be surprisingly easy and fun. Yes, the trainer needs to know the material and, certainly, the seminar agenda must be planned in great detail. BUT the actual training component is relatively easy because the slides help guide you through the process.

Figure 3.5

You would probably prepare for the seminar's opening by moving to the very top of the network and accessing the *Main Switchboard,* the slide described earlier containing hidden menus. One of the thumbnail-based menus available there is shown as Figure 3.5.

Five minutes before start time, you are conversing with attendees. One of them has been reading the program guide and is really curious to know how Relational Presentation handles bullet points. If you were a typical presenter, you might answer her question verbally or say, "You know what, we'll talk about that in a couple of hours." Not being a typical presenter, you look at your watch and think, "Hey, I still have three minutes. Let's just SHOW her right now." You then pull up the thumbnail menu and find the link you need (Figure 3.5), which by sheer coincidence just happens to look exactly like the show it will open. In this case, you access a section of the network called *Components,* where the 500 training slides are located.

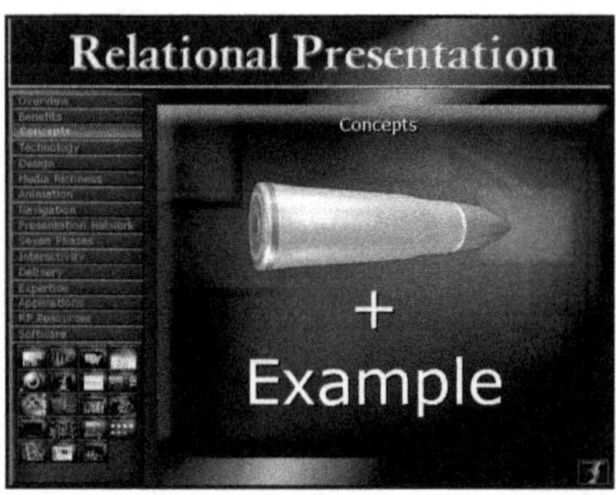

Figure 3.6

Think back to the example of the grocery store. In that case, we used hierarchical design to simplify selection of content. The same process applies here. You are looking for a particular slide discussing bullet points. Starting from the Main Switchboard, there are thousands of slides available. Even so, you don't need to think about all those slides because the one you want is in a subset of 500. A single click on the Components link greatly simplifies the search.

Once inside the Components section, you have 16 categories available. Another click will eliminate 15 of those categories. Again you are using the navigation as a road map that guides you to the slide needed. There is no reason to think about the other slides at the moment because they are irrelevant. The only detail to remember is that the required slide is in the *Concepts* category.

Upon opening the Concepts category, thumbnail links in the bottom left menu allow you to quickly see and select the target slide. Unlike Bill, who probably has little idea at any moment what content happens to be on slide 48 in his show (or how to access that content), you can walk your way directly to any slide needed by using Visual Clues.

The navigation process just described takes only seconds and is performed while you are talking. There should be as little break in continuity as possible. You will briefly break eye contact with the audience to click links, but that connection should be re-established right away.

To recap this benefit, Relational Presentation techniques allow a speaker to continually see a bird's-eye view of topics available in the network, as well as other slides approaching within a particular show. Less mental energy is wasted trying to remember exactly which slide is coming up after this one, or what topics remain. Effective slide design can provide regular reminders. As a result, the presenter is mentally preparing for upcoming subjects and transitions, even while discussing the current slide. This subtle assistance can make a huge difference in performance quality.

3.6 Stress Reduction

A guided approach to finding content, in addition to enhancing audience interest, has a marvelous effect on speakers. Because we are not forced to constantly remember exactly what content is where and can adjust message flow by using what amounts to a *user interface*, presentation becomes much easier—and less scary. Stress levels decrease because we feel more in control of topic selection and timing.

Once when we were demonstrating these concepts and talking about the fear factor, we mentioned research showing that people in surveys consistently rank fear of public speaking even higher than the fear of death. One wise guy in the back of the room raised his hand and said, "Yeah, well I fear dying WHILE I'm public speaking!" Take courage. Change is near.

Relational Presentation methods essentially guarantee we are no longer trapped by our computer. Feeling in control produces confidence. Confidence leads to a higher perception by viewers that you know what you're talking about, leading to more engagement, resulting in higher confidence, and so forth. It's a wonder cycle that feeds upon itself.

Although there is no definitive research yet to show exactly how this process works, we have seen it happen over and over again and are convinced. Random, dynamic selection of subject matter, while presenting, greatly reduces the fear of public speaking.

This assertion may be hard to believe at first. The tendency is to equate random selection with potential chaos. Novice relational presenters are wary of not being able to find content or of forgetting how the pieces should fit together. These concerns are valid when first starting out and should be taken seriously. Eventually though with practice, navigable, visually rich slide shows provide confidence and security that is impossible to replicate in any other way.

3.7 Handling Objections, Closes and Obstacles

Something Bill probably would love to avoid if he could is having people challenge the validity of his claims. Nevertheless, such challenges are inevitable and are a normal part of conversation. Relational Presentation treats challenges as a welcome and expected part of presentation as well.

Let's say, in Bill's case, someone in the audience doesn't agree with his interpretation of data or his conclusions on a particular topic. They may have their own argument or perspective and politely (or in some cases not so politely) challenge Bill to defend his position. Standard presentation formats typically fail dismally in this situation.

A smart and agile presenter actively hopes for challenges because they increase audience engagement and give the presenter a chance to offer more detail in a focused direction. A salesperson would call this process *objection handling*. Once an objection is made, it gives the speaker a chance to better know how audience members are thinking and reacting to the content being delivered. Furthermore, these objections often are quite predictable based upon prior audience interactions. They can be anticipated with the availability of appropriate slides. If a particular objection comes up, the objection-handling slides for that issue are shown. Otherwise, the audience never knows those slides exist.

In this sense, relational techniques allow a speaker to sincerely educate viewers, professionally addressing their concerns and misconceptions (both verbally and visually) in a timely manner. A network's design should anticipate as many objections as possible. Acknowledging and answering such situations on the spot can be very valuable. Remember that challenge often reveals opportunity. An objection or question raised is an open invitation for connection, assuming you are adequately prepared to provide visually meaningful feedback.

3.8 Additional Thoughts

Notice that most, if not all, of the benefits discussed in this chapter somehow revolve around presenter adaptability. Being able to adjust to feedback within speaking environments is a critical component of relational methodologies. Nevertheless, flexibility does not in any way equate to disorganization or lack of planning. Relational presenters must be extremely well-organized at all times and always know exactly where they are during the progression of their performance.

We suggest approaching speaking events with a delivery strategy called the *Content Ladder*. Plan your overall talk in exquisite detail, yet view it in terms of discrete mini-messages, like the rungs of a ladder. Gradually work your way up the ladder, from message to message, checking along the way for misunderstandings, questions, objections and so forth. If you have an hour to speak, plan only 45 minutes worth of content. Leave the rest of the time free for interactions DURING the talk, not just at the end.

It's quite common for viewers to ask questions about issues you planned to address anyway within your Content Ladder strategy. So be prepared to take pieces out of order if appropriate. Also plan in advance for situations where audience members are inert and don't interact with you, despite all your efforts to the contrary. In such cases, fill the time with extra (bonus) material along the way. The main idea here is to strike a balance between meticulous planning—you know exactly where you will start, what will be covered throughout, and where you will end—and the agility to respond to audience interests. Perfecting that balance is an art and, not surprisingly, takes practice.

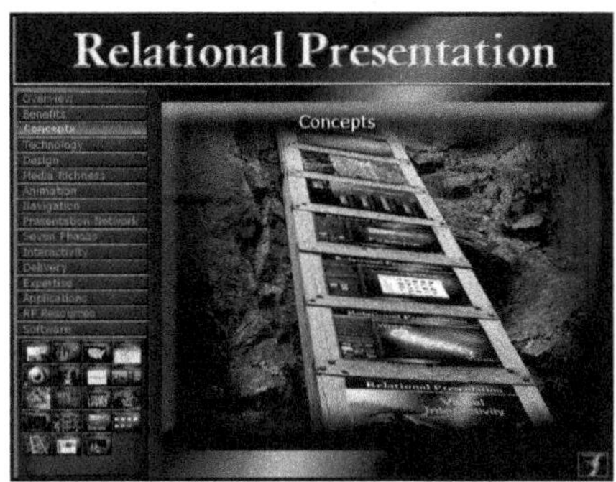

Figure 3.7

As we now launch into the "how to" portion of this book, keep in mind the overarching value of what you will be learning. If you are like many learners who have gone before, the upcoming techniques will completely transform your conceptions of what it means to give a presentation. What used to be one-way, rigid lectures will become conversational, flexible, natural and customizable exchanges. We can almost guarantee your fear of public speaking will decrease and enjoyment will increase. You probably will approach digital communication with a new appreciation for its power.

Amusingly, some have described this process as being so rewarding as to accuse us of creating a new addiction. So be it. The enjoyment comes from the fact that you basically are building a model of your personality and wisdom in digital form. You are molding a structure that displays your contributions to the world, your knowledge, your opinions, and your accomplishments. Now, that is rewarding!

"PowerPoint is a lot more powerful and flexible than people realize. All the tools to create a visually interactive presentation are right there, just waiting to be used. The key is knowing they're there and having the imagination to see their potential."

Echo Swinford, Microsoft PowerPoint MVP

Introduction and Setup

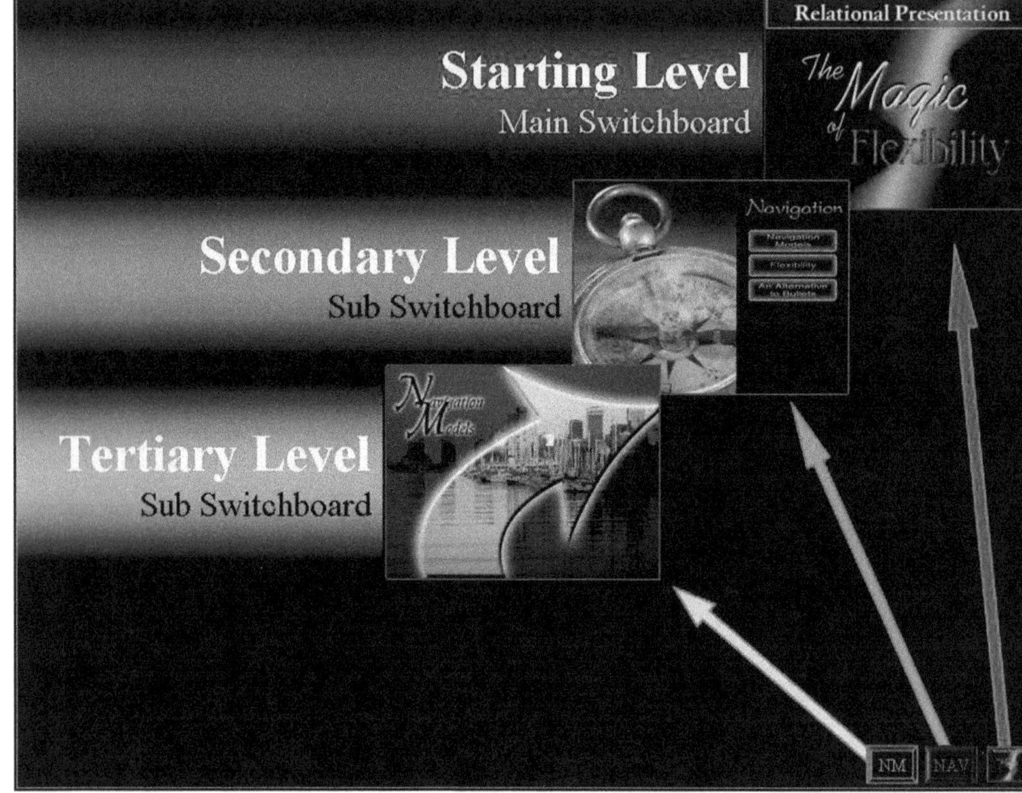
Relational Presentation
The Magic of Flexibility
Starting Level
Main Switchboard
Navigation
Navigation Models
Flexibility
An Alternative to Bullets
Secondary Level
Sub Switchboard
Navigation Models
Tertiary Level
Sub Switchboard
NM
NAV

4.1 The Big Picture

The Relational Presentation concept is based on use of PowerPoint software. Are there particular reasons why? Yes. PowerPoint is very easy to use, most people have it on their computers as a part of Microsoft's Office Suite, and it is a very stable and dependable platform. Will visually interactive methods work using other presentation software? Certainly. In fact, theoretically you could reproduce most of the PowerPoint-specific techniques we discuss in this book using html or Adobe Flash. Such endeavors would be mind-numbingly more difficult compared to working with PowerPoint but are possible. If you do prefer another platform, make sure you understand the underlying principles behind the Relational Presentation concepts discussed in this book, and then explore mechanisms for accomplishing the same effects with different software. Overall, relational methods are quite universal.

You will notice also that the PowerPoint interface graphics from here on are taken from PowerPoint 2003 for PCs. A version of this book will be available for PowerPoint 2007 as well in the near future. If you are still using PowerPoint XP (2002), practically all the directions on the following pages apply exactly the same for you. There will be small differences in the appearance of graphics for toolbars, dialog boxes, and such, but the functionality is the same. For those of you who are Mac users, your graphics will look substantially different sometimes, and your functionality will vary somewhat from the directions given here. We have chosen to include PC-based PowerPoint directions only, for simplicity sake. Realize, however, that Mac users can do everything we discuss in this book by modifying the directions accordingly for Mac protocols.

Finally, in addition to Relational Presentation methods being based on PowerPoint, keep in mind they also require NOTHING BUT PowerPoint. No other software applications, plug-ins, or add-ons are needed. To the surprise of many, relational methods have been in use, in one form or another, since PowerPoint 97, with no supporting software or special equipment added. Visual Interactivity is not a hi-tech concept available only to the *geekiest* among us. It's just a different way of approaching presentation.

Because many learners are unfamiliar with PowerPoint's more robust features, we begin by exploring available tools. Advanced use of PowerPoint is not difficult. All you need to know is which tools do what. The first step is to prepare PowerPoint's work area for maximum efficiency by displaying helpful toolbars. The following four toolbars (shown in Figure 4.1) should appear at the top of your PowerPoint work area: **Standard (1), Formatting (2), Drawing (3),** and **Picture (4).**

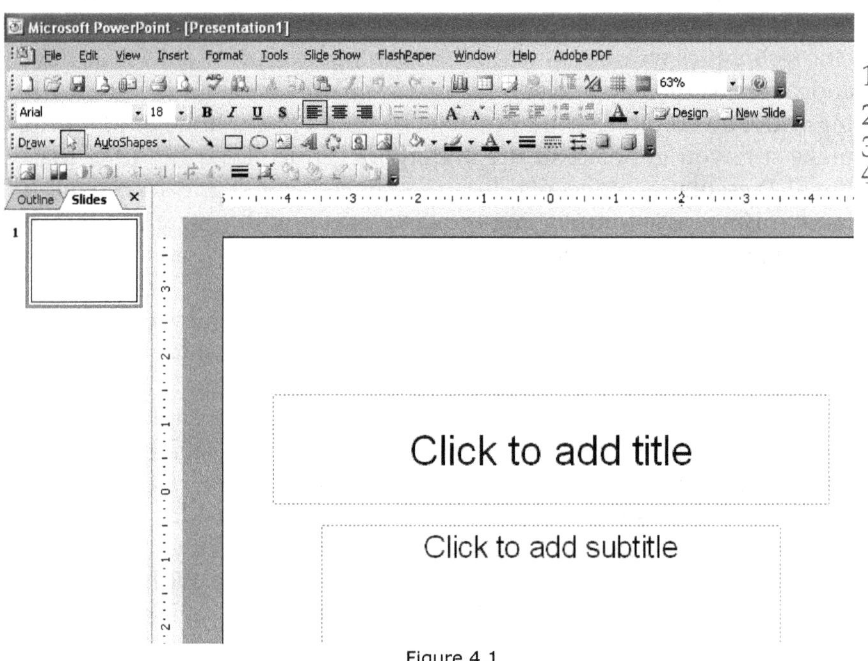

Figure 4.1

4.2 Customizing the Work Area

If you do not see all four toolbars on your screen, click the View menu and hold your cursor over the **Toolbars** option. Make sure those four toolbars have a check mark beside them. Note that by default, your **Drawing** toolbar probably is already visible but is anchored at the bottom left side of your screen. You can leave it down there if you like but it's a good idea to anchor it at the top with the rest of the toolbars, to avoid confusion with screenshots in this book. You will use this particular toolbar often.

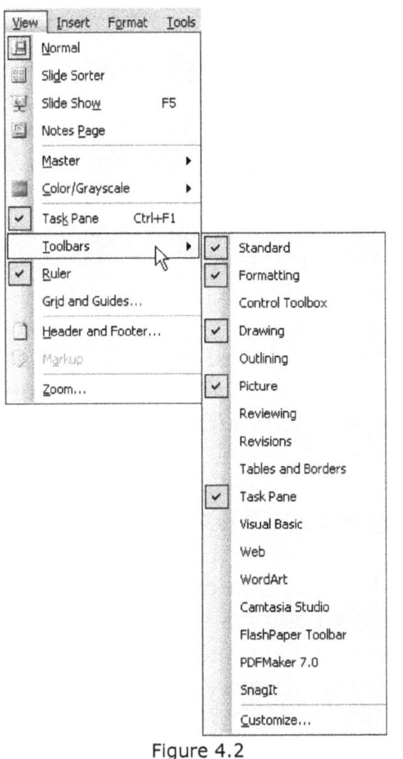

Figure 4.2

To move the **Drawing** toolbar to the top of your screen, hold your cursor over the vertical dotted line on the far left side of the toolbar.

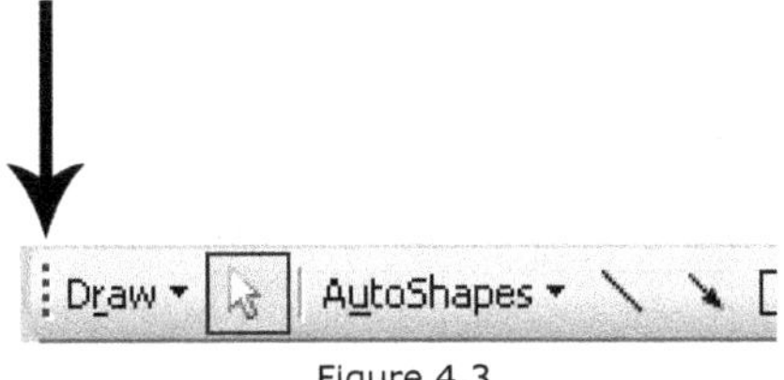

Figure 4.3

Notice when the cursor is over the dotted line, it changes to four opposing arrows. At this point, you can click and drag the toolbar to the top. A toolbar that is visible but not anchored at the top, bottom, or side of the work area is said to be *floating* and appears with a blue bar above it (Figure 4.4). Once the toolbar is anchored again, the top blue bar disappears. If you accidentally release the mouse while dragging, simply click the blue bar and continue to drag.

Figure 4.4

Once all toolbars are anchored at the top, make sure each is on its own line so that it is fully expanded (you can see all the icons each contains). If more than one toolbar exists on the same line, tools on those toolbars may be compressed out of view and, therefore, seemingly are no longer available. To avoid this situation, simply make sure all toolbars are on separate lines, as in the screenshot on the previous page.

4.3 Getting Rid of the Text Boxes

Here is one more tip that will come in handy as we begin working with AutoShapes and pictures: Because Relational Presentation places so much emphasis on visual information as opposed to text, PowerPoint's default text boxes in the slide pane often just get in the way. In fact, they can be quite annoying sometimes when inserting pictures on slides.

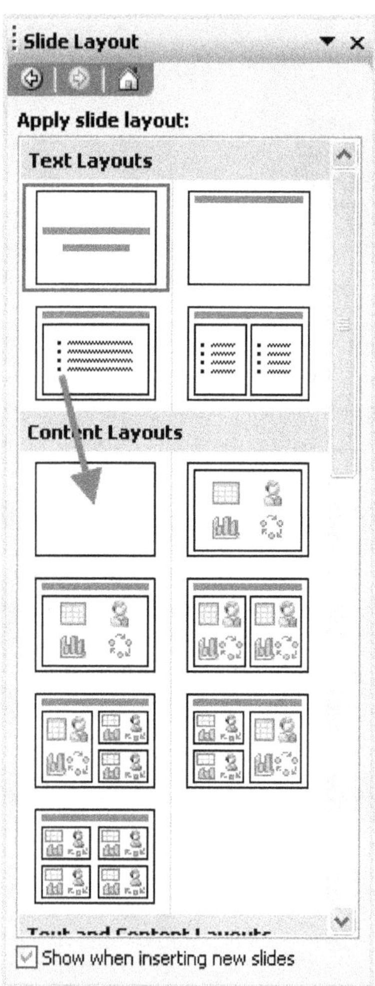

Figure 4.5

Therefore, in most of the exercises to come it's a good idea to develop a habit of getting rid of these boxes when creating new slide shows. This can be accomplished by selecting the boxes and deleting them. Or, an easier way to remove the boxes is to click the **Blank** option on the **Slide Layout** task pane (as shown here with an arrow). Doing so removes all the default text boxes at once. Note that this action DOES NOT remove AutoShapes, pictures, custom text boxes you add, or any other content on the slide—only the default text boxes controlled by the Slide Master.

These boxes were especially annoying in the past when working with pictures because pictures tended to be inserted inside the boxes instead of directly onto the slide pane. It seems Microsoft has fixed that problem with PowerPoint 2003; we still recommend eliminating the textboxes from the slide pane if not used.

That's not to say we never incorporate text as labels or content. We frequently do. For the most part, however, AutoShapes serve as a text container rather than text boxes. They are more versatile.

A note to presentation professionals: Some of you who work in presentation-related professions (helping others create and effectively deliver presentations) probably react strongly to discouraging use of the master-controlled text boxes. Such a reaction is certainly understandable considering the many hours you spend fixing disastrous text-oriented presentations that were not based on the Slide Master.

Remember, though, that what we are emphasizing here is a strong reliance on visual media, an environment where text plays a minimal role. Here there is little use for master-controlled text, or at least not in the traditional sense. Most visually interactive presenters, frankly, have little need for the default text boxes.

"A successful presenter is able to make a real connection with an audience, achieving clear communication of ideas and concepts. By following the methods detailed in this book, you'll learn how to prepare and deliver a visually-rich, non-linear presentation—one that truly connects with, and engages, your audience."

Julie Terberg
Principal, Terberg Design
Microsoft PowerPoint MVP

Chapter 5

Working with AutoShapes

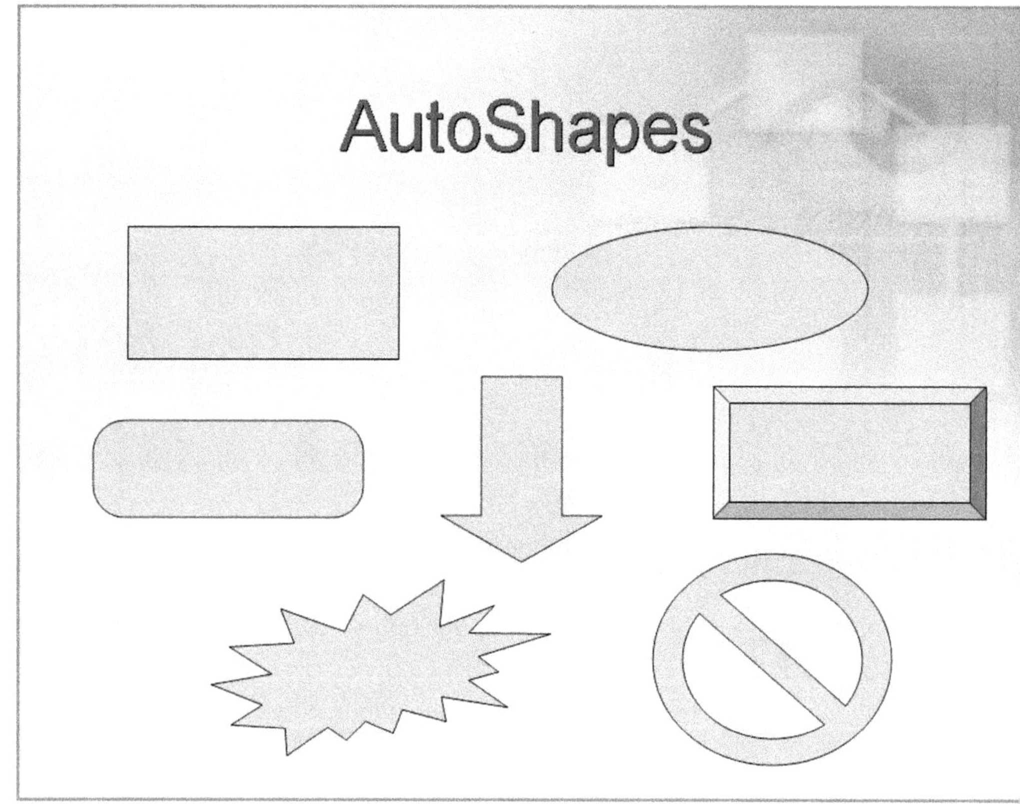
AutoShapes

5.1 Thinking Outside the Software

In a conversation with one of Microsoft's Web masters, the topic turned to how people have a knack for applying software (especially PowerPoint) in ways the designers never intended or imagined. Such may well be the case with methods you will be learning throughout the rest of this book. From this point forward, you will mold, stretch, contort, and otherwise push PowerPoint beyond its envisioned limits. As wonderfully and effectively as PowerPoint *does what it does,* we must ask for more. We need greater flexibility and control.

To that end, we treat PowerPoint almost as though it could design Web sites, or at least we put up a good pretense. Optical illusions help us create the impression the software can do more than it actually can. At the same time, we make PowerPoint hide what it actually is doing so that the presenter can manipulate the message without undue distraction. Such artistry sounds complicated, perhaps, but it's really quite easy and deliciously fun.

Working with AutoShapes gives us a wealth of options for creating such effects. These innocent-looking objects can be used in countless ways you may never have learned in PowerPoint class, or in help files for that matter. They help us harness digital presentation's full potential. To begin, make sure the **Drawing** toolbar is displayed at the top of the work area, as previously discussed.

5.2 What Is an AutoShape?

AutoShapes are part of PowerPoint's built-in functionality. In a sense, they are nothing more than fancy text boxes and have similar features. They can contain text but also play many other valuable roles. In standard presentations, they typically are included as slide labels or as parts of diagrams. We will expand their usages.

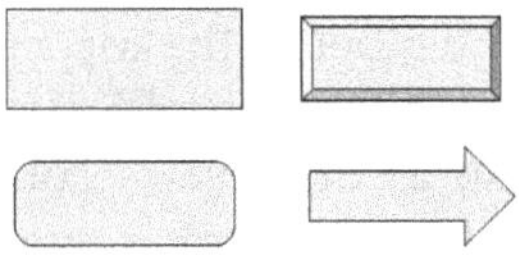

By default, AutoShapes created in PowerPoint 2003 have a starting appearance like these pictured but they can be formatted in countless ways to be more attractive, versatile, and pragmatic—or they can be completely invisible. AutoShapes are so important to Relational Presentation that considerable time will be spent exploring all aspects of their creation, design, and utility.

Figure 5.1

5.3 AutoShapes and Flexible Presentation

The following categories demonstrate some of the most common AutoShape applications for visually interactive presentation:

Navigation: AutoShapes are a mainstay of relational design, especially in the formation of *Navigation Elements*. Navigation Elements are collections of hyperlinked objects (usually AutoShapes or pictures) that enable a presenter to jump from one place to another. Shown here is a *Navigation Panel* made of several AutoShapes stacked on top of each other. The result is a menu of navigation options. Once hyperlinks are added, clicking on a shape transports the presenter to a specific location, perhaps another slide or slide show.

Figure 5.2

Such devices are similar to navigation components found on most Web sites. For that reason, audiences normally don't pay much attention when seeing them in your slide shows. Navigation Elements can, of course, be made more or less obvious, and their look and feel will vary considerably with designer preference and functional purpose. Chapters 9 and 10 cover navigation in much more detail.

Text Holders: AutoShapes can serve as text boxes. In fact, a text box is basically a rectangular AutoShape that contains no fill (color) and no border. We tend to use AutoShapes for holding text because of their available shapes, along with robust and easy formatting features. In the Navigation Panel above, the shapes contain meaningful labels that indicate where the links will lead.

In the slide to the right, shapes are used to form an alternative to a traditional PowerPoint table. The label at the top has a gradient fill to provide visual interest, as does the secondary label below it. Another gradient-filled shape supplies a divider line further down. Otherwise, shapes here are transparent so that they resemble standard text boxes.

Multiple Intelligences

Category	%
Visual / Spatial	25-35
Logical / Mathematical	10-15
Kinesthetic / Hands-on	10-15
Linguistic	20-35
Musical / Auditory	20-35
Interpersonal / Social	
Intrapersonal / Reflective	

Figure 5.3: Courtesy University of Arizona, DISCOVER

As a rule, if your slide shows will contain a substantial amount of text, consider sticking with the default text boxes because of their connection to the Slide Master. Otherwise, explore having AutoShapes hold text. You may find they are more versatile.

Design: AutoShapes enable many decorative design options. They work well for creating multicolored gradients, lighting effects (if using a dark background), and shadows (if using a light or medium-colored background).

Figure 5.4

In the example to the right, multiple AutoShapes are filled with progressively changing gradient colors and laid next to each other in the background, giving the impression that color is gradually changing. The design also has the effect of drawing your eyes toward the lighter color at the top, emphasizing the material featured there. It's a simple and effective idea for displaying products.

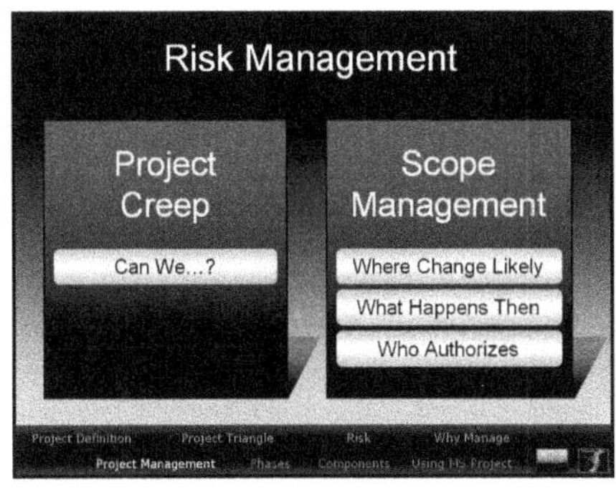

Figure 5.5

All objects on the slide to the left are AutoShapes except for the two tiny thumbnail pictures in the bottom right corner. Notice in particular the shadows behind the vertical rectangles. These effects were built in PowerPoint and are nothing more than parallelogram AutoShapes with a partially transparent, dark gradient fill. Parallelogram shapes can be skewed sideways to the desired angle, for realistic shadow appearance. Shadows also can be formed using elliptical shapes, giving the impression that spheres and other curved objects are hovering. Such techniques do not require graphic arts knowledge per se because they can be accomplished with PowerPoint alone.

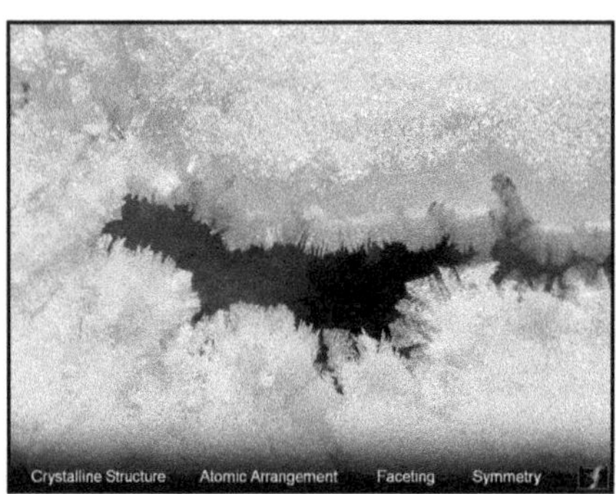

Figure 5.6 Courtesy Dawn Allynn

Figure 5.7

Also in a design context, we sometimes place AutoShapes behind text menus (Figure 5.6) to clarify the text against background images that are either dark or light.

AutoShapes can even create star effects (Figure 5.7) and add subtle or colorful decorative interest to slides. With creative application, many attractive and useful design ideas are possible, without needing to be an artist. Being able to add transparency to shapes is the key. Overlapping semitransparent shapes allows color blending, which gives the effect of producing color gradients.

Figure 5.8

Organization: AutoShapes also frequently come in handy for visually laying out objects on slides, especially when dealing with complex navigation styles such as Showcase Switchboards (Figure 5.8). In the example pictured, there are 49 links. Finding one appropriate link during a presentation would take awhile if thumbnails were randomly distributed on the slide, with no obvious groupings. As is, AutoShapes appear behind groups of related links and form what amount to colored zones. That way a presenter's eye is directed to stay within the zone when searching a category. If he is looking for a building here, 70 percent of the thumbnails on the slide can be ignored because only the *Structures* zone (the two right-most columns) is applicable. Shape, color, and placement of AutoShapes can be used to define categories of links that naturally belong together. This strategy is another example of using *Visual Clues* in slide design.

Figure 5.9

A related concept is to group individual AutoShapes by their color, design, or shape. Perhaps all shapes (or links) representing subjects relevant to boys are blue and those for girls are pink. Again, the network user's eyes are directed to stay within the appropriate cluster when searching for a defined subject. If color or fill varies or AutoShapes contain picture fill, categories can be formed by relying on the actual shape of the AutoShapes. In the case shown, rectangles might represent vegetable-related links and rounded rectangles fruit-related links.

Whatever strategy is chosen, consistent use is the critical guidance a presenter needs. The goal is to automate the search for material as much as possible and reduce the amount of time and thought energy required to locate individual links.

Emphasis: Finally, we use AutoShapes to emphasize specific numbers or sections of text by outlining the material, pointing to it (using an arrow shape for example), coloring the background, or in some other way drawing attention to detail. An oval AutoShape with no Fill Color and a thick border makes a nice emphasis effect. We typically add animation to such shapes so that they can be viewed or hidden, as needed.

If a shape is invisible but contains text, an effective optical illusion is to cause the font color to change, or at least appear to change. Thus a table filled with black numbers can be set up to change the color of individual numbers to red on demand.

5.4 Creating AutoShapes

At this point we enter the hands-on section of this book where gray text indicates steps to complete in PowerPoint. Working through all the hands-on components in this and following chapters will give you practical experience needed for restructuring your own materials later. We'll start by making a few basic shapes, and then proceed into more complexity.

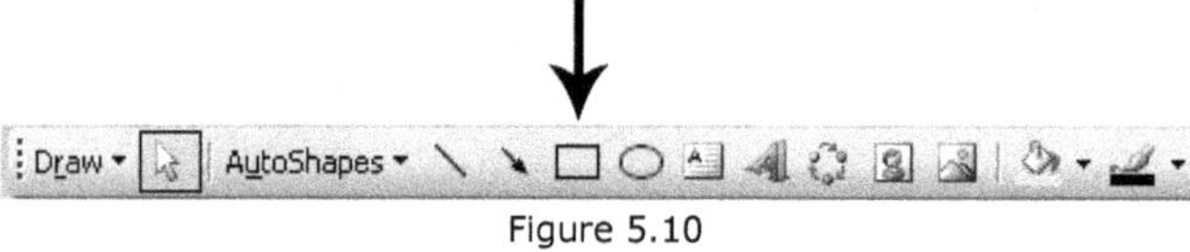

Figure 5.10

1. Open PowerPoint.
2. Remove the default text boxes on the beginning white slide that appears by selecting the blank option on the **Slide Layout** task pane. If you don't see the **Slide Layout** task pane, click the **View** menu, select **Task Pane**, and then select **Slide Layout**.
3. Click the **Rectangle** icon on the **Drawing** toolbar (Figure 5.10). Your cursor changes to a "+" sign. Click and drag anywhere on the slide pane of slide 1 to create a rectangular AutoShape.
4. Create another shape by clicking the **AutoShapes** button on the **Drawing** toolbar, selecting the **Basic Shapes** option from the pop-up menu, and clicking the shape called **Rounded Rectangle** from the submenu. Again, your cursor changes to a "+" sign. Click and drag on the slide pane to make the shape.
5. Experiment with creating other shapes.

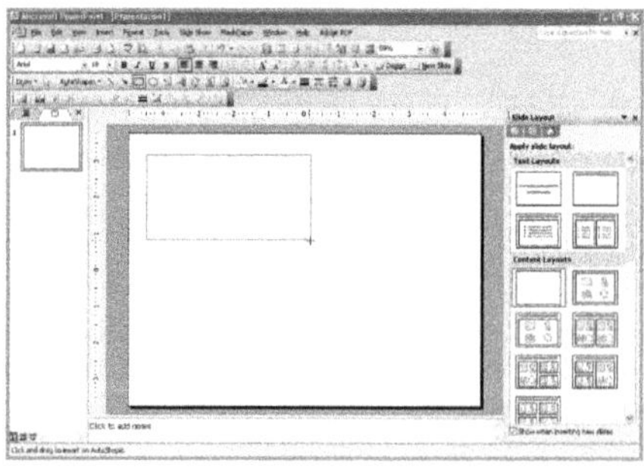

Figure 5.11

5.5 Selecting AutoShapes

An existing shape must be *selected* (made active) before it can be changed in any way. One way to select a shape is simply to click it. Upon selection, a shape has small white circles at its corners, top, bottom, and along its sides. These circles are called *selection handles* and allow size adjustment. Practice selecting shapes using the procedures described below. Also note that clicking the slide pane anywhere outside a shape's area deselects the shape.

1. Select a single shape by clicking it. Notice the small white circles that appear around its border.
2. To select multiple shapes, hold down either the **Shift** or **Ctrl** key while clicking the desired shapes.

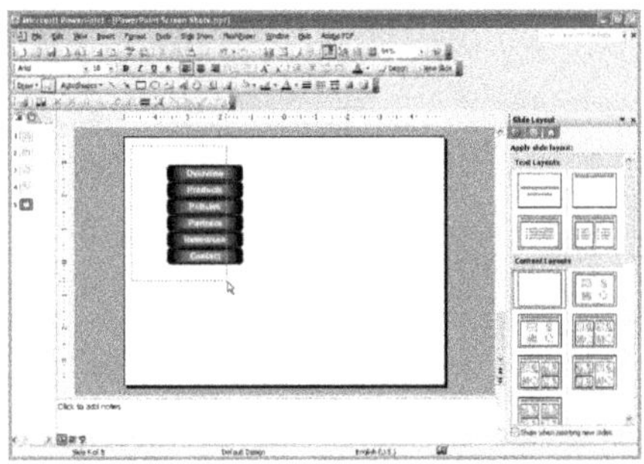

Figure 5.12

3. Multiple selections are even easier by forming a selection net (see Figure 5.12): Left click and drag somewhere on the slide pane to surround the desired shapes. Make sure you begin by clicking off to the side of (outside) a shape. Anything fully contained within the dotted rectangle that forms will be selected.

5.6 Moving AutoShapes

You can move shapes from one area of the slide pane to another by three different methods. Practice all of the following:

1. Click the shape and, with the mouse button held down, drag it.
2. Click the shape to select it, and then press the keyboard **Arrow** keys.
3. Specify an exact target position on the slide by double-clicking the

Holding down the **Ctrl** key while pressing an **Arrow** key moves any selected element in smaller increments.

shape to open the **Format AutoShape** dialog box.

a. Click the **Position** tab if it is not selected.

b. Type **.5** in the **Horizontal** box and **.5** in the **Vertical** box.

c. Click **OK** to close the dialog box. This action moves the shape to the upper left corner of the slide, a half inch from the top and left boundaries.

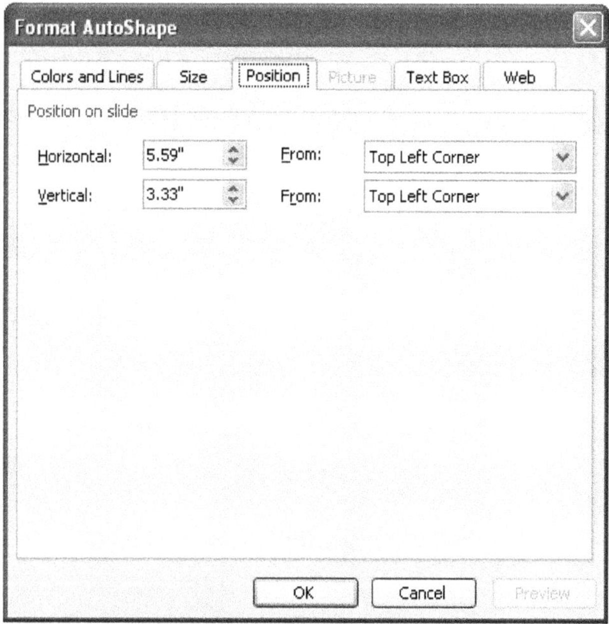

Figure 5.13

5.7 Resizing AutoShapes

You can resize AutoShapes by "eyeballing" or being specific. Practice the following:

1. Select a shape; then click and drag one of its selection handles (small white circles). Dragging from a corner resizes both height and width simultaneously in any direction. Dragging from the

top, bottom, or sides changes only one dimension at a time. Try making the shape approximately 0.5 inch tall and 2 inches wide.

2. Now double click the shape to check its exact dimensions. The **Format AutoShape** dialog box appears.
3. Click the **Size** tab. How close were you? If your estimate was off, make the shape's dimensions exactly **0.5** tall and **2** wide by entering those values. You do not need to enter the inches symbol ("). Simply entering the number automatically defaults the value to inches.
4. Click **OK** to close the dialog box and set the size.

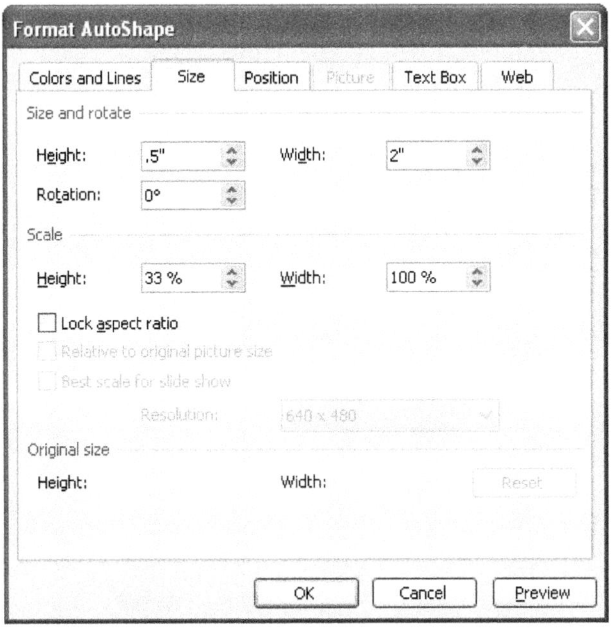

Figure 5.14

5.8 Adding Fill Color to AutoShapes

AutoShapes can be formatted extensively, giving you as a designer considerable freedom of expression. It's important to know all the possible options because unattractive or improperly formatted shapes give your presentation materials an amateurish or distracting appearance. As a general rule, especially when building shapes used by Navigation Elements, coordinate shape design with the look and feel of slides the shapes appear on. In other words, shapes used for navigation should not unduly stick out from the background unless there is a particularly good reason they should.

We'll begin exploring formatting options with a look at **Fill Color**, the color existing inside the shape's borders:

1. Double click a shape to open the **Format AutoShape** dialog box.
2. Click the **Color and Lines** tab. We will use this tab quite often.
3. Click anywhere in the **Fill Color** bar to open a palette of colors.

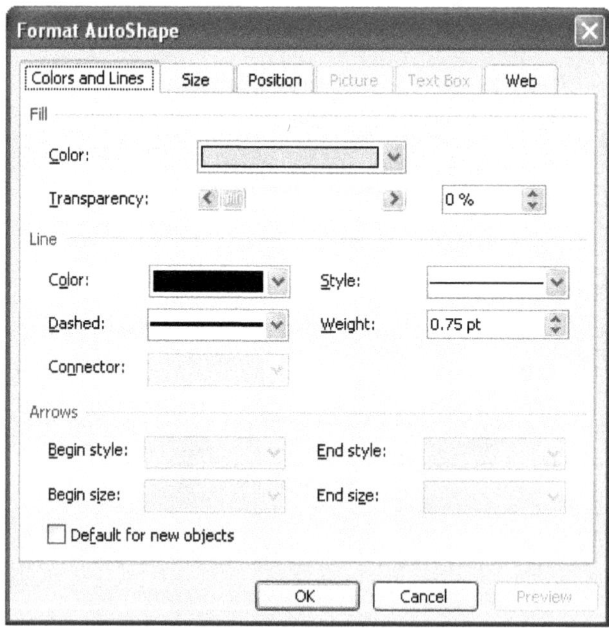

Figure 5.15

4. Click **More Colors** for a larger selection. Preset options are available in the color wheel on the **Standard** tab, or you can create your own colors in the **Custom** tab. If your company requires specific branding colors, exact RGB definitions can be entered into the boxes shown. You also can click anywhere in the color gradient displays (either the large or the skinny box) or move the slider up and down to change lightness/darkness. The before and after colors are displayed in the **New/Current** box in the bottom right corner of the **Colors** dialog box.

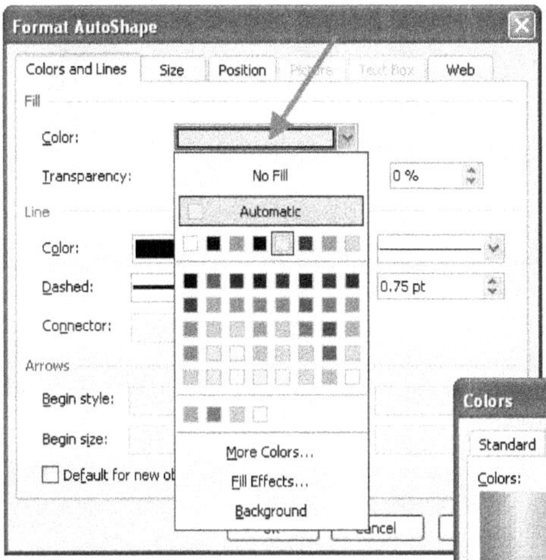

Figure 5.16

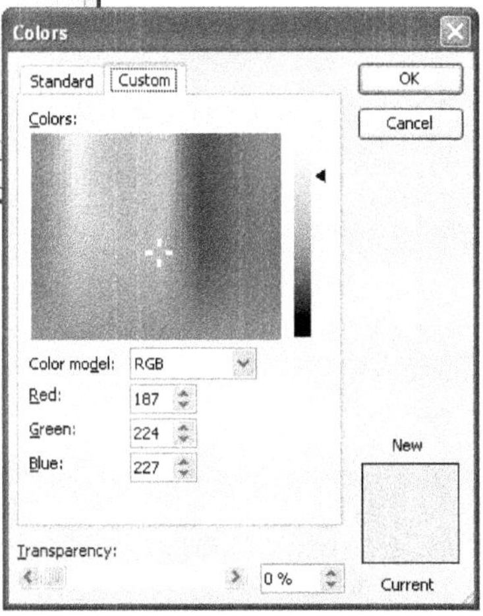

Figure 5.17

5. Change the **Fill Color** to a dark red of your choice.
6. Click **OK** to close the **Colors** dialog box.
7. Click **OK** again to close the **Format AutoShape** dialog box and complete the shape's color change.

5.9 Adding Fill Effects to AutoShapes

Shapes filled with solid, uniform color are rather boring. They can be made more attractive and given the appearance of having dimension using Fill Effects. Let's create the shape shown here:

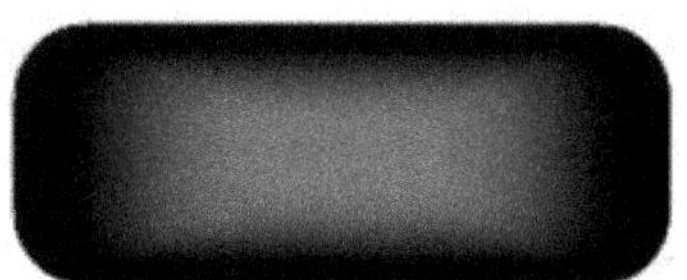

Figure 5.18

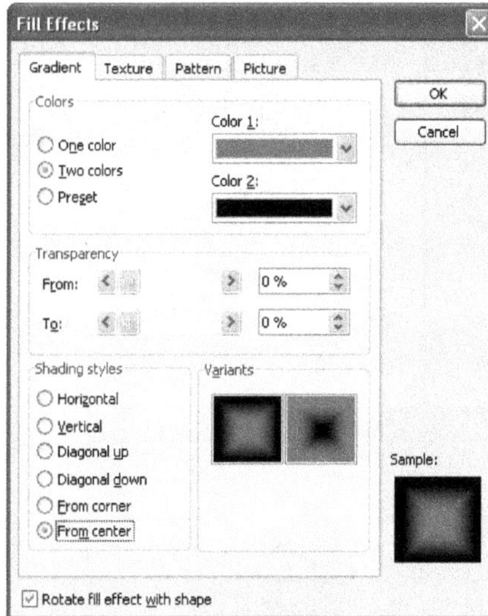

Figure 5.19

1. Make a **Rounded Rectangle** AutoShape on your slide, if one does not already exist.
2. Double click the shape to open the **Format AutoShape** dialog box.
3. Click the **Color and Lines** tab.
4. Click anywhere in the **Fill Color** bar to open the color palette.
5. Select **Fill Effects** (at bottom).
6. In the **Fill Effects** dialog box, make sure the **Gradient** tab is selected and choose the T**wo Colors** option. Click the respective color bars to make one color **red** and the other **black**.
7. Under **Shading Styles**, select the option **From Center** and make sure the black is the outside color displayed in the **Sample** thumbnail.
8. Click **OK** twice to close the dialog boxes and complete the formatting.
9. If this shape is to appear on a dark background, you might also want to give it a red border so that the shape is more defined against the background.

5.10 Adding a Border to AutoShapes

If you wish to give AutoShapes a border so that they are better defined, do so using the Color and Lines tab:

> **TIP**
>
> When adding a border, increase the **Line Weight** to at least **1.5 pt** for best display when projected.

1. Double click the shape to open the **Format AutoShape** dialog box.
2. Click the **Color and Lines** tab.
3. Click the **Color** bar in the **Line** section and change the line color to the same red used for the shape's inner fill.
4. Change the **Line Weight** to **1.5 pt**. This increase in line weight produces a better display when the slide show is projected, especially with older projectors.
5. Click **OK**.

5.11 Transparency and AutoShapes

Being able to make AutoShapes semitransparent or entirely invisible is extremely important to Relational Presentation design and delivery strategies. Invisible AutoShapes, for example, can contain hyperlinks just like visible shapes, enabling the speaker to control the delivery process without the audience knowing what options are available—or that any options are possible. Such functionality and the reasons for using it are explored in detail throughout upcoming chapters. Suffice it to say, invisible navigation has many practical benefits.

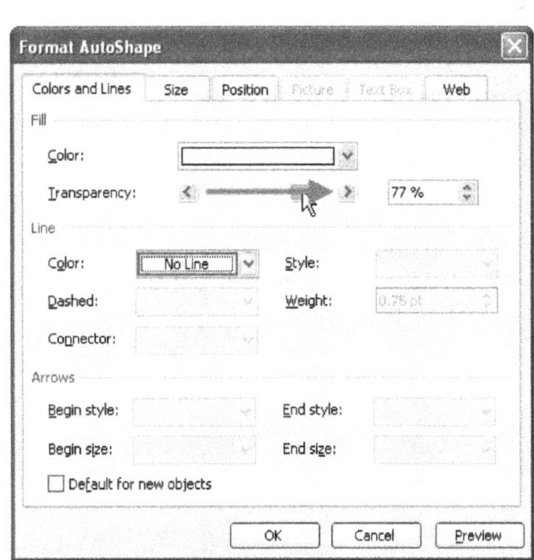

Figure 5.20

Follow these steps to make a shape invisible:

1. Create a new shape next to the existing red and black shape.
2. Double click the new shape to open the **Format AutoShape** dialog box.
3. The first step in making the shape transparent (invisible) is to remove the border: Click in the **Line Color** bar to open the palette and select **No Line** at the top.
4. Complete the transparency by sliding the transparency bar (in the **Fill** section) to **100 percent**.
5. Click **OK** to view the results. Notice the white selection handles are still visible but the shape itself is invisible. If you click away from the shape, somewhere on the slide pane, the shape is deselected and becomes completely invisible. It can be reselected at any time, as normal, with a mouse click.

CAUTION: Most learners when first experimenting with shape invisibility (not having received the previous instructions) are tempted to remove the Fill color just like we removed the Line color. Removing the Fill does make the shape invisible but adjusting the transparency instead is a superior approach. Not having Fill causes problems later when working with hyperlinks. It also makes attempts at selecting the shape with a mouse click difficult. There is one exception where we definitely DO want to remove the Fill, and that situation is covered at the end of this chapter. Otherwise, always leave the Fill in the shape and make it transparent.

Note that making a shape invisible is slightly more complicated when it contains a gradient such as a two-color fill. In this case, adjusting the transparency as described previously only changes the transparency of one of the colors, leaving the other opaque. To make both colors transparent, follow the steps below:

1. Repeat the previous transparency process using the red and black shape (the shape containing a red and black, two-color, from center Fill Effect).
2. After clicking **OK**, notice that the transparency procedure in this case affected either the black or red Fill, leaving the other unaffected.

3. To make a Fill Effect-formatted shape invisible, you must manually move both fill colors to 100 percent transparency. To do so, return to the **Format AutoShape** dialog box, select the **Color and Lines** tab, click the **Fill** color bar, and click **Fill Effects**. Notice in the **Fill Effects** dialog box that a transparency bar now exists for each color. Move both transparency bars to **100 percent**.
4. Click **OK** twice to close the dialog boxes and complete the formatting. The shape now should be entirely invisible (assuming you also removed the line).

Working with invisible shapes, not surprisingly, can be a bit tricky considering they disappear when deselected. One technique for quickly finding invisible shapes on a slide is to click and drag across the slide to form the selection net described previously, thereby displaying the selection handles of all existing invisible shapes on the slide.

5.12 Filling AutoShapes with Texture

In addition to color **Fill**, shapes can be filled with **Texture** to provide more visual interest. **Texture Fill** often results in attractive, professional-looking **Buttons** for navigation.

1. Start from scratch by creating a new shape.
2. Double click the shape to open the **Format AutoShape** dialog box.
3. Click the **Color and Lines** tab.
4. Click the **Fill Color** bar to open the color palette.
5. Select **Fill Effects**.
6. On the **Fill Effects** dialog box, click the **Texture** tab, select a desired texture, and click **OK** twice.

Figure 5.21

5.13 Filling AutoShapes with Pictures

Filling shapes with pictures opens up all kinds of creative possibilities. Doing so can result in very attractive buttons and can be highly useful in certain applications of PowerPoint animation. You can choose to force the picture within the dimensions of the shape, or keep the picture in its original form and let it show through the shape unaltered (see TIP).

1. Create a new shape.
2. Double click the shape to open the **Format AutoShape** dialog box.
3. Click the **Color and Lines** tab.
4. Click in the **Fill Color** bar and select **Fill Effects**.
5. In the **Fill Effects** dialog box, click the **Picture** tab. Click the **Select Picture** button and navigate to where a picture is stored in your computer.
6. Double click the picture to insert it as a background in your AutoShape. Click **OK** twice to complete.

TIP

Leaving the **Lock Picture Aspect Ratio** unchecked in the Fill Effects dialog box squeezes a picture into shape boundaries and can result in the picture being distorted. If you place a check mark in this option, the picture dimensions will not distort but the entire picture may not be visible, depending upon the picture size compared with shape dimensions. If the picture must exactly fill the shape without distortion, make sure the shape and picture have identical dimensions.

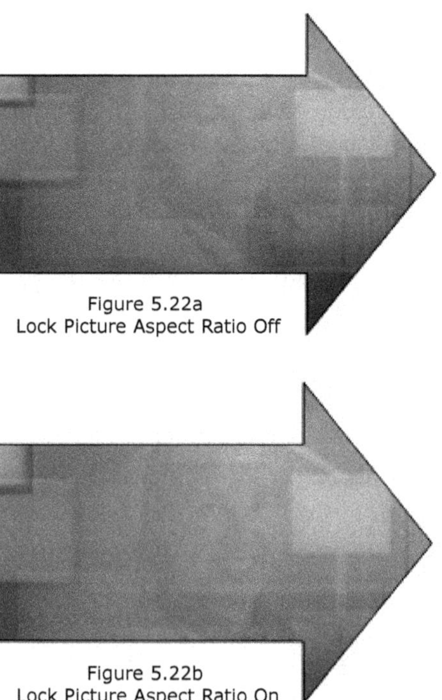

Figure 5.22a
Lock Picture Aspect Ratio Off

Figure 5.22b
Lock Picture Aspect Ratio On

5.14 Adding Text to AutoShapes

A well-formatted AutoShape that contains text makes a perfect building block for navigation. When used for this purpose, we call it a **button**. In the instructions below, you build from what we have done so far and create a button that can be part of any number of navigation styles. In effect, this single button will serve as a master (pattern) for creating additional identical buttons, all of which together eventually make up a Navigation Element.

1. Make your red and black shape fully visible again, or create another shape like it by adding similar Fill Effects.
2. Adding text to a shape is easy. Select the shape and type **Slide 1**.
3. Notice the text you entered is black and, therefore, barely visible. Change the text to white by selecting the text, and then clicking the arrow next to the **Font Color** icon on the **Drawing** toolbar.

Figure 5.23

4. Choose **white** from the color options that appear. The text in the shape turns white.
5. Make any additional desired changes to the text, such as making it **Bold** or changing the alignment.
6. For horizontal alignment, use the **Align Left**, **Center**, or **Align Right** icon on the **Formatting** toolbar.

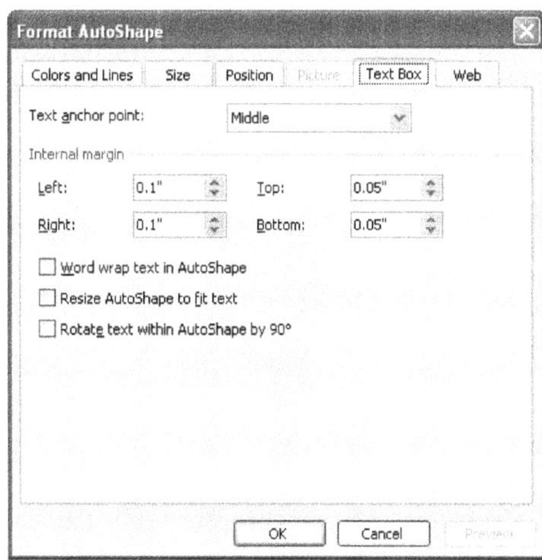

Figure 5.24

7. For vertical alignment, double click the shape to open the **Format AutoShape** dialog box. Click the **Text Box** tab. Make desired adjustments to the **Text anchor point** and **Internal margin**. Notice by default that the **Text anchor point** is set to **Middle**. When the shape is large and contains a lot of text, it's a good idea to get in the habit of setting the **Text anchor point** to **Top**. This is especially true if using AutoShapes as text boxes across multiple slides. By anchoring text at the top of the shapes, it will not appear to jump up and down when moving between slides.
8. Also notice you can have text wrap automatically within a shape by selecting the **Word wrap text in AutoShape** check box. If you do not select this box, text will spill out beyond the shape's borders and continue in a straight line.
9. Click **OK** to close the dialog box when finished.

Take a moment to notice that adding text to the shape changes its characteristics. The shape now has two selection modes instead of just one. You can select either the text or the shape. This distinction becomes very important later when working with hyperlinks.

Clicking or selecting text places you in **text edit mode**. When in this mode, either the text is highlighted or there is a blinking cursor in the text. Another way to recognize this selection state is that the shape's selection handle boundary appears as slashed lines (Figure 5.25).

Figure 5.25

Clicking the shape somewhere away from the text (toward the outer border) places you in **shape edit mode**, where the shape is directly selected instead of the text. In this mode the shape's selection handle boundary appears as tiny dots (Figure 5.26).

Figure 5.26

Establish a habit right away of noticing which selection mode is active at any given moment. Unless specifically making changes to the text, you normally will want the shape—not the text—selected, ESPECIALLY when hyperlinking.

5.15 Changing Shape Characteristics

Some AutoShape categories, such as **Basic Shapes**, **Block Arrows**, and **Stars and Banners**, allow adjustment of shape characteristics, including the amount of curvature, head size, point extension, and other aspects that affect appearance. For example, a **Rounded Rectangle** can be adjusted to have a very slight round on the corners or have a fully semicircular round.

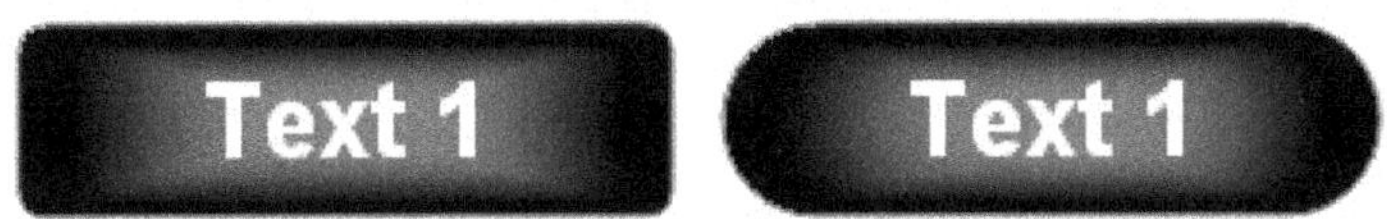

Figure 5.27

1. Select your **Rounded Rectangle** shape and notice the small yellow diamond that appears along with the shape's selection handles.
2. Click and drag this yellow diamond to change the curvature of the rectangle's corners.
3. Some shapes display more than one yellow diamond when selected. Anytime you see this, it means this shape is multiadjustable. **Arrows** are an example because both the thickness of the body and the width of the arrowhead are adjustable. Make an **Arrow** shape and experiment with its adjustment options.

5.16 Changing to a Different Shape

Perhaps you create a shape, with all the desired formatting and characteristics, and then change your mind about the particular shape chosen. Rather than starting over, simply change the existing shape to a different shape. Few PowerPoint users know about this functionality because finding it is not obvious. The menu you need is on the **Drawing** toolbar within the category labeled **Draw**. Do the following to change your **Rounded Rectangle** to a **Bevel** shape:

1. Select your **Rounded Rectangle** and click **Draw** on the **Drawing** toolbar.

Figure 5.28

2. From the menu that appears, select **Change AutoShape**, and then hold your cursor over the **Basic Shapes** category (Reference Figure 5.29).
3. Choose the **Bevel** option. This particular shape, by the way, is a good choice for making navigation Buttons.

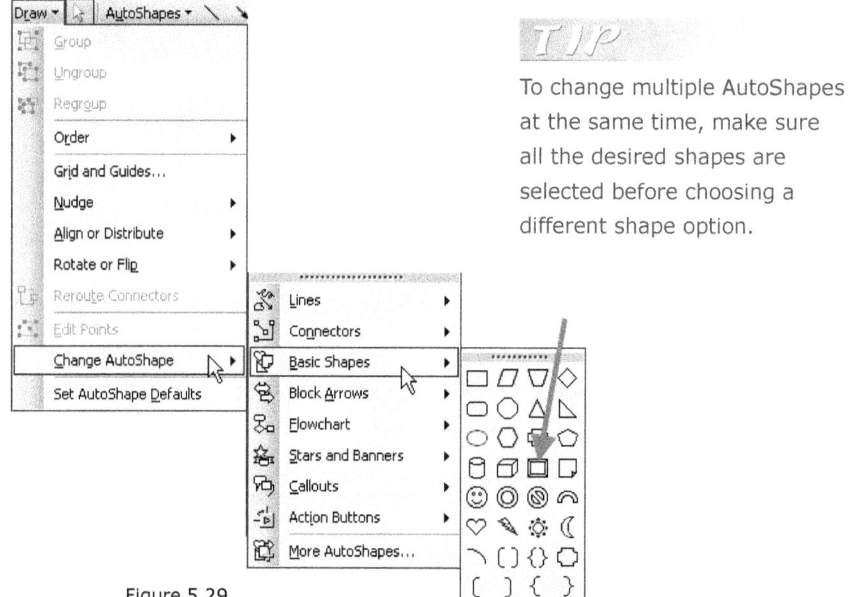

Figure 5.29

TIP

To change multiple AutoShapes at the same time, make sure all the desired shapes are selected before choosing a different shape option.

5.17 Copying and Pasting AutoShapes

Copying and pasting elements on the slide pane is critical to efficiently building Presentation Networks. Wherever possible, duplicate items rather than starting from scratch. For example, you might wish to have what amounts to the same hyperlinked shape available on hundreds of slides. Rather than creating the shape and link for each slide, copy the linked shape from an existing slide and paste it onto others. There are some important considerations to keep in mind when pasting links but, in general, copying and pasting is the way to go.

One of PowerPoint's wonderful features is that it respects original positioning when pasting. If you want a shape to appear in the bottom right corner of every slide in a show, copy a shape that is in that position, and then paste it onto remaining slides. The duplicate will appear in exactly the same place on every slide as it appeared on the original, even if pasted onto slides in other shows. The only exception is when a shape is duplicated on top of itself, on the same slide. The duplicate is pasted but PowerPoint offsets the copy slightly, vertically and horizontally, so that you can still see the original.

You can copy multiple elements at the same time if they are selected before the copy operation.

Shapes add very little to file size of a PowerPoint show. Don't worry about having many shapes or many copies of shapes. The number of shapes has minimal impact on performance. Also realize that PowerPoint, unlike some software, does not have any kind of functionality resembling a library object. With library objects, one can create a desired object and apply it throughout a document. One can also change an original object, which then cascades the changes through all applied instances. But in PowerPoint, there is no way to change one shape and have the change cascade through all copied/pasted shapes.

Four copy and paste methods are given below. We use the last two most frequently because they are the fastest, but try all four to make several copies of your red and black shape.

1. Right click the shape and select **Copy** on the shortcut menu. Then right click again anywhere on the slide pane and repeatedly select **Paste**. Notice the copies overlap and line up on an angle.

2. With the shape selected, from the **Edit** menu select **Copy** and then **Paste**.
3. With the shape selected, hold down the **Ctrl** key and type the letter **C**. Then hold down the **Ctrl** key and type the letter **V**.
4. The fastest way to copy a shape and place it anywhere on the slide pane is to hold down the **Ctrl** key while left clicking and dragging the shape. To constrain this copy method to a straight line, either horizontally or vertically, hold down both the **Ctrl** AND **Shift** keys while clicking and dragging.

Figure 5.30

Copying and pasting a shape is a quick way to create Navigation Elements. By making one shape first, and then copying/pasting it, you will save considerable time. In fact, we have found that learners who pursue such efficiency strategies are more likely to succeed with a Relational Presentation approach. The TIPs scattered throughout these and upcoming pages highlight such strategies. Try them all and learn to work efficiently. These suggestions have been compiled through years of experience and lessons learned, across thousands of designers and presenters.

5.18 Applying the Format Painter

A fast way of providing uniform formatting across multiple shapes is to use a clever tool called the **Format Painter**, located on the **Standard** toolbar. The Format Painter gives you the ability to copy and paste only the formatting associated with a shape, rather than the entire shape itself. Applying the Format Painter affects a shape's fill, line, and text characteristics, such as font and font color.

Figure 5.31

Let's say, for example, you already have a group of shapes created, positioned, and linked. Then you decide a red and black Fill Effect is not what you want after all, and a Texture Fill is more appropriate. In this case, copying and pasting entire shapes probably is not the most efficient way of making the change. Instead, reformat the existing shapes using the Format Painter.

The Format Painter looks like a paint brush. Notice that the tool appears dimmed ("grayed out") in the toolbar screenshot displayed above (Reference Figure 5.31), meaning the tool is unavailable. The tool will appear unavailable until you select a shape that is to be used as the tool's formatting source; then it becomes active.

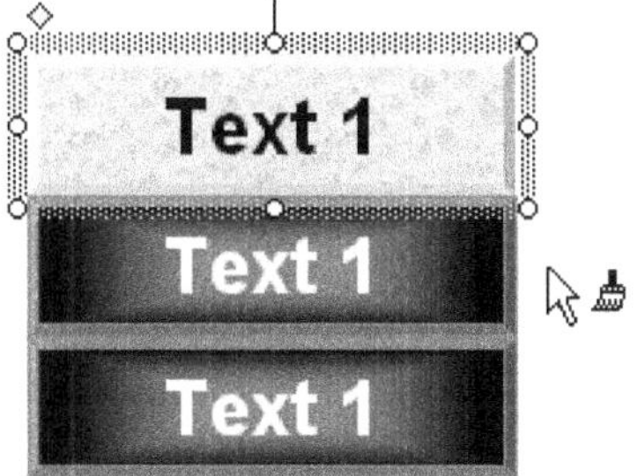

Figure 5.32

1. The **Format Painter** copies formatting. So the first step is to find formatting you want to copy, or create that formatting. Start by making a formatting change to one of your **Bevel** shapes, such as adding the **Texture Fill** shown.
2. Make sure this newly formatted AutoShape is selected, and then click the **Format Painter** icon on the **Standard** toolbar. The cursor displays a paint brush.

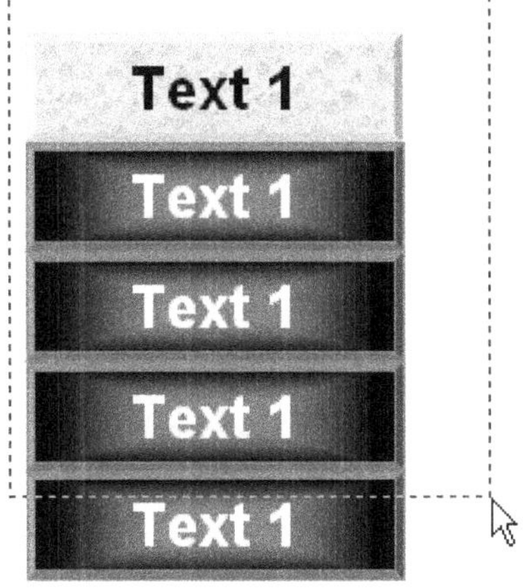

Figure 5.33

3. Click another AutoShape. That shape immediately takes on the formatting of the source AutoShape.
4. If you wish to format multiple shapes at the same time, repeat the above procedure but begin by double clicking rather than single clicking the Format Painter. Doing so places it in "sticky mode," meaning it stays selected, allowing multiple shapes to be clicked. Sticky mode remains active until you again click the Format Painter icon. Practice now.
5. A related method is to click the Format Painter, and then click and drag on the slide pane, beginning outside the shapes and surrounding them with the dotted-line selection box that forms. Anything contained within the borders of the selection box will be reformatted when you release the mouse button (Figure 5.33).

5.19 Alignment Using the Draw Menu

Navigation components in Relational Presentation typically are made up of groups of shapes or pictures that are all aligned and evenly distributed, vertically or horizontally. Perhaps your shapes are not neatly organized initially. Aligning and distributing manually by moving individual shapes one at a time is possible, but there is a faster way. First we'll consider alignment:

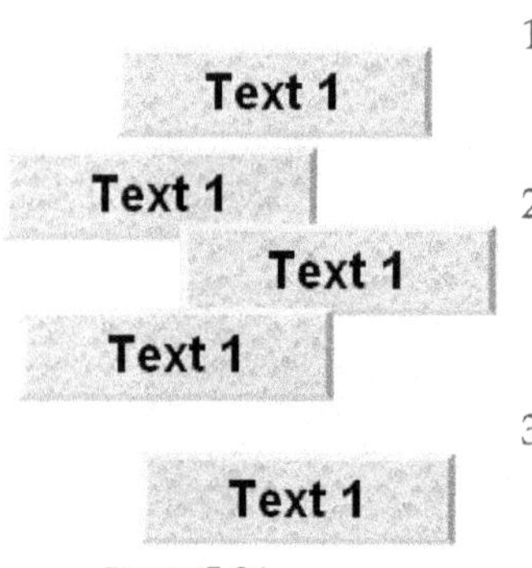

Figure 5.34

1. Move your shapes around so that they are randomly placed (out of alignment and unevenly distributed).
2. To align multiple shapes, either horizontally or vertically, you must select all the shapes to be aligned, and then click **Draw** on the **Drawing** toolbar.
3. From the menu that appears, select **Align or Distribute**, and then select one of the alignment options available. In this case we want to align the shapes on their left sides, so choose **Align Left**. The shapes line up vertically.

4. By default, shapes are aligned relative to one another. Another option is to align the shapes relative to the **top**, **center**, **bottom**, **right** or **left** side of the slide. To do so, select the **Relative to Slide** option before selecting one of the alignment choices. Uncheck this option to return to the default alignment method.

5.20 Alignment Using Guides

Another way of aligning shapes makes use of PowerPoint's **Guide** feature. A guide is a nonprinting, nonprojecting line (either vertical or horizontal) that is visible only when the slide show is in edit mode and only if you turn the guide feature on (it is off by default). This line acts like a magnet if you move a shape within its vicinity, snapping the shape to itself. Such functionality comes in very handy, especially if you have shapes on multiple slides and want each shape to be in exactly the same place on each slide.

1. Turn guides on by clicking the **View** menu and selecting **Grid and Guides**. Select the **Display drawing guides on screen** check box.
2. Click **OK**. A horizontal guide and vertical guide initially appear at the center of the slide, like a crosshair. Experiment with moving your shapes next to these guides.
3. The positioning of a guide can be changed by holding your cursor exactly over it, and then clicking and dragging it sideways (vertical guide) or up and down (horizontal guide). Note that you must click EXACTLY on the guide to select it.
4. You also can create up to four additional guides (either vertical or horizontal) by holding down the **Ctrl** key while clicking and dragging the guides. Keep in mind that guide positioning and configuration are specific to individual slide shows and are saved along with the show. If you open a different slide show, guides are displayed in their default positions, unless you previously changed them and saved the show.

5.21 Distributing AutoShapes

After shapes are aligned, they may also need to be distributed. Distribution refers to placing an equal amount of spacing between all the shapes, either vertically or horizontally. When dealing with a small number of shapes, manual distribution using arrow keys on the keyboard is reasonably easy, but the automated process available on the **Drawing** toolbar may be faster and more accurate. This functionality is located in the same area where the alignment options are found.

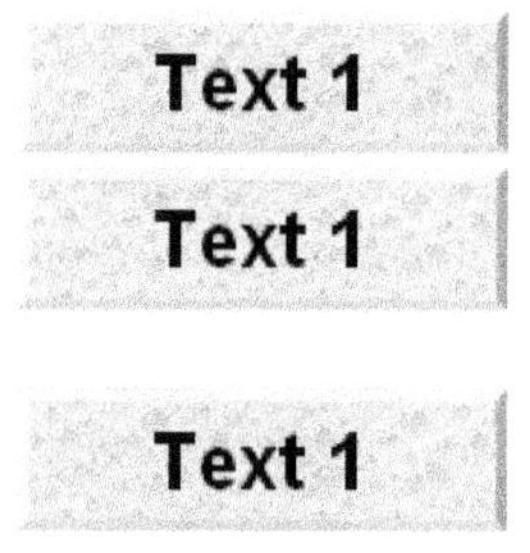

Figure 5.35a: Non-Distributed

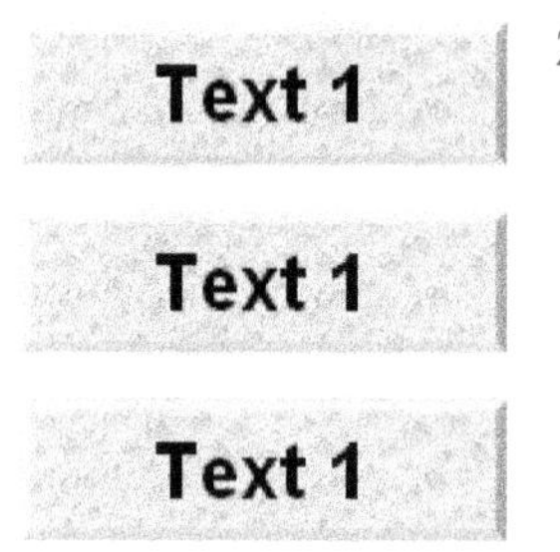

Figure 5.35b: Distributed

1. From the menu that appears, select **Align or Distribute**, and then select one of the distribution options available. Note: You MUST have at least three shapes selected; otherwise, the distribution options will be dimmed and unavailable. This makes sense, if you think about it: There must be at least three shapes in order for two or more spaces to exist so that spaces can be compared.
2. If distributing vertically, the function looks at the position of the top shape compared with the position of the bottom shape, and evenly spaces other selected shapes in between. Similarly, if distributing horizontally, the function looks at the position of the left shape compared with the position of the right shape, and evenly spaces other selected shapes in between.
3. After distributing your shapes, practice moving either the top or bottom shape (or left or right shape) and then redistributing the collection. Use this method to make fine adjustments to the spacing between Navigation Elements in a column or row.
4. Distributing more than one column or row at a time usually produces unsatisfactory results. Therefore, distribute only one column or row at a time. The same is true, by the way, when aligning AutoShapes.

5.22 Changing Stacking Order

AutoShapes can be stacked on top of each other like pancakes. Think of each shape as existing on its own transparent layer. A shape on top of the pile covers shapes below. This positioning is known as **Stacking Order**. Frequently, you may find yourself wanting to change this order and bring a shape on top of, or behind, another. Changing a shape's stacking order moves it higher or lower in the pile.

Although we have not yet discussed pictures, realize pictures have a stacking order also. In fact, the same stacking order functionality applies equally to shapes and pictures. In other words, you can bring a picture on top of a shape or vice versa. Note that this is NOT true of some other Microsoft Office applications, such as Word; pictures and shapes are treated differently and do not always have the same amount of flexibility as in PowerPoint. The fact that PowerPoint does treat pictures and shapes the same is very good news for relational designers. It greatly magnifies design possibilities.

TIP

If selecting a shape to change its stacking order is difficult because other shapes cover it, try selecting any shape and then pressing the **Tab** key. The **Tab** key will progressively cycle through the **Stacking Order**, just like form fields on a Web site. When the shape you want is selected, right click exactly on one of its selection handles to open the shortcut menu for changing **Stacking Order**.

By default, any new shape or picture added to the slide automatically goes on top of the stack. In some cases this may be the desired effect, but often the new arrival's position belongs behind already existing shapes or pictures. For example, you may decide to place a decorative background behind Navigation Elements or content on a slide. In this case, you must send the new shape to the back of the stacking order.

More than one change of stacking order may be necessary as well, such as sending one item to the back, and then bringing other items to the front. Stacking order becomes particularly important (and more challenging) when dealing with transparent or semitransparent shapes. Make sure transparent shapes do not unintentionally cover hyperlinked objects because the links then will be unavailable. Always bring linked objects to the top of the stacking order.

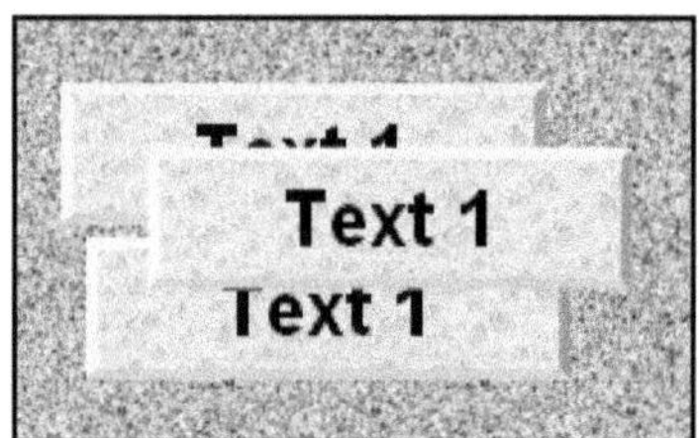

Figure 5.36

1. Move your shapes around so that several overlap each other.
2. Change a shape's position in the stack by right clicking it and choosing **Order** from the shortcut menu.
3. Four reordering options are available. As a general rule, the **Send to Back** and **Bring to Front** options are the most useful.
4. Practice reordering your shapes, and then practice adding a decorative background by placing an additional shape behind the originals and formatting it with Texture Fill. If necessary, perform more than one reordering operation.

5.23 Grouping AutoShapes

Multiple shapes can be locked to each other so that they behave as a single entity called a **group**. Doing so makes the process of rearranging complex collections of shapes on a slide easier and can be useful in certain animation applications. With rare exception, we never group shapes used for navigation. Grouped shapes are more difficult to hyperlink and grouping adds no tangible benefit in this case.

1. To group shapes, select the desired shapes, and then right click one of them. Make sure to right click inside one of the selected shapes; otherwise, you will inadvertently deselect all.
2. From the menu that appears, choose **Grouping/Group**.
3. To ungroup the shapes, repeat the process and choose **Grouping/Ungroup**.
4. Practice grouping and ungrouping your shapes.

5.24 Rotating AutoShapes

AutoShapes in a Relational Presentation context normally are not rotated, but occasionally doing so can provide a nice decorative accent to side design. A case in point is when shapes with partial transparency are used to create lighting effects.

There are two main ways to rotate an AutoShape. Experiment with both methods:

Figure 5.37

1. Click a shape to select it. Move your mouse cursor over the small green circle that appears with the shape's selection handles (white circles). Clicking and dragging near this green circle turns the shape.
2. Double click the shape to open the **Format AutoShape** dialog box. Click the **Size** tab. Enter a rotation angle value in the **Rotation** box. Click **OK**.

Figure 5.38

An example of rotation is the *star effect* shown at right. This effect was created by overlaying two rectangular AutoShapes and rotating them somewhat in relation to each other, and in relation to the text. The design technique uses shapes that have a **white/white, Two-Color Fill Effect** set at **From Center**, with the outer color taken to **100 percent** transparency. Notice also that one of the semi-transparent shapes, the one on top, is smaller.

5.25 Creating Lighting Effects

Transparency in AutoShapes can be used to create numerous useful lighting effects. The previous *star effect* is one of them. The slide shown in Figure 5.39 has a subtle glow in the upper right corner, as though ambient light is being thrown across the background. This particular example is made by using an oval shape that has a **white/white, Two-Color Fill Effect** set at **From Center**, with the outer color taken to **100 percent** transparency and the inner color set at about **70 percent** transparency.

As you probably can guess, most of the oval is positioned off the slide pane in the gray area. Only a small piece of it overlaps the visible area. Experiment with creating the effect shown here.

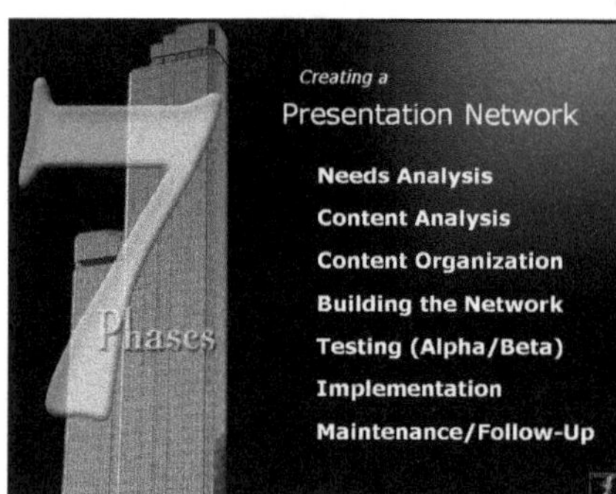

Figure 5.39

Use **Two-Color Fill Effects** by taking one of the colors up to **100 percent** transparency and adjusting the other color's transparency as well.
Overlap multiple semitransparent shapes of this kind to produce even more interesting and complex effects.

3. Make overlapped shapes different colors. The combination of different colors, different shapes, different rotations, and different transparency levels leads to practically endless combinations. Be creative.

5.26 Adding Shadow to Text

Adding shadow to text in PowerPoint helps the text pop out from the background and is especially important if the background is busy or if the text color does not strongly contrast with part or all of the background. One method (NOT RECOMMENDED) for adding shadow to text is to right click the text, select **Font** from the menu options, and then select the **Shadow** check box. This method works but is limited and allows no adjustment to shadow characteristics. A better method is as follows:

Figure 5.40

1. Create a new AutoShape and type the word **Text**.
2. Increase the font size of the text to **120 pt**.
3. Make the font color **White**.
4. Click the shape to select it. Make sure to click the shape away from its text region so you are selecting the shape, NOT the text. If you see a cursor blinking in the text, click the shape again

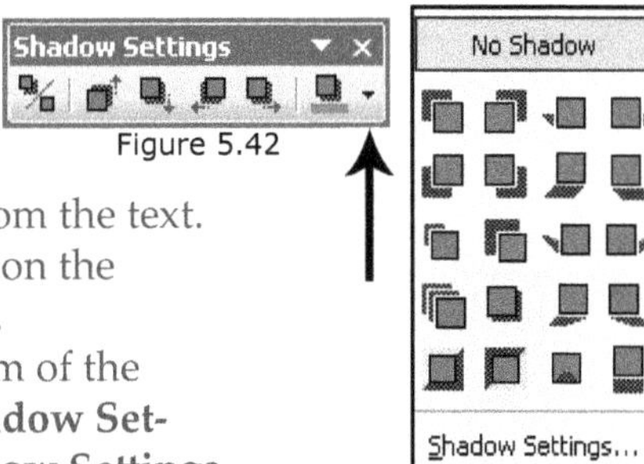

Figure 5.42

Figure 5.41

closer to its border—away from the text.

5. Click the **Shadow Style** icon on the **Drawing** menu (Figure 5.40).
6. Select the option at the bottom of the resulting menu that says **Shadow Settings** (Figure 5.41). The **Shadow Settings** toolbar appears (Figure 5.42).
7. On this toolbar, change the shadow color to black by clicking the arrow next to the **Shadow Color** icon and selecting the black square. This action adds a black shadow to your SHAPE.

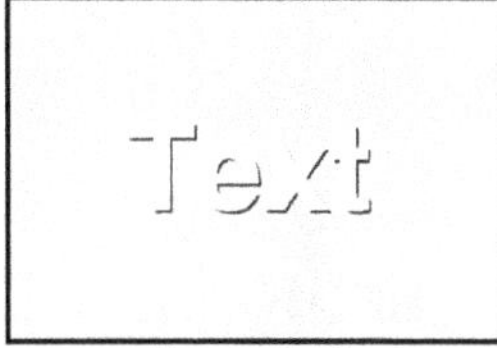

Figure 5.43

8. Now here is the trick. Technically, you want the shadow to be on the text rather than the shape. Therefore, double click the shape to open the **Format AutoShape** dialog box.
9. Click the **Line Color** bar and select **No Line**.
10. Click the **Fill Color** bar and select **No Fill**.
11. These two actions make the shape invisible, all except the text. Notice that the shadow now is applied to the text only.
12. Depending on the size of your text, you may wish to adjust the shadow in or out and up or down. Do so by using the nudge icons on the **Shadow Settings** toolbar (Figure 5.44).

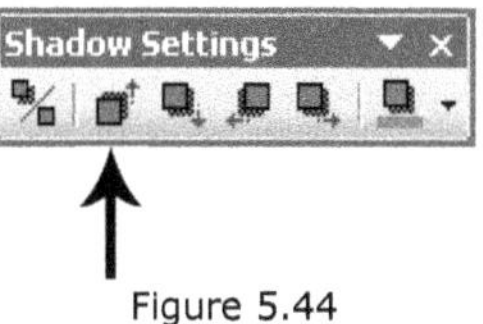

Figure 5.44

Recommendations: This technique allows adjustment to shadow characteristics, compared with putting shadow directly on the font. It works best when the text is large so that the shadow does not overpower the text. Also keep in mind this technique normally is reserved for text used as a label, such as the title of a slide or slide region. AutoShapes with no Fill should NOT be used for purposes of navigation (that is, contain a hyperlink). The reason is that when you place a hyperlink on an AutoShape that contains no Fill, and then copy and paste that shape, the hyperlink exists only on the border and text, and nowhere else in the shape. In other words, it does not exist where there is no Fill in the shape. Avoid this scenario by always leaving transparent Fill in hyperlinked AutoShapes—which means, of course, you cannot use the above technique when creating navigation.

"Digital presentation has to go this way. Visual media affects just about every area of our lives today. We must learn to use it dynamically in our communications."

John Hall, PhD,
Associate Director, Department of BioMedical Communications,
University of Arizona, USA

Chapter 6

Working with Pictures

96 dpi

6.1 The Roles of Pictures

Pictures in Relational Presentation either accentuate speakers' verbal communication or they *speak* on their own. Visual imagery enables expression of ideas with far more impact than is possible with words alone. While it is true an excellent storyteller can paint images in your mind with merely verbal expression, the quality and interpretation of such mental images varies from person to person. A better way to more predictably cement visual concepts is to be both a storyteller AND show meaningful pictures during talks. A relational approach takes this concept a step further by making sure this imagery is always available on demand.

Why do many speakers fail to take full advantage of picture-based presentation? In most cases, it's simply a matter of their never having made the effort to explore it. Even though PowerPoint greatly simplifies inclusion of rich media, especially pictures, the average presenter seems content to rely mostly on text.

In all fairness, there is another reason. Being an EFFECTIVE visual communicator doesn't just happen by accident and involves more than merely dropping random pictures onto slides. It requires knowledge, experimentation, practice, and skill. Graphical expression of thoughts, when done well, literally entails learning a new language where visuals serve as vocabulary.

Many people struggle here. Translating abstract concepts into meaningful imagery can be challenging. Presenters and designers alike frequently lack graphic design skills that otherwise could help produce pictures better customized to their needs. Furthermore, these individuals often do not know where to find appropriate pictures to help express ideas and may be confused by copyright issues once they do find them. This chapter touches on these issues and other important subjects that can assist your efforts in taking visual expression to a higher plateau.

As we move through upcoming topics, keep in mind Relational Presentation's two most important foundational pillars: *Flexibility* and *Visual Expression*. This chapter focuses mostly on developing the second component. Remember our goal is to connect *What We Say* with *What We Show*. For most of us, that means using a lot of pictures, maybe hundreds or even thousands. It's easier then you may suspect. Start thinking now about how some or most of your bullet points can be replaced or embellished by using pictures. Begin to develop *Visual Thinking*.

6.2 What Is a Picture?

Notice in the screenshot below that, ironically, we use visuals on slides to describe the process of including visuals on slides. At the same time, you will see that our messages don't always abandon the use of text altogether; they often supplement it with visual examples. Basically, the slide here contains four bullet points, but each point features a visually expressive element as well.

Figure 6.1

We begin our look at visual expression by exploring the basics of how PowerPoint handles pictures and what actually is meant by the term *picture*. PowerPoint treats pictures and AutoShapes the same in many respects. As a result, much of what is covered in the previous chapter applies almost identically to pictures. For example, you use the same methods to copy and paste pictures as you use to copy and paste AutoShapes. On the other hand, there are quite a few differences between pictures and AutoShapes. It is important for you to know these differences and to feel comfortable working with pictures in all respects before continuing to the next chapter.

PowerPoint has a rather broad definition for *picture*. In Relational Presentation, however, four major categories of visual imagery are applicable: clip art, photo, graphic, and screenshot.

Clip Art: Clip art is a type of image that can be inserted onto a PowerPoint slide. It usually has a *cartoonish* look and is composed of vector graphics (lines) rather than the tiny dots that make up bit-map images (what most people would call a photo). A majority of digital presenters use clip art in their slide shows, far more than the other three forms of imagery. We hope this book helps to reverse this trend and encourages designers to move away from clip art, replacing it with higher forms of visual expression. At the risk of stepping on toes, we adamantly discourage people from using clip art (ESPECIALLY animated clip art) in any form unless it is very well-designed and specifically tailored to a company's (institution's) purposes. Despite its prevalence of use, presentation experts generally concur clip art imagery gives slide shows a cheap and unprofessional appearance. We couldn't agree more and believe clip art contributes to the overall perception of presentations being produced by amateurs, like dining by candlelight with silver and linens, yet having dime store plastic flowers as the table's centerpiece. Include clip art if you must but more realistic imagery is almost always superior.

Photo: Our definition of a photo is any still image someone captures with a camera, usually—these days—a digital camera. Photos in digital format are composed of potentially millions of tiny dots and are called bit-map images. Bit-map images, when used in a presentation context, typically are (or should be) electronically compressed to reduce their file size.

Using photos in your messages is enormously important, particularly because of the significant role visual information plays in our everyday lives. At any rate, our brains crave rich, visual imagery. The more your presentation materials depict real, meaningful scenes people potentially can relate to as part of their own experiences, the better.

Graphic: We define a graphic as an image, perhaps originally based upon a photo, that has been digitally created, enhanced, or altered in some way. Notice the third image on the previous slide (Figure 6.1). It's the same photo of the light bulb but three changes are apparent. First, the overall picture was given a color adjustment. Then text was added on top and given its own special effects. Finally, the entire image was enhanced with a bevel on the outside edge, so that it has a three-dimensional appearance. This type of visual manipulation typically is accomplished using graphics editing software such as Adobe Photoshop.

It's a good idea, if you are serious about becoming a relational presenter or designer, to learn at least some basic graphic design skills. Otherwise, your creativity will be hampered. Having these skills, and thus being able to create your own customized graphics for slides, is valuable. It saves money and allows you to produce what is needed on the spot, the way you want it. Certainly one can get by without graphics skills, but knowing this aspect of visual communication will likely transform your entire approach. Photos and graphics often serve separate roles in Relational Presentation, so you will need both. Photos alone really are not enough.

Screenshot: One other type of image we find ourselves using often is the ever-humble screenshot. You may be surprised how helpful these images can be, and how versatile their use. A screenshot, in essence, is a photograph of whatever appears at any moment on your computer screen and is taken by your computer itself. It is whatever you see on your monitor, converted into a picture that can be inserted into PowerPoint. Screenshots are important to presenters in several ways. For instance, they provide a marvelous source for navigation because the presenter sees a preview of what the link will open.

Figure 6.2

Other Visual Elements: Certainly, other visual elements can appear on slides as well, such as graphs, diagrams, and tables. These kinds of visuals are important but are mentioned here only in passing because they typically are handled differently than pictures. The term *pictures*, as used throughout the rest of this book, refers specifically to the four categories: clip art, photo, graphic, and screenshot.

Figure 6.3

PowerPoint's Perspective: From PowerPoint's point of view, the different visual categories mean relatively little. Whether you are working with clip art, a photo, a graphic, or a screenshot, PowerPoint sees everything as just a picture. Inserting a picture refers to inserting any of the four image types.

Image format is far more important than image type. Format refers to the last three letters accompanying a picture's name. Typical image formats used in PowerPoint include **Jpg**, **Png**, **Bmp**, **Tif**, and **Gif**. In general, avoid using Bmp, Tif, and Gif formats. Insert only Jpg and Png images if at all possible because these formats use compression algorithms that substantially reduce file size, usually without a noticeable loss in image quality. Bmp and Tif files, on the other hand, are not compressed and tend to be very large compared with their counterparts. Gif files are compressed and usually have a small file size (they work fine in PowerPoint), but they tend to be low-quality because of the color restrictions associated with Gif format. Jpgs usually have the highest quality-to-file-size ratio and should be your default choice.

Figure 6.4

Png-formatted images tend to have a larger file size than Jpgs but offer the powerful advantage of allowing you to save an image with transparency. As an example, notice the model in Figure 6.4. Her image has no background—that is, the background in her image is transparent, allowing the slide's background imagery to show through around her. To create this effect, the background of the original photo (below on a black slide background) was erased in Photoshop and the graphic saved in Png format. The resultant image can be inserted onto any slide in PowerPoint and transparency will be retained.

Figure 6.5

The technique for removing the background was fairly simple. The photo was opened in Photoshop and a filter called **Extract** applied to remove the extra white behind the model. The process required several steps and took perhaps 10 minutes total, but the

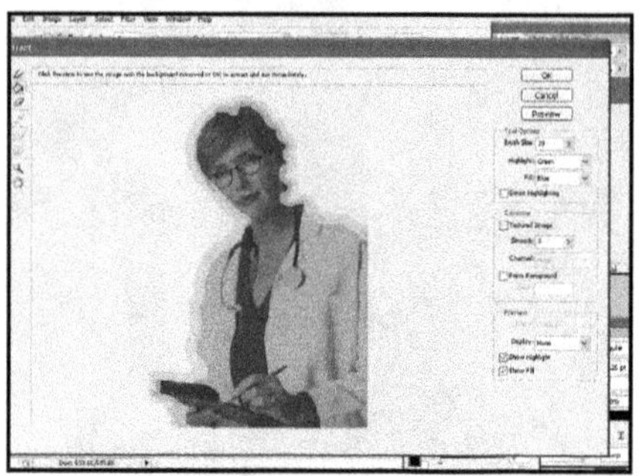

Figure 6.6

final outcome is a professional looking graphic that sets a slide apart from those displaying standard photos. Knowing graphic design skills can enable you, too, to use such techniques.

We use transparency all the time. It adds a whole new dimension to the quality of graphics. It's important to note, however, that transparency does come with a price: The file size of images containing transparency can be three or four times larger than their standard Jpg cousins. This difference normally is not a problem except in cases where your shows hold a large number of images. To keep file size of PowerPoint shows as small as possible, we save images in Png format only when transparency is required and, otherwise, stay with Jpg format. Again, consider enhancing your graphic design skills.

A side note to readers who consider themselves, well, technically challenged: This book does, at times, focus on technical details associated with digital presentation. A certain amount of such focus is necessary to give you bearings on what is going on behind the scenes in your network. Realize, however, that this book does not cover media creation skills to any great depth. For that subject matter, a separate book will be needed and we encourage you to explore the last chapter of this book for ways of expanding your experience with media creation. Eventually you may want to go beyond this text and experiment with graphics, audio, video, and animations. What you will see in this chapter and beyond is just the tip of much larger potential waiting for you to discover.

6.4 Picture Size, File Size, and Resolution

Three characteristics of digital pictures—*physical size, file size,* and *resolution*—are related to each other and cause much confusion. How does one affect the other and what do the terms actually mean?

The **physical dimensions** of a picture denote how big the picture will be (physically) if printed or placed on a PowerPoint slide. PowerPoint's slide pane area is set by default to hold pictures that are 10 inches wide and 7.5 inches tall (a 4-to-3 ratio). If you create an image in a graphics program and give it dimensions of 10 inches by 7.5 inches, it will completely and exactly fill the slide pane when projected. So how big is a 10-by-7.5 (full-screen) picture in terms of **file size** (the amount of space it requires on a disk or thumb drive)? Well, that answer depends on the picture's **resolution**, what can be thought of as the image's quality.

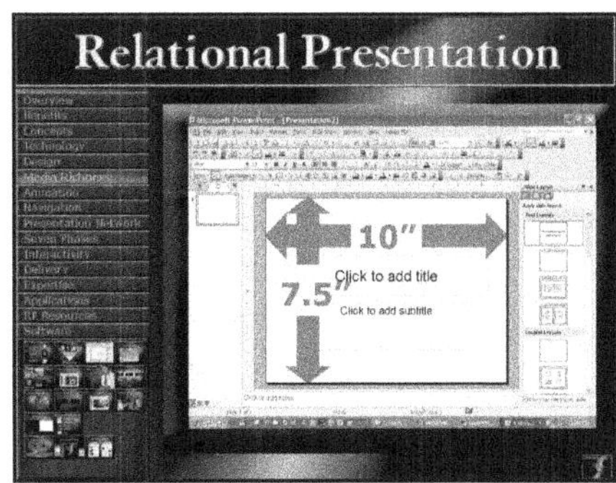

Figure 6.7

Digital photos, graphics, and screenshots are made up of tiny colored dots (known as pixels). At a distance, these dots are undetectable. Viewed at higher magnification, however, seemingly smooth pictures show the individual dots as distinct squares of color. The more dots a picture contains, the smaller these dots seem to be, and pixel detection is less likely when the picture is magnified. Therefore, the more dots there are in an image, the higher the resolution and quality will be. Dots per inch (dpi) is a standard measurement denoting how crisp an image will appear in print or when projected through Powerpoint.

In the blown up screenshot at right (Figure 6.8), we zoomed in on the R in the Relational Presentation banner shown in Figure 6.7. The zoom amount is 1,600 percent, or 16 times closer than print size. The red rectangle represents a half inch of physical space. At this magnification, notice the lettering becomes jagged; individual squares making up the lettering become visible. These squares are the dots (pixels).

Figure 6.8

Knowing this image has a resolution of 96 dpi, we can guess the letter contains approximately 48 pixels from one side to the other. If, on the other hand, this image had a resolution of 200 dpi, the letter's physical size still would be approximately a half inch wide, but now would contain roughly 100 dots from one side to the other. Squeezing double the number of squares into the same linear space means the squares must be smaller, resulting in finer variations of color between squares and a sharper image. At the same time, recognize that having more squares translates into exponentially more information the computer must keep track of, resulting in larger file size (storage on disk) for the image. Computer graphics are always a balance between file size and quality.

So, if a picture has low resolution, it will have a smaller file size compared with the same picture with a higher resolution. In either case, the physical size might remain exactly the same. Both the low-resolution and high-resolution picture will print out at the same size, but the low-resolution image may look blurry, whereas the high-resolution image will be sharp and clear.

What if you wish to decrease the file size of the picture but don't want to sacrifice any quality? That is you don't want to lower the resolution. In that case, the only option is to decrease the physical size of how the picture will print or display.

Are you beginning to notice a pattern? If we keep one of the variables constant and change another, the third variable will change accordingly—either up or down. Thus, if you keep the physical dimensions constant and lower the resolution, file size will go down. If you want the file size to remain constant but want a higher quality display (higher resolution), the picture must decrease in physical size.

At this point you may be wondering what resolution is most appropriate for images inserted in PowerPoint. Not many PowerPoint users know the answer. Most people add pictures that are much larger, in terms of file size, than needed. However, there are rules of thumb for deciding the optimal combination of these three variables. Consider the following dpi standards.

Graphics that are intended for professional paper printing should be around 300 dpi. Web designers work with graphics at 72 dpi. What about images for presentation? PowerPoint graphics actually should be no larger than 96 dpi. A little-known fact is that PowerPoint has a 96-dpi cutoff. This means you can, if desired, insert visuals that have a resolution higher than 96 dpi. Doing so, however, only increases the slide show's file size without providing any additional visual benefit. In PowerPoint, a 96-dpi picture will look just as good as the same picture at 300 dpi, yet the file size difference between the two will be substantial. In a large presentation containing many pictures, this difference might be a serious issue. Therefore, a good practice is to take pictures down to 96 dpi before bringing them into your slide shows. This resolution is considered *optimized*, or ideally suited for PowerPoint. Resolutions considerably less than 96 dpi produce displays that look blurry, especially when projected on a large screen.

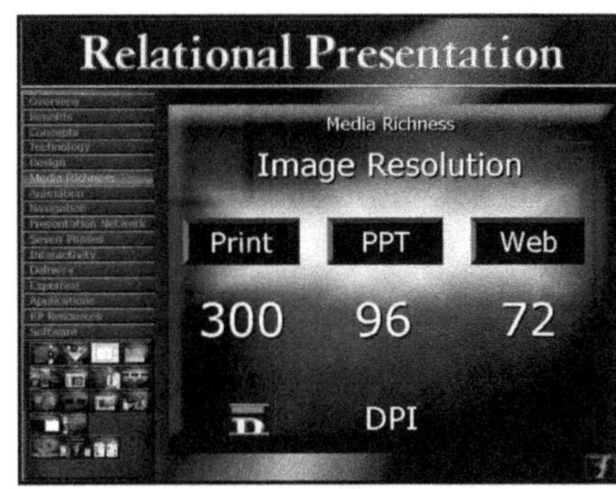

Figure 6.9

Full-screen Jpg images properly optimized for PowerPoint should fall in the file-size range of 100 to 150 kilobytes. If your images are 200 kilobytes or more, probably the resolution is unnecessarily high or physical size too large. Consider decreasing either with graphics editing software or take advantage of PowerPoint's compression feature (discussed later in this chapter).

That said, most of the time there is little need to be overly concerned with picture file size. Modern computers handle large PowerPoint files very well. If your shows have only a few pictures, picture file size or resolution is of little concern. Some of our slide shows approach 30 megabytes and still work fine. However, file size can become an important issue when your shows contain many pictures, in particular if using hyperlinks to open these shows. File size also adds up over time across your Presentation Network, with each individual show contributing. We like to keep our core network (the collection of regularly used shows) less than 2 gigabytes so that we can easily back it up on a memory stick in case we have to present from someone else's computer. Considering the Aspire network contains many thousands of slides, we surely do monitor file size.

Our recommendation to you, therefore, is simply to use common sense when adding pictures. Don't be overly concerned about the resolution of every picture but, for the most part, get in the habit of optimizing images.

Having spelled out all the above parameters, a vital clarification is in order. Everything said so far in this chapter about image **file size, physical size**, and **resolution** is true from the perspective of graphics editing software such as Photoshop. PowerPoint, to some extent, operates according to different rules. Relationships between the variables *seem* to behave differently. For example, one might reasonably expect that decreasing the physical size of a picture on a slide will correspondingly decrease that picture's file size and, therefore, decrease the overall file size of the presentation, right? Not true.

Although this rule universally applies to graphics software, downsizing an image in PowerPoint only gives the appearance the image is becoming smaller. No change is made to the actual image itself and, therefore, file size does not change. Likewise, making multiple copies of the same image once it's inserted does not increase file size of the presentation by an appreciable amount. PowerPoint often tricks your eyes into thinking more or less is happening, when such is not really the case.

6.5 Inserting Pictures

To place a picture on a PowerPoint slide, you must **Insert** the picture onto the slide pane. Pictures can be inserted in three ways. Experiment with all three:

TIP

You can insert more than one picture at a time onto a slide by selecting multiple pictures before clicking the **Insert** button.

1. On the **Insert** menu, select **Picture/From File** and search for a picture. Double click the picture to insert it or click it once, and then click the **Insert** button.
2. Click the **Insert Picture** icon on the **Drawing** toolbar (Figure 6.10). This method directly opens the **Insert Picture** dialog box (eliminating steps from the above procedure)

Figure 6.10

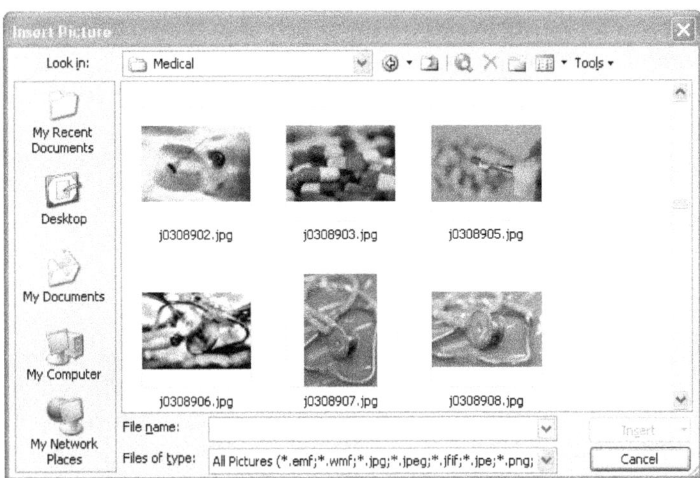

Figure 6.11

3. Open a window for **Windows Explorer** and another window for **PowerPoint**, side by side. Select one or more pictures in Windows Explorer and drag the picture(s) onto the slide pane in PowerPoint.

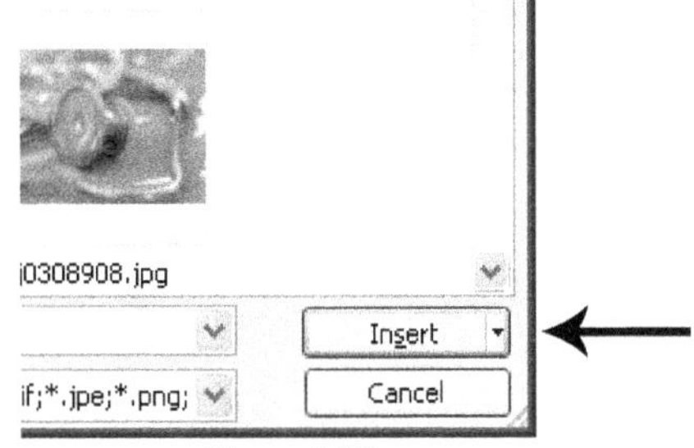

Figure 6.12

Notice on the **Insert Picture** dialog box that the **Insert** button has a small arrow next to it. This arrow allows you to select the option **Link to File**. DO NOT CONFUSE THIS *LINK* WITH A HYPERLINK. Furthermore, unless there is a specific reason to do so, DO NOT USE THIS OPTION. The **Link to File** option allows you to link to a picture's location on your computer, rather than actually inserting (embedding) it in your slide show. Selecting this option means the picture will look like it actually exists on your slide but, in reality, PowerPoint is only referencing it. Referencing a picture rather than inserting it is not a good idea.

Inserting pictures is better because you may wish to place a presentation on a memory stick, another computer, or make it downloadable from a Web site. Doing so when the pictures are not actually embedded means the pictures will not display unless you likewise physically transfer them to the stick, computer, or server as well. If the pictures are inserted, they become part of that particular slide show and are copied (transferred) along with the show. When using modern computers, especially if your images are properly optimized, the **Link to File** option is obsolete and should be avoided. By the way, if you drag and drop pictures onto a slide from Windows Explorer, they are automatically inserted rather than linked-to-file.

6.6 Resizing and Constraining Pictures

Adjusting picture size is a frequent part of relational design. We frequently decrease the size of pictures (or copies of pictures) until they appear as tiny thumbnails, usually about a half inch wide. These thumbnails then are used for navigation, providing a perfect link source to access other slides. Thumbnails give a presenter visual meaning, a preview of where the link will lead. Practice resizing your inserted pictures by first selecting one or more, and then using any of the following methods:

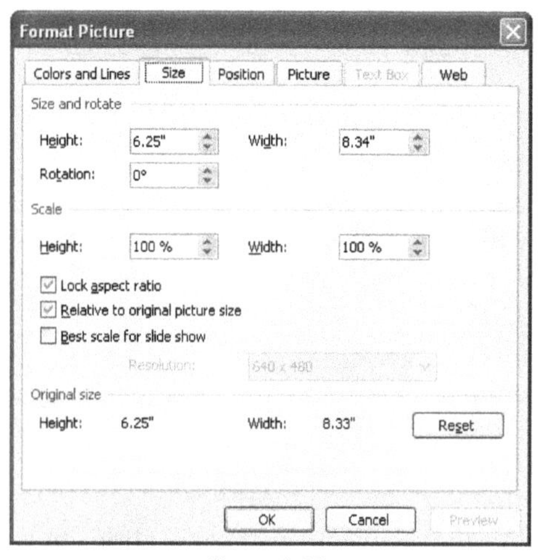

Figure 6.13

1. On the **Format** menu, select **Picture** to open the **Format Picture** dialog box. Then click the **Size** tab. Enter the desired dimensions.
2. A faster process is to double click a picture to directly open the **Format Picture** dialog box. Click the **Size** tab and enter the desired dimensions. All you need to enter is a number. PowerPoint assumes you mean inches and adds the inches symbol automatically.

3. Click and drag a picture's selection handles (the white circles). Note that dragging from a corner keeps the picture constrained, meaning its dimensions will scale proportionately and the picture will not distort. Dragging from either side, top, or bottom distorts the picture because resizing occurs only vertically or horizontally.
4. Select more than one picture and then drag the selection handles of one of the pictures. Notice the resizing action affects all selected pictures proportionately, at the same time.

By default, pictures scale proportionately when they are resized by dragging the corner handles or by entering a number in one of the **Format Picture** dialog box dimensions. You can change this characteristic by doing the following:

1. Double click a picture to open the **Format Picture** dialog box, if not already open.
2. Click the **Size** tab and uncheck the **Lock aspect ratio** check box.
3. Click **OK**. Now, dragging a corner selection handle allows free-form resizing.
4. You can manually constrain the proportions again, even with **Lock aspect ratio** unchecked, by holding down the **Shift** key while clicking and dragging a corner selection handle.

Thumbnails used for navigation are merely small pictures and often represent the link's destination. Navigation based on pictures is relatively easy to create, visually appealing, and incredibly helpful to a presenter. There are no set guidelines on how big or small to make navigation thumbnails, although for most applications we prefer the following guideline:

> Downsize one of your pictures to thumbnail-size. The standard we prefer for most thumbnails is 0.5 inch wide by 0.37 inch tall. This size seems large enough for a speaker to easily see the thumbnail's visual meaning, yet small enough not to unduly distract from slide content. Occasionally we make thumbnails 0.7 inch wide or more, depending

on the style of navigation desired. Thumbnails may be much larger indeed if they also provide a decorative effect. Experiment and decide your own preferences. Larger thumbnails are easier to click too.

6.7 Adding a Border to a Picture

We sometimes add a border to thumbnail pictures, so that they stand out somewhat from background graphics on slides.

1. To add a border, double click a picture to open the **Format Picture** dialog box and make sure the **Color and Lines** tab is selected.
2. Click the **Line Color** box (that contains the words "**No Fill**") to open the color palette, and then select a color—or select **More Colors** to specify a different color option.

6.8 Cropping Pictures

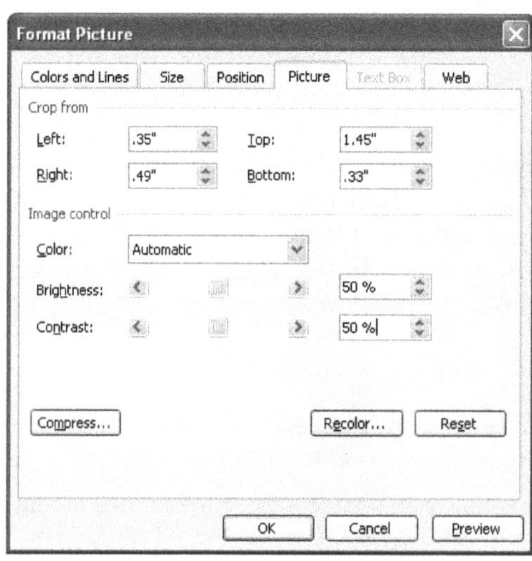

Figure 6.14

To remove unneeded or undesirable portions of images, they can be **cropped**. Cropping an image in PowerPoint, as with resizing, does not actually change the underlying image or in any way throw away pixel data. The cropped area instead is basically hidden from view. Cropping does not decrease file size of either the picture or the slide show that holds it.

To crop an image, use either of these two methods:

Method 1: Dimension Cropping

1. Double click a picture to open the **Format Picture** dialog box and make sure the **Picture** tab is selected.
2. Enter values in the **Crop From** boxes. Note that values can be to the hundredth of an inch, allowing fine adjustments.
3. If you decide later not to crop the picture or to modify the amount of cropping, simply open the **Format Picture** dialog box and click the **Reset** button to restore the original picture, or enter different values in the **Crop From** boxes.

Method 2: Manual Cropping

1. Select the picture to be cropped.
2. Click the **Crop** tool on the **Picture** toolbar.
3. Click and drag one of the black crop handles that appear around the image. Notice that this action crops the image in increments (jumps).
4. To crop with finer detail, hold down the **Alt** key while clicking and dragging one of the crop handles.
5. To undo cropping later, drag the crop handles back out again.

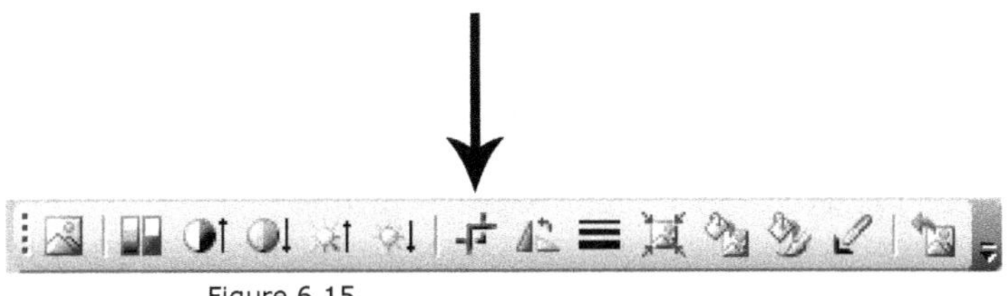

Figure 6.15

Figure 6.16

6.9 Compressing Pictures

Although it's better to decrease the file size of pictures before bringing them into PowerPoint, the **Compress** feature on the **Format Picture** dialog box can downsize picture resolution to **96 dpi,** either for one picture at a time or for all pictures in a slide show. A MAJOR caveat in using the Compress feature, however, is that shows should not be compressed more than a few times because repeated compression has the potential of corrupting the entire file, rendering it unusable. Always back up a file before using this feature.

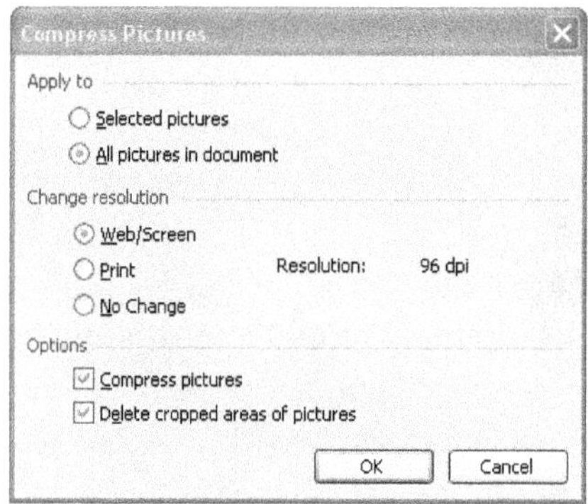

Figure 6.17

1. Double click a picture to open the **Format Picture** dialog box.
2. Click the **Compress** button. The **Compress Pictures** dialog box opens.
3. To decrease a picture's resolution to **96 dpi**, select the **Web/Screen** option.
4. Also decide whether the compression should be applied to this picture only or to all pictures in the show.
5. Finally, notice that you can delete the cropped area of a picture. Putting a check mark in this option DOES throw away the extra pixel data that was cropped. Compression throws away downsized pixel data no longer needed as well.

6.10 Moving Pictures

Pictures can be moved manually by dragging, by using the keyboard arrows, or by specifying the exact position. Practice moving a picture by all of the following:

1. Click and drag it.
2. Select the picture, and then press the keyboard **Arrow** keys.
3. Specify an exact position by double-clicking the picture to open

the **Format Picture** dialog box, clicking the **Position** tab, and typing the coordinates. Type **.5** in the **Horizontal** box and **.5** in the **Vertical** box. Click **OK** to close the dialog box. The picture moves to the upper left corner of the slide, a half inch from the top and left boundaries.

Holding down the **Ctrl** key while pressing an **Arrow** key moves the picture in smaller increments.

6.11 Flipping Pictures

Flipping pictures horizontally is useful in certain design situations. For example, you generally want lighting angles across multiple pictures to be similar. Observe the pictures in the image below. The sun angle is completely different in the two photos. If these two people were together in the same space, such lighting inconsistency would be physically impossible. Inconsistent lighting tends to cause a subconscious *something is wrong with this picture* feeling.

Simply flipping one of the pictures horizontally creates a more physically plausible environment, yet does not change the realism of the pictures at all in this case. Of course, one needs to be careful when flipping pictures. If the image has a clock, text, or anything else in the background that might appear clearly backwards when flipped, such a transformation is not a good idea.

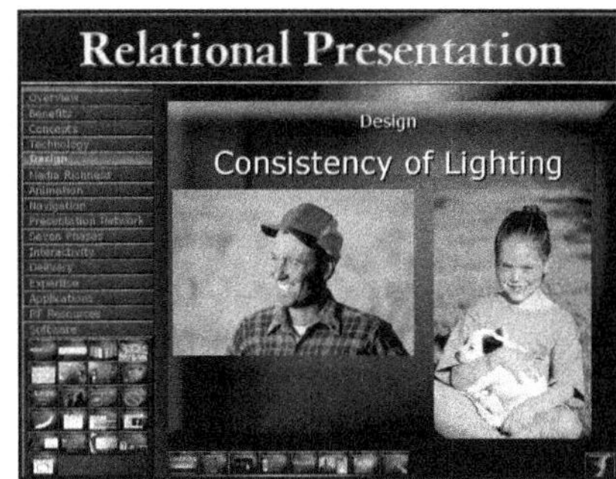

Figure 6.18a

Do the following to flip a picture horizontally:

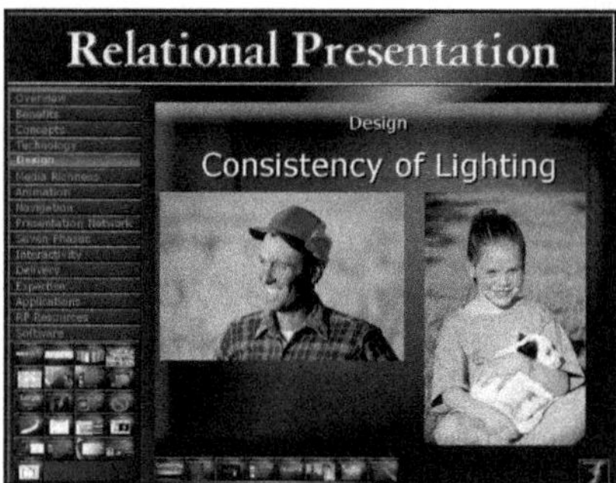

Figure 6.18b

1. Select the picture.
2. Click the **Draw** button on the **Drawing** toolbar.
3. From the menu, select **Rotate or Flip/Flip Horizontal**.

Flipping pictures vertically is also possible but rarely produces usable (realistic) results, unless the flip is intended for artistic effect.

6.12 Copying and Pasting Pictures

For relational designers, the most common reason for copying and pasting pictures involves building navigation. A picture on a slide might be copied, and then pasted onto another slide and downsized into a thumbnail. A wonderful aspect of PowerPoint's design is that such copies do not increase file size. You can copy and paste a picture practically an unlimited number of times, within a single show, and the impact on file size is minimal. This fact is useful for making what we call Primary Navigation, where identical thumbnails are pasted onto every slide in a show.

If, on the other hand, a picture is copied from one show and then pasted into another show, the action does increase the file size of the second show. The file size will increase by approximately the same amount as that picture's size.

Practice making several copies of a picture doing all of the following:

1. Right click the picture and select **Copy** from the shortcut menu. Right click again anywhere on the slide pane and select **Paste**.
2. With the picture selected, from the **Edit** menu select **Copy**, and then **Paste**.

3. With the picture selected, hold down the **Ctrl** key and type the letter **C**. Then, while holding down the **Ctrl** key, type the letter **V**.
4. The fastest way to copy a picture is to hold down the **Ctrl** key while left clicking and dragging the picture. To constrain the copy in a straight line, either horizontally or vertically, hold down both the **Ctrl** AND **Shift** keys while clicking and dragging.

6.13 Alignment Using the Draw Menu

PowerPoint's alignment mechanisms are especially useful when there are many pictures on a slide. If aligning only a few pictures, manual alignment is relatively easy using keyboard arrow keys or clicking and dragging shapes into place. In some situations, though, automated alignment produces better results, particularly when space is limited. Each time we add thumbnails to our blocks of thumbnail navigation, we typically have PowerPoint align the new thumbnail with the existing ones; otherwise, the alignment ends up being slightly off after pasting. The **Draw** menu alignment synchronizes pictures exactly, whereas manual alignment sometimes is inadequate.

To align multiple pictures, either horizontally or vertically, do the following:

1. Select the pictures, and then click the **Draw** button on the **Drawing** toolbar.
2. From the menu that appears, select **Align or Distribute**, and then select one of the alignment options.
3. Experiment with aligning your pictures so that their left sides are lined up vertically.
4. Move pictures around manually and try aligning them horizontally.
5. By default, the **Align or Distribute** functions align the pictures relative to one another. Another option is to align the pictures relative to the **top**, **center**, **bottom**, **right** or **left** side of the slide. To do so, select the **Relative to Slide** check box before selecting one of the alignment options. Uncheck this option to return to the default alignment methods.

6.14 Alignment Using Guides

Another way of aligning and positioning pictures is to use PowerPoint's **guide** feature. A guide acts like a magnet, snapping pictures to either a vertical or horizontal line when the pictures are moved within close proximity. This method is indispensable when you want different pictures in exactly the same position on multiple slides within a show.

Figure 6.19

For example, as shown in this slide we often place a medium-size screenshot on a slide to introduce a concept. This screenshot then links to a separate show available for displaying more detail if needed. We want all such screenshots to be exactly the same size, and in the same position, on all slides. Why? Because doing so provides smooth consistency when moving between the slides in the show.

Without this consistency, screenshots in different locations relative to one another would appear to jump around with every slide transition. Aligning them with guides gives the impression each screenshot replaces the other during slide transitions, in gradual succession.

When creating such an effect, lay out the guides at the beginning when first making the show. They then appear in the same position on all slides. Graphics can be dropped into place on each slide and all will be positioned properly, both vertically and horizontally.

1. Turn on guides by clicking the **View** menu and selecting **Grid and Guides**. Select the **Display Drawing Guides on Screen** check box and click **OK**. (Remove the check mark in the future to turn the guides off again.)
2. A horizontal guide and a vertical guide initially appear at the center of the slide, like a crosshair. Experiment with moving your pictures next to these guides.
3. The positioning of a guide can be changed by holding your cur-

sor exactly over it, and then clicking and dragging it sideways (vertical guide) or up and down (horizontal guide).

4. You also can create up to four additional guides (either vertical or horizontal) by holding down the **Ctrl** key while clicking and dragging the guides. Note that guide positioning and configuration are specific to individual slide shows and are saved along with the show. If you open a different slide show, it will display the guides in their default positions, unless you previously changed them and saved the show.

6.15 Distributing Pictures

After pictures are aligned, they may need to be distributed. Distribution refers to placing an equal amount of spacing between pictures, either vertically or horizontally. When dealing with a small number of pictures, as with shapes, manual distribution is relatively easy, but the automated process available on the **Drawing** toolbar can be faster.

1. To distribute multiple pictures, either horizontally or vertically, select all the pictures that need to be distributed, and then click the **Draw** icon on the **Drawing** toolbar.
2. From the menu that appears, select **Align or Distribute**, and then select one of the distribution options. Note: You MUST select at least three pictures in order to create at least two spaces for comparison; otherwise, the distribution options will be dimmed (unavailable).
3. If distributing vertically, the function looks at the position of the top picture compared with the position of the bottom picture, and evenly spaces other selected pictures in between. Similarly, if distributing horizontally, the function looks at the position of the left picture compared with the position of the right picture, and evenly spaces other selected pictures in between.
4. After distributing your pictures, practice moving either the top or bottom picture (or left or right picture) and then redistributing the collection. Use this method to make fine adjustments to spacing between navigation elements in a column or row.

6.16 Adjusting Picture Stacking Order

Each picture exists on its own transparent layer. Thus, as with shapes, they can be stacked on top of each other. You can also change the order, even put a picture on top of other pictures and AutoShapes. A common scenario is adding an AutoShape that will be a background behind a group of shapes on a slide, yet needing ALL these shapes to be on top of the slide's background picture. In such a case, the easiest way of getting the shapes and background picture in their proper positions is to first send the new background shape all the way to the back of the staking order. Then send the background picture to the back of the stacking order.

1. Move your pictures around so that several overlap.
2. Change a picture's position in the stack by right clicking it and selecting **Order** from the shortcut menu.
3. Four reordering options are available. In general, the **Send to Back** and **Bring to Front** options are the most useful.
4. Keep in mind you can select multiple pictures and apply the reordering commands to all selected pictures simultaneously. Experiment with placing various pictures on top and bottom of the stack.

6.17 Grouping Pictures

Multiple pictures can be locked to each other so that they behave as a group. Doing so makes the process of rearranging complex collections of pictures on a slide easier and can be useful in certain animation applications. Note that we normally do not group clusters of thumbnails that are used for navigation. Grouping pictures makes hyperlinking more difficult and offers no usable benefit.

If you do group pictures, and then want to perform an individual action on a picture such as adding a hyperlink, click the group once to select it as a whole (white selection handles). Then click a specific picture to select it individually from the group (gray selection handles).

1. To group pictures, select the desired pictures, and then right click one of them, making sure to right click ON one of the se-

lected pictures to avoid deselecting all.

2. From the menu that appears, select **Grouping/Group**.
3. To ungroup the pictures, repeat the process and select **Grouping/Ungroup**.

6.18 Rotating Pictures

There are two ways to rotate a picture. Experiment using both methods below:

1. Click the picture to select it. Move the mouse cursor over the small green circle that appears with the picture's selection handles (white circles). Click and drag near the green circle to rotate the picture.
2. Double click the picture to open the **Format Picture** dialog box. Click the **Size** tab. Enter a rotation angle value in the **Rotation** box. Click **OK**.

6.19 Darkening or Lightening Pictures

Increasing or decreasing the brightness of a picture can help it blend into a slide's background. Such adjustment is useful for making navigation components less distracting.

1. Click a picture to select it.
2. Click the **More Brightness** or **Less Brightness** icon on the **Picture** toolbar to change the lightness or darkness.

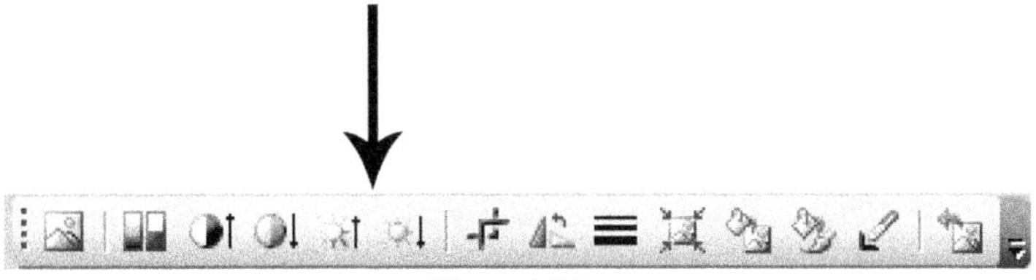

Figure 6.20

6.20 Making a Picture Semitransparent

Making a picture semitransparent in PowerPoint is impossible. However, a roundabout method exists for accomplishing the same effect. Here we turn a picture into a watermark background:

1. To make a picture semitransparent in PowerPoint, first create an AutoShape that has the same dimensions as the picture.

Figure 6.21

2. Fill the AutoShape with the desired picture, using the AutoShape's **Fill Effects** (topic 5.9).
3. Once the shape is filled with the picture, you can adjust the shape's transparency, which, in turn, changes the transparency of the picture it contains.

6.21 Full-Screen Display

We wonder why most presenters using pictures in their presentations are content to leave those images small and inconsequential, off to the side of text. Very few allow pictures to cover entire slides, even though the effect is considerably more dramatic. It's almost as though some kind of unspoken rule mandates that slides must contain text and pictures should be an afterthought.

Allow visuals to jump out at the audience, as though they were watching a large-screen TV. Include pictures that have a high enough resolution to cover entire slides and still look crisp. Normally, such files when properly optimized have a file size between 100 and 150 kilobytes.

Full-screen display of pictures gives a much more visually powerful impact compared with picture-text combinations. In fact, images often say what words alone can never fully express. Therefore, let the picture say what it will, and then verbally expand upon the impression made. That is, give audiences the opportunity to strongly encode visual messages from the slide content and, at the same time, supplement that information with additional verbal detail.

Our brains process visual information very quickly because we are used to receiving constant streams of such data all day long. Showing a full-screen visual thus allows the audience to quickly scan the slide for meaning, and then return focus right away to the presenter. This enables the speaker to maintain better contact with viewers, considering full-screen visuals do not break concentration the way reading text on a slide often does.

Figure 6.22

For pictures to cover a slide, remember they must have a physical size of 7.5 inches tall by 10 inches wide, assuming default PowerPoint settings. If parts of the picture are larger than the slide (the width, for example), don't worry about the portions that hang off the slide pane into the gray area. That material won't display when projected and can be left hanging. If you still feel an urge to place text on the slide even with a full-size picture, try making the text large with only one or two words. Lay it directly on the picture, or on a bar (AutoShape) at the top or bottom of the slide.

6.22 Creating Picture Stories

A *picture story* is one of the most essential tools available to a relational presenter. Your network should contain many, if not hundreds, of these devices, allowing you to visually display a story as it is told.

Picture stories are short, linear slide shows that progressively and visually help a presenter communicate ideas or demonstrate a point. Think of them as being similar to movie trailers. If you were to describe a movie verbally, the effort might not be as successful as giving someone a quick screening preview of actual scenes in the movie. Likewise, picture stories provide the audience a rapid visual tour of a topic, as details unfold verbally. Again, think back to the Dual Coding process discussed previously. Our goal is to *say* the same thing both verbally and visually, at the same time, bringing clarity and deeper meaning to a message.

Picture stories normally contain less than seven slides and often no more than one to three slides. Each slide features an image or something visually relevant to the topic at hand. Moving through a picture story is like gradually adding pieces to a puzzle. The final meaning comes into view along a timeline.

Picture stories are randomly accessible at all times. They typically require only 30 to 90 seconds to complete. In a sense, they bear resemblance to a commercial because a speaker can say, "Oh, here, let me show you something," jumping into, and then out of, the story.

Figure 6.23 Courtesy National Gypsum Company

Paul Kinney is a national accounts manager with National Gypsum Company and uses picture stories to spontaneously highlight proper use of products. Their new XP wallboard product, for example, is designed to resist mold and mildew. Visual stories show examples of what can happen when regular wallboard is applied (as opposed to the XP product) around windows, doors, in bathrooms, or in other locations where moisture content is high. His before and after visuals are simple and to the point.

Other stories sequentially show the steps involved in correct installation and product selection. When a customer or vender asks a question during a trade show, these stories give the feeling of actually *being there,* stepping through installation techniques, time-saving strategies, and best practices. A similar approach, by the way, involves using short video clips to accomplish the same goals. Such devices, not surprisingly, are *video stories.*

Picture stories (and video stories) work well for handling objections, explaining processes or guidelines, giving how-to examples during trainings, and enhancing persuasion in sales environments. They facilitate immediate customization of a message to the interests of viewers.

Picture stories often follow patterns or formulas, any one of which might be more or less appropriate for a given situation. Think about your message contexts and consider which of these patterns might be useful. Perhaps your stories will follow other sequences altogether. That's fine. Keep in mind also that just because a formula has a certain number of steps does not necessarily mean the picture story must have the same number of slides. The number of slides is more a function of whatever it takes to smoothly and effectively show and tell the story.

Before/After formulas display starting conditions, the approach taken, and the outcome. A civil engineering company building bridges might showcase various technical aspects of past projects. Questions arising during design or approval stages then can be answered visually and responses customized according to real past examples. Several related picture stories might feature soil conditions at different construction sites, the kinds of support structures required, shots of projects in progress, and final results.

Projection formulas are similar, yet future-oriented. They explain the current situation, recommend an approach, and then predict the results. The idea is to give viewers a visual sense of what they can expect, what options are available, and perhaps what you can do for them. Returning to the engineering company example, their network might feature different projected cost outcomes, based upon initial design parameters and recommendations for minimizing time expenditure and costs. All of these components, of course, are displayed visually.

A **Progression** formula is exactly what it sounds like. Sequential visuals show the unfolding of events or the steps of a process while the presenter says, "When we have soil type A, the typical procedure is to take a core sample, analyze bedrock composition and stability, calculate foundation depth based upon bridge span, and determine the required support structure. If the soil type is B, the process is similar but an additional stress analysis is necessary as well." Viewers should see progressive displays of images that depict the stages of the process, as though they were present when the photos were taken. Such sequential, on-demand imagery helps an audience member or learner break down complex subjects into manageable pieces. As might be expected, this particular formula works especially well in a training context and for explanatory demonstrations.

This or That formulas are along the lines of the mechanic's mantra "Either pay $25 for an oil change now or see me later when your engine needs replacing." Picture stories in this context might powerfully depict calls to action or warn of potential dangers, showing possible consequences. This formula lends itself well to sales situations and other arenas where persuasion is important—perhaps in politics, consulting, or charitable work. The engineers, in this case, might have a battery of information available to deal with objections arising due to design-quality costs.

Comparison/Contrast formulas can take several forms. The point is to understand, through interaction, your audience's perspectives, and then suggest an alternative approach, give alternative perspectives, or correct misconceptions. This type of picture story applies well across a range of contexts, particularly in sales, training, and education. The underlying message is "I know you think it is THAT way, but it's actually THIS way, and let me show you why." Visuals can be extremely effective in backing up your perspective because they show it like it is, or at least how it seems to be.

One of our most frequently used picture stories is the former grocery store example that illustrates the information architecture process. We could attempt to describe this procedure verbally, calling it organization. It is merely organization, after all. Even so, the example and the pictures bring a simple understanding to an otherwise potentially confusing subject. By literally (visually) walking the viewer though the store in search of the desired apple, the underlying lesson takes on more meaning because of the situation's familiarity. The concrete nature of the scene turns an abstract concept into a workable model. The more you can implement similar approaches, the better viewers will relate to your messages.

In some cases, picture stories are added to a network as isolated accents to specific topics. For example, a story might be used as an illustration, or an expansion of a bullet point. In other cases, stories are organized in categorical collections so that a presenter can choose the most appropriate illustration to make a point. She might have what amounts to a visual database of picture story examples, allowing customization of topics according to disparate contexts and clients.

Not surprisingly, these devices vary considerably from presenter to presenter in look and purpose, depending on the intent of the designer and the field focus. When designing your own, ask yourself, "What do I see through my eyes, or in my mind, during these situations?" Then find appropriate, sequential visuals to show others the same views.

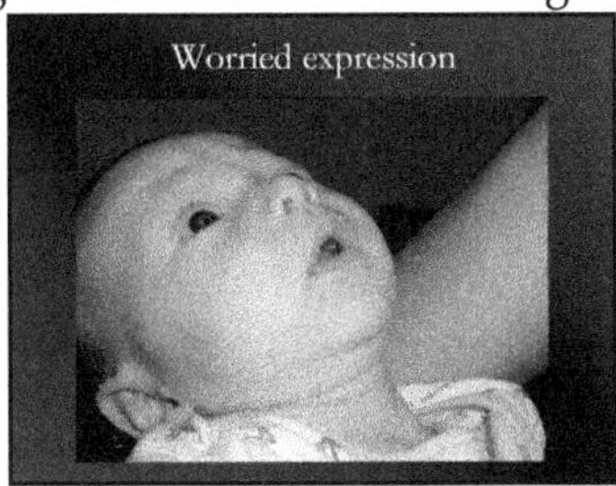

Figure 6.24 Courtesy Catherine Watson Genna, IBCLC

Catherine Watson Genna is an IBCLC lactation consultant who helps parents, doctors, and other medical professionals recognize early symptoms of conditions adversely affecting an infant's feeding ability. Most of her talks are technical and medical in nature, to meet demanding standards for continuing medical education (CME) events.

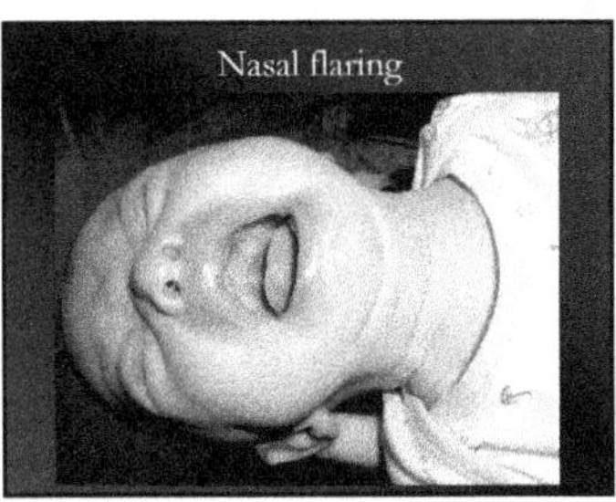

Figure 6.25 Courtesy Catherine Watson Genna, IBCLC

Even so, over the years she has taken literally thousands of pictures that visually illustrate what she verbally describes. Catherine was drawn to visually interactive presentation out of a desire to enhance the usefulness of these photos. Rather than letting them sit in long linear presentations full of duplicate slides, she has begun the process of arranging her collection into small, modular presentations—picture stories that are all conveniently accessible when needed.

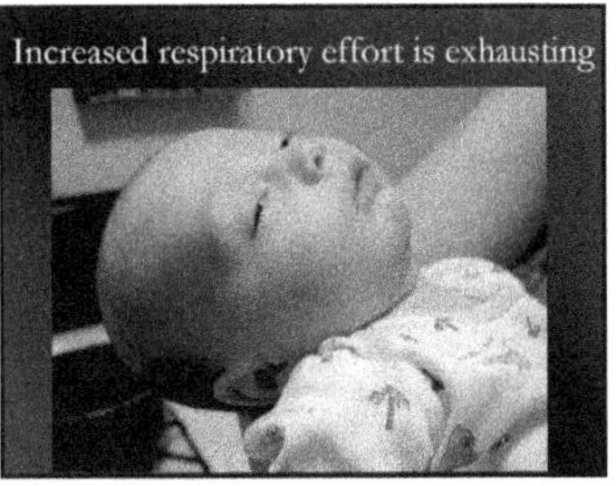

Figure 6.26 Courtesy Catherine Watson Genna, IBCLC

The story shown here is used when talking about respiratory disorders and breastfeeding. Feeding is aerobic exercise for infants. They need good heart, lung and airway function to have enough energy and oxygen for the process. The little one in this example has a condition called laryngomalacia, which causes the upper airway to close up as the baby is breathing in.

When Catherine displays these photos, her goal is to show some of the subtle signs that indicate a baby has a respiratory disorder—the nostrils flaring as the baby fights to breathe, a worried look, and exhaustion from how much effort it takes to force air through a collapsing airway.

Her strategy in this case is to use a combination of a picture and simple text. There are no navigation devices, branding elements, and few design features. The pictures effectively say what needs to be said, without the need for bullet points per se. Each succeeding picture adds appropriate depth and detail. Often this kind of design simplicity is the best approach for visual communication.

After these slides, she follows with a video of the same baby, to illustrate dynamic symptoms of the condition. She then teaches how to help babies with this condition to breastfeed.

Picture stories in their purest, most basic form are nothing more than full-screen pictures delivered in short, sequential bursts. Brian Woolsworthy incorporates pictures when discussing climate change and its effects on alpine vegetation. He might show sequential pictures of a glacier's disappearance over the years, or how a particular variety of plant gradually has become dominant and affected the ecological balance of a region.

Figure 6.27 Courtesy Brian Woolsworthy

We use maximum visual display frequently because of its powerful effects. In this case there is nothing distracting to draw attention away from the message. Whatever supplemental information needs to be added to the visual component can be accomplished verbally. A well-told story in this context places the listener in the scene, as though he or she were really there.

Keeping in mind all that has been said so far about the different styles and formulas for picture stories, realize you are never locked into a particular option. Different stories might feature various combinations of branding, text, or navigation. There is no rule saying everything must have a uniform appearance or follow a set pattern. Audiences, in fact, appreciate variety and creativity of design.

Think about the possibility of being creative with picture stories in non-obvious ways. Any picture on a slide, whether full screen or not, might be set up as an active link that pulls up supporting detail. Brian, for example, might have invisible animation available on demand, to highlight specific plants or show related facts. Similarly, he might have invisible, animated navigation available, or pictures might open another slide show entirely or play a hidden video clip. While it's true picture stories are normally short, simple, and linear in nature, they can be as complex as desired and include any Relational Presentation functionality.

Still, it's a good idea to keep designs basic at first. The struggle for most of us is getting used to the idea of tearing apart large shows and building these kinds of modular story units in the first place.

6.23 Incorporating Screenshots

Relational presenters often use screenshots in at least four different ways to visually augment their Presentation Networks. Earlier we mentioned that a screenshot is basically a picture of what someone would see if looking at your computer screen. Screenshots allow you to show people your screen in picture form, as part of the regular presentation materials.

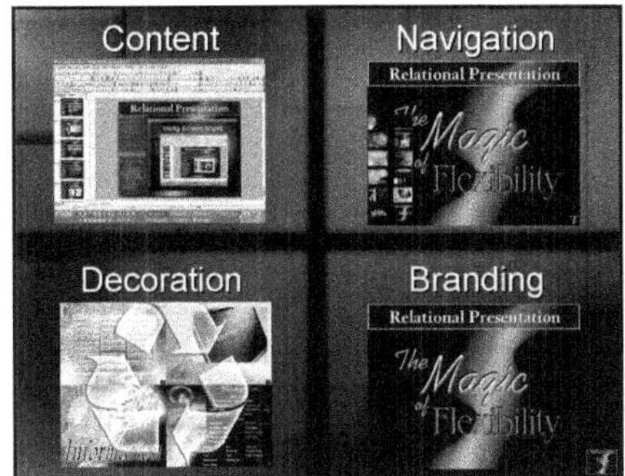

Figure 6.28

You may, for example, wish to display a Web page at a speaking venue but there is no live Internet connection. In that case, it's necessary to have still shots of the site pages available on PowerPoint slides. Or, the software you want to showcase is not installed on the show computer. Screenshots let you bring viewers right to your desktop computer, so to speak, and help them see what you see. Think about how such approaches might apply to your needs.

Screenshots as Content: There are practically unlimited opportunities for using screenshots as actual content in slide shows. Figure 6.28 is actually a screenshot of screenshots we use as both visual content and as a linked switchboard to explain the concept of screenshots in presentation. The screenshots ARE the message, or at least part of it.

Maybe you wish to show various layouts generated in a CAD program but aren't familiar with operating the software yourself. Screenshots of the software in action can be added to a Presentation Network; no extra knowledge is necessary. Another advantage of using these kinds of displays in a training situation is that portions of the screenshot can be highlighted, emphasized, or even enlarged so that people in the back of the room can see it better. The same is true of Web page captures.

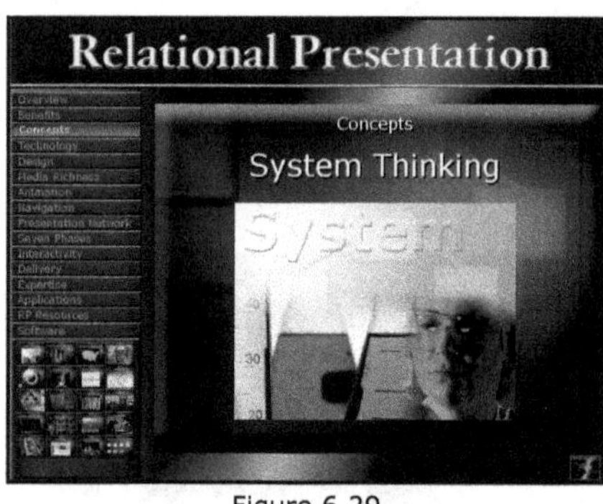

Figure 6.29

We recommend incorporating medium-size screenshots (3.5 inches by 4.67 inches) onto slides, as shown at left. Doing so enables an effective dual-messaging strategy where a speaker has the option of staying with the current slide or accessing related content.

Here's how it works: The slide shown here introduces a discussion of systems theory. The *system* picture is actually a screenshot of the first slide in an external slide show containing more systems theory detail. Not surprisingly, the screenshot hyperlinks to that external show so that we can open it at any moment if more information is needed. Often we don't need the extra detail. During review sessions, or while making a passing comment on system dynamics, we might display only the original slide, and then move on to other topics. The screenshot gives us the option of either staying at a summary level on the original slide or diving into much more depth with the external content.

Another way of thinking about this approach is that the screenshot slides act as title slides for introducing extra relevant material. Integrating this concept throughout the network gives you the option of staying shallow or going deep at any time, depending on the circumstances.

Screenshots as Navigation: We earlier mentioned advantages of using thumbnails as the basis for navigation. Frequently these small pictures are simply screenshots that give a preview of what the link will open once clicked. The image at right is a shot of our Main Switchboard. A close inspection of the thumbnail-based navigation reveals a representation of the next image below. Clicking the link on the Main Switchboard opens the connected Brain Switchboard, a categorical collection of additional links we use for discussing brain-related topics.

Figure 6.30

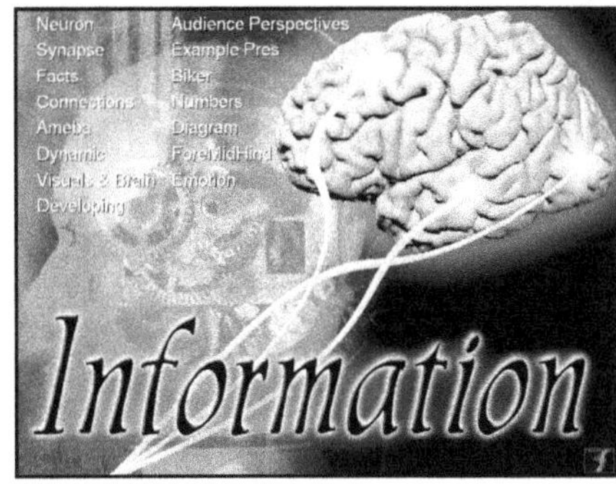

Figure 6.31

Turning screenshots into navigation components gives the speaker easily recognizable Visual Clues for finding information. In this case, we know exactly where to go to find brain-related content while training; it's all right here. The network user learns to associate images with the content they represent, simplifying the search process.

A related benefit of screenshots in navigation is the fact that they remind the presenter of what content actually exists—not a trivial matter when under pressure or nervous. In other words, he or she does not need to constantly keep track of, and remember, all the potentially thousands of slides in the network. Visual reminders in the form of screenshots are like bread crumbs on the trail to the gingerbread house. They help us remember where we are going next and what content is waiting. They are, in effect, our notes, our cheat sheets.

Screenshots as Decoration: In some cases, screenshots make a pleasant decorative background for a slide when discussing concepts. In the example shown here we wanted to emphasize the importance of Relational Presentation content being reusable. A small amount of effort produced four screenshots that were then overlaid with recycle arrows. The same can be done with Web site material or any other computer images, perhaps even as a faded watermark image behind other primary content.

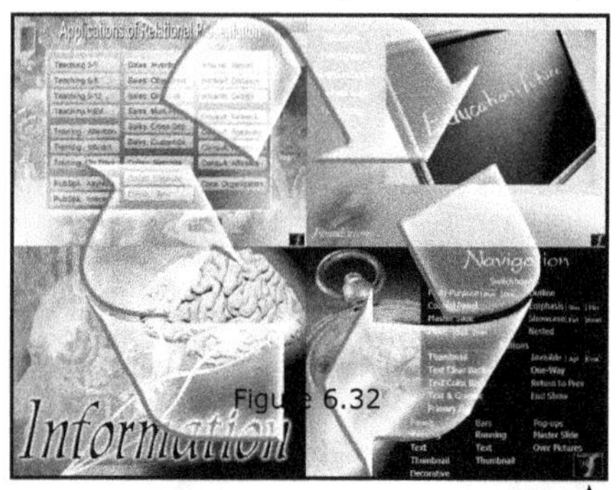

Figure 6.32

Screenshots as Branding: You may have noticed the small thumbnail that appears in the lower right-hand corner on most of the slides printed in this book (see Figure 6.32). This image is a screenshot of the Aspire Main Switchboard and, not surprisingly, links back to the Main Switchboard from every slide in our network. Its secondary purpose is to be a branding element, like a miniature logo on every slide. In this sense, the image has both a functional and a symbolic role.

To make a screenshot, follow these procedures:

1. Select a slide you want for a screenshot and start the slide show at that slide (**Shift F5** keys).
2. Press the **Print Screen** key on your keyboard. Note that on some computers you must press the **Ctrl** or **Fn** key along with the **Print Screen** key. Pressing the **Print Screen** key places a copy of the screen image into your clipboard (meaning you are now able to paste it, like making a copy of your screen).

3. Select the PowerPoint slide where you want the screenshot to appear (click on the slide pane) and press **Ctrl V** to paste. The image that appears is a picture like any other picture and can be downsized, cropped, and so forth.

Depending on what is being captured, screenshots tend to have a fairly large file size when pasted directly into PowerPoint. If incorporating many screenshots within a single show, you may want to reduce their size in graphics editing software first, before inserting them onto slides.

6.24 Strategies for Stock Photos

A stock photo is taken by a professional photographer and made available for sale, or it may be downloadable free as royalty-free art. Stock photography is a wonderful way of visually augmenting your presentations because someone else has taken the pictures you need, in just about every imaginable category. Usually these images are searchable, either as part of a DVD collection or via the Web. The downside of working with stock material is that you are not the only one searching for images in a particular category. Perhaps hundreds, if not thousands, of other people have already used those photos in their newsletters, brochures, presentations, and so forth.

Figure 6.33

Using such generic content is acceptable, but your slide shows will look more professional if viewers cannot easily recognize imagery as something they have seen before. A best practice when using stock photos, therefore, is to change the pictures in some way to make them less recognizable. In the very least, flip them horizontally if you can get away with it or, perhaps, try to combine more than one image into a collage.

Major changes require graphics skills. If you have such skills, consider removing backgrounds, adding transparency, adding bevels and glows, changing colors, and even adding filters to make the image look different. Anything you can do to alter the original view will decrease the likelihood of someone seeing it as familiar. The image shown in Figure 6.33 combines two pictures. The younger child was flipped horizontally and parts of both images were removed. Both pictures were made semi-transparent and the overall final graphic was faded on all edges. We saved the final graphic in Png format, with transparency, so that the red slide background shows through.

The last segment of this chapter lists numerous sources where you can obtain inexpensive or free photos. No doubt, many other people are looking there, too. Again, it may be worth the investment of time to learn at least some basic graphics skills. That way, making changes to photos is easy. Of course, the best way to guarantee someone won't recognize your photos is to take them yourself. Never underestimate the usefulness of a digital camera for visually supplementing slides. Pictures don't always have to be *super professional.* They just have to communicate.

6.25 Using the Photo Album Feature

A little-known feature of PowerPoint that lets you make a *photo album* has an alternative purpose in Relational Presentation. In fact, this feature can substantially reduce the amount of time necessary to create certain forms of picture-based navigation. It automates the process of building slide shows used for *Showcase* and *In-line* navigation where slides usually contain single, full-screen pictures.

1. On the **Insert** menu, hold your cursor over **Picture** and, from the pop-up menu, select **New Photo Album**. A **Photo Album** dialog box appears.
2. Click the **File/Disk** button.
3. On the **Insert New Picture** dialog box that appears, browse to find where you have a collection of pictures in a folder on your computer.

4. Open that folder and select all the pictures you want to insert. To select multiple pictures, click one and hold down the **Shift** key while clicking another picture further down the list. Or, while holding down the **Ctrl** key, click multiple pictures.

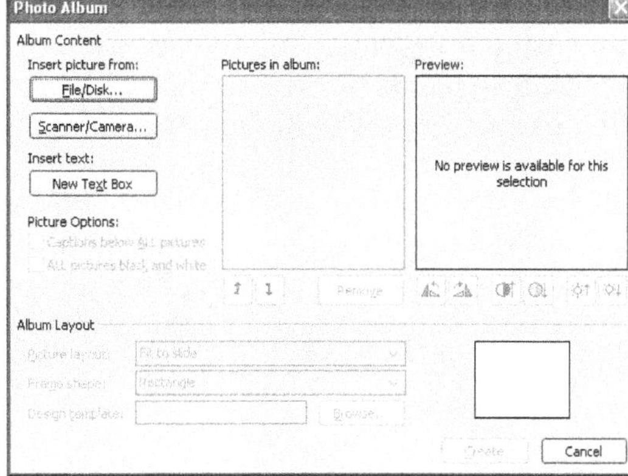

Figure 6.34

5. When finished, click the **Insert** button and notice that a list of the pictures to be inserted appears in the **Photo Album** dialog box.

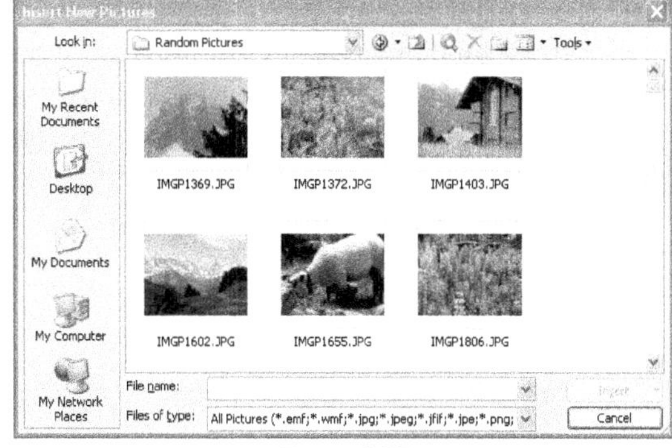

Figure 6.35

6. You can change the order of the pictures if desired by clicking a picture's name in the list and using the arrow keys provided.
7. Click the **Create** button to finish the process. Doing so creates a new show containing a blank slide at the beginning, along with full-screen pictures (one per slide) on remaining slides.

Notice a key characteristic of the **Photo Album** feature. It doesn't merely place pictures on slides. It actually inserts them as **Picture Fill** inside AutoShapes. The AutoShapes inserted match the proportions of the pictures and are as tall as the slide or as wide as the slide (or both), whichever dimension is first reached. Keep in mind that because PowerPoint automatically expands pictures in this situation to fit the slide, regardless of their quality, low-resolution pictures might look fuzzy as a result.

Also consider that as useful as the Photo Album feature may be, there is one drawback: Pictures inserted into AutoShapes as Fill cannot be compressed. If your pictures are already optimized before assembling a photo album, no problem. Otherwise, realize that if the pictures end up causing file size to be large, PowerPoint's compression feature will not help in this situation.

6.26 Where to Find Pictures

The following recommendations point you in the direction of all the photos and graphics you could ever want. Most available pictures have few restrictions, but respect license restrictions where applicable. Some images in this book were obtained from the sources below and we requested use approval first. You can always send a courtesy e-mail asking for permission. Most sources gladly grant it.

Microsoft: On the Microsoft Office Online Web site, thousands of royalty-free pictures await. Be sure to select **Photos** in the search category at the top, to avoid all the clip art. Photographs are arranged by category and are of reasonable quality for presentation. The link to the download site, as of the writing of this book, is:

http://office.microsoft.com/clipart/default.aspx?lc=en-us

Search Engines: Most major search engines such as Google, Yahoo and MSN allow search for images in addition to Web sites. Click the **Images** tab. Note that you can search by size of image, to ignore tiny Web images that are of little value to presentations.

Flickr: Flickr is a fascinating modern phenomenon, where millions of people all over the world upload their photos to share with others. You can find just about anything imaginable at this site and download the desired images. If you need it, somebody, somewhere, has posted it. Most images are for public consumption, with few if any restrictions, and the site is searchable by key words. The site also allows you to e-mail individuals who post photos, for use permission if required. Here is the Web site:

http://www.flickr.com/

Photoshop Tutorials Blog: And now for the *biggie*. This site lists nearly 70 other sites that offer free stock photography. If you don't find what you're looking for at one of these sites, it probably doesn't exist in the physical world.

http://pstutorialsblog.com/?p=44

You and Your Colleagues: Again, use your digital camera. Some presenters are reluctant to include their own photos for fear they will not be professional enough. On the contrary, if your pictures help others see through your eyes and into your thoughts, that is EXACTLY what the audience needs.

"I have begun re-working a presentation for delivery to a client, and am implementing the relational presentation concepts into it. I'm really enjoying it! More importantly, I believe it will make it much easier for him to present. "

R. J. Gosselin, Sr., Ph.D.
President, Acumen Development, Inc., USA

Chapter 7

Working with Hyperlinks

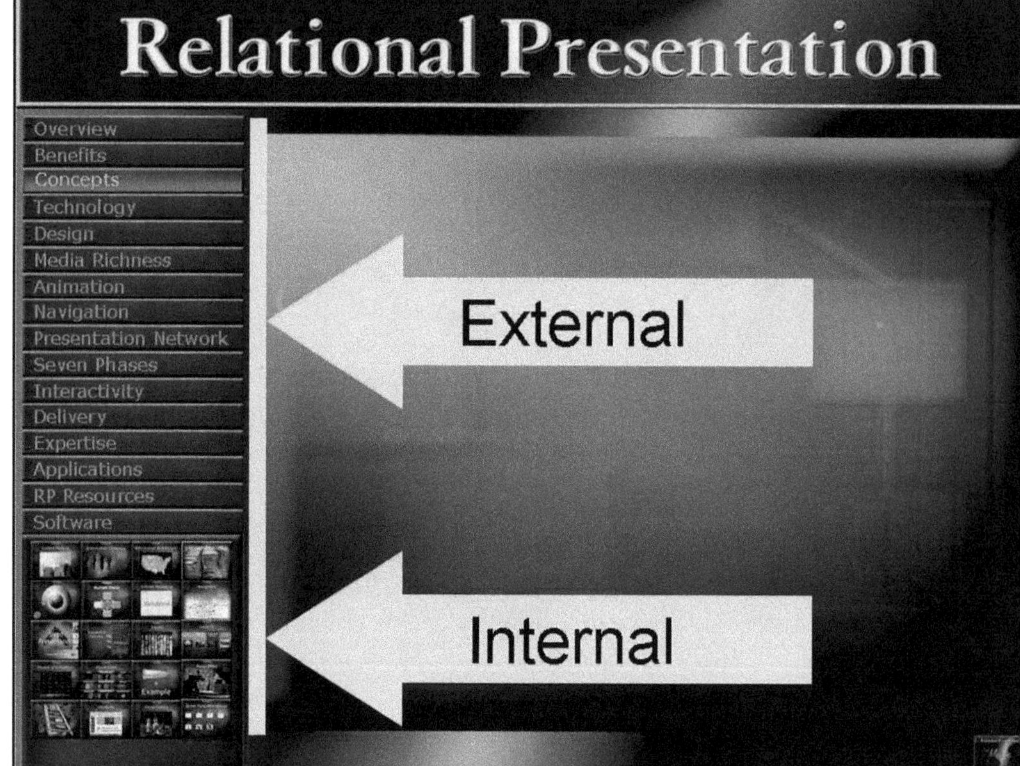
Relational Presentation
Overview
Benefits
Concepts
Technology
Design
Media Richness
Animation
Navigation
Presentation Network
Seven Phases
Interactivity
Delivery
Expertise
Applications
RP Resources
Software
External
Internal

7.1 Introducing Hyperlinks

Hyperlinks are the glue that holds a Presentation Network together. They are so easy to use and so powerful in their potential that it's amazing more presenters don't apply them on a regular basis. Most presenters seem unaware that hyperlinks even exist in PowerPoint.

Indeed, the average person, when asked to explain a hyperlink, thinks first of Web sites. Hyperlinks have revolutionized access to information on the Web. By clicking a link at a Web site, we can be transported almost instantly from one piece of content to another, and then another. A world of knowledge literally waits at our fingertips. The purpose of this chapter is to explore how hyperlinks can bring the same power of interactivity to digital presentation. Just as hyperlinks have changed the way we access information online, we predict they will also revolutionize the way we communicate with each other using digital media.

In reality, at the moment however, very few speakers use or even have experimented with hyperlinks. And those who have experimented tend to constrict their focus to single slide shows. The idea of linking together many separate presentations and pursuing dynamic navigation strategies is practically unheard of. Hopefully, that fact will change as we demonstrate how easy it is to develop network-based thinking.

7.2 What Is a Hyperlink?

The function of a hyperlink in PowerPoint is to initiate an action, such as transporting the user from one place to another. Hyperlinks in presentations have much broader applications than their Web counterparts. PowerPoint links can perform multiple tasks. They might, for example, transport you to another slide in the current show, open a separate slide show, open other types of files such as an Excel spreadsheet, or directly access the Web. Special kinds of hyperlinks called **Action Settings** can even execute Visual Basic code or run internal PowerPoint commands. A closely related form of link called a **Trigger** can start animations and play media (video and audio). In other words, hyperlinks in PowerPoint are highly versatile and useful, perhaps even more than Web links.

As with hyperlinks on the Web, PowerPoint links cause the cursor to change to a pointing hand. In this way you can easily tell which parts of your slides contain active links and which do not. You can set up links to fire off either with a mouse click or by moving the cursor over the link (called a *mouse over*). In general, we discourage presenters from using the mouse over option because it's too easy to accidentally activate a link when randomly moving the mouse. Hyperlinks requiring a mouse click give the user more stability and control.

7.3 Hyperlink Roles in Relational Presentation

Hyperlinks, in their basic use, give presenters choice and control while speaking. Relational Presentation methods expand their potential by making them a part of various optical illusions. Relational presenters frequently take advantage of visual *tricks* that seemingly push PowerPoint beyond what it was designed to do. These fun techniques greatly extend PowerPoint's normal paradigm.

A case in point is a particular link we call the *Magic Back Button*. It works exactly like a back button in a Web browser, but there is no *back button* in PowerPoint per se. This marvelous and extremely simple illusion enables a speaker to jump out of the middle of any bullet point list at any time, access external presentation materials on the fly, and then instantly return to the bullet list and continue. If you try to find such a button in PowerPoint, or read about it in help files, it will be your life's quest because it does not exist! Nevertheless, it can be built. All you need is illusion and an **Action Setting**.

Hyperlinks, in addition to their obvious navigational contributions, give relational presenters valuable organizational frameworks. Each click represents drilling down into more and more specific detail so that other less relevant information can be temporarily ignored. Hierarchical structures of linked content provide invaluable forms of content management that will help you reduce complexity and stay oriented within your message.

7.4 Hyperlink Sources and Destinations

A Presentation Network is composed of information clusters. Slides in one cluster often are related in some way to slides in another cluster. Hyperlinks bridge the gap between the two and form meaningful connections.

Think of a hyperlink as similar to the wireless signal between two cell phones. For communication to occur, both telephones must be *connected* to each other. At any given moment, one sends and the other receives. In the same way, a hyperlink must always have a ***source*** and a ***destination***. If either the source or destination is removed, the link does not function and is said to be *broken*. The source is the object you click (such as an AutoShape or picture) and the destination is the item the link affects in some way.

Sources: In Relational Presentation, the two most common starting points (sources) for a hyperlink are AutoShapes and pictures. Other items can be sources as well, such as OLE objects, tables, graphs, and the like, but this chapter focuses exclusively on the use of AutoShapes and pictures. Realize that a slide itself CANNOT be a source; you cannot directly hyperlink one slide to another slide. You must always hyperlink something ON a slide (a picture or AutoShape) to something else (the destination). It would be nice if a slide could be a source because then we could click anywhere on a slide and automatically follow the link, no matter what content the slide happened to contain. However, such functionality does not exist in PowerPoint. We can, nonetheless, employ another optical illusion to effectively fake this technique.

Destinations: Interestingly, a destination CAN BE a slide, or an entire show, or any of the other items listed below. A destination is something the link acts upon. Destinations can be:

- A slide within the current show or a separate slide show
- A Custom Show (within the current show)
- A specific slide in a separate slide show
- A Web site
- An OLE object (for example, a Word or Excel file)
- A video or audio clip
- An animation
- Visual Basic code (a macro)
- Functions internal to PowerPoint

7.5 Helpful Facts to Know about Hyperlinks

Fact 1: Hyperlinks are active only after starting the slide show. This situation is a frequent area of confusion. New designers sometimes add hyperlinks to their shows, and then wonder why the links don't work as expected when clicked. When adding a hyperlink, you must enter Slide Show Mode before the link becomes available and active. If, on the other hand, you click a linked source while in Edit Mode, all you are doing is selecting that source, just like clicking any other AutoShape or picture.

Fact 2: If your link source is an AutoShape that contains text, placing the link on the shape is better than placing it on the text within that shape. Recall that AutoShapes containing text can have two selection modes—either the text or the shape can be selected. It is possible, therefore, to attach a hyperlink to either the text or the shape. We never place the link on the text because doing so involuntarily changes the text's color to dark teal and underlines it. This probably is not the effect you want. Placing the link on the shape instead leaves the look of the shape unaffected (including the appearance of the text) and the link functions perfectly. If you want to simulate the look of a pure text link, place the link on the shape, and then make the shape totally transparent, so that only the text remains visible.

Fact 3: Once a source contains a link, the source can be copied and pasted as many times as desired. In almost all cases the link remains valid. For example, you can add a hyperlink to a shape that points to Slide 1 as its destination. That shape then can be copied and pasted onto all other slides in the show, giving the presenter the option of returning to Slide 1 at any time. This situation is common because often the first slide is a switchboard controlling other slides, or a link to external shows. When the shape is pasted, the link continues to point to the absolute position of Slide 1, regardless of where the shape is pasted. Pasting links does not always work smoothly, and links can break in the process.

Fact 4: Links can be edited or removed. Once a link is in place, it can be edited or removed by right clicking the source and selecting the appropriate option from the shortcut menu.

Fact 5: Web hyperlinks transfer into PowerPoint. Know that if you copy a picture from a Web site and that picture has a hyperlink associated with it, pasting the picture onto a PowerPoint slide will paste the link as well. If this result is not intended, right click the picture in PowerPoint (after pasting) and remove the Web-based link.

7.6 Inserting Hyperlinks

To add a hyperlink to a shape or picture, you **Insert** it:

1. To insert a hyperlink, right click the desired source (such as an AutoShape or a picture).
2. From the shortcut menu, select Hyperlink. The **Insert Hyperlink** dialog box appears.

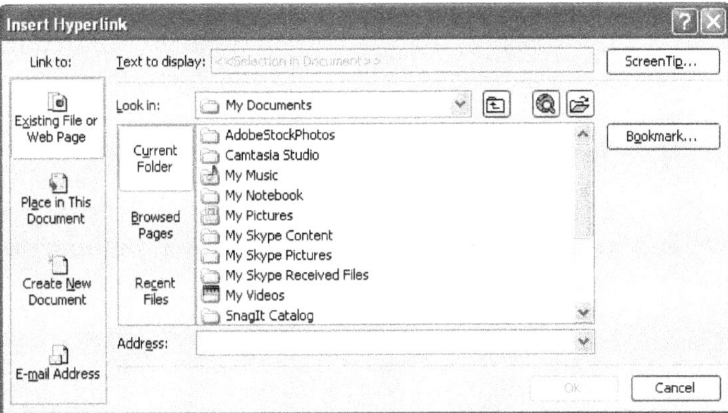

Figure 7.1

3. At this point, you need to decide if your link is internal—within the same slide show—or external—to a different slide show or to some other object or destination such as a Web site. For an internal link, in the **Link to** column, select **Place in This Document**. For an external link, select **Existing File or Web Page**.

7.7 Internal Hyperlinks

The terms ***internal*** and ***external*** hyperlinks are distinctions made in this book; they do not necessarily appear in PowerPoint help files or other books. For our purposes, assume any kind of linking activity that involves a single slide show is considered internal linking.

Internal links are a crucial part of Relational Presentation. They facilitate showing any slide, in any order, within a single show. That is, internal navigation gives the presenter the option of picking and choosing content on demand, without having to drag an audience through unnecessary or irrelevant slides.

Think of internal navigation in this way: Perhaps a realtor has a mammoth linear slide show (200 slides—don't laugh—it does happen) and each slide features a picture of a different house, along with details associated with the property. Does he need to show every house to every potential buyer? Probably not. Perhaps only 20 of his featured houses fit a given buyer's purchase parameters. So why show 180 houses that are irrelevant?

Internal hyperlinking enables instant and effortless selection. Any slide can be chosen in any order, as if providing *information customer service* to viewers. For the most part, internal hyperlinking is nothing more than linking a source (picture or AutoShape) on a slide to another slide in the same show.

1. To create an internal hyperlink, right click a source.
2. From the shortcut menu, select **Hyperlink** to open the **Insert Hyperlink** dialog box, and then select **Place in This Document**. The slides in your show are listed below **Select a place in this document**. If your slides contain text in the default title text box (the **Title Box** that is based on the **Slide Master**), this title is displayed as the **Slide Title**. Otherwise, individual Slide Titles are displayed as the default **Slide 1**, **Slide 2**, and so forth.

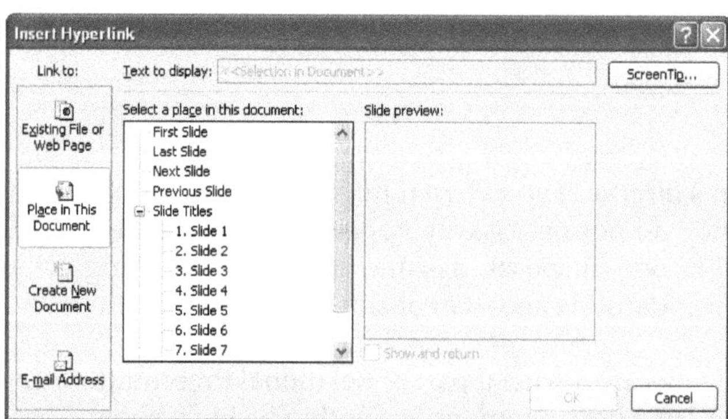

Figure 7.2

3. To complete the link, either click the appropriate **Slide Title** once to select it, which displays a thumbnail view below **Slide preview**, and then click **OK**, or simply double click the desired **Slide Title**. For example, if you want to link your source to the third slide in the show, double click **Slide 3** under **Slide Title**. Double clicking is faster but doesn't provide a thumbnail view of the slide.
4. The dialog box then disappears. You can check whether the link is working by starting the slide show (at the slide containing the source) and clicking the link.

7.8 External Hyperlinks

External hyperlinks are slightly more complex than internal hyperlinks because there are more linking options available. However, they are just as easy to create. An external link jumps outside the current show and acts on something else. Therefore, you need to tell PowerPoint where to jump and how to find the desired destination. These directions are called the external link's **path**. The path is like a road map, pointing to the right place on your computer, or to an address on the Internet. It may look something like this:

C:\ASPIRE\RELATIONAL PRESENTATION\Relational Presentation Shows\Components\COMPONENTS CONCEPTS Switchboard.ppt

Fortunately, you do not have to manually type the directions; you can browse to find and select the destination—just like finding anything else on your computer—and PowerPoint automatically fills in the path.

1. To create an external hyperlink, right click a source.
2. From the shortcut menu, select **Hyperlink** to open the **Insert Hyperlink** dialog box. Make sure **Existing File or Web Page** is selected, and then select the appropriate option below **Look in**. The resulting display depends on what folders exist on your computer and what software is installed. The following diagram describes the features in this dialog box that most likely will be important to you as a relational presenter.

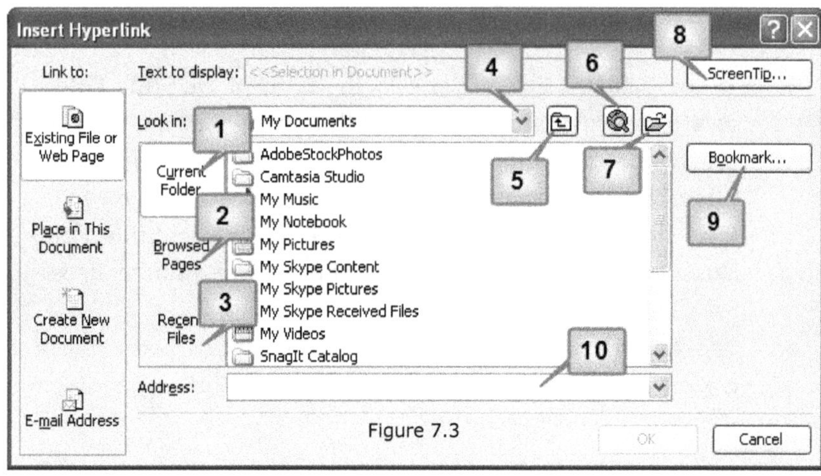

Figure 7.3

1 Most of the time you will leave **Current Folder** selected. This allows you to browse through files on your computer and find the one needed—usually a PowerPoint file. To browse, start by using item 4 or 5 in the above diagram to view the contents of your computer's hard drive, and then double click through the folders in the main window until you locate the desired file. This process is just like browsing in any other software, or inside Windows Explorer. Notice that as you browse through folders, the path you are creating appears in the **Address** box (10). When you find the desired file, either click it once and then click **OK**, or simply double click the file to complete the link. The dialog box disappears.

2 If linking to a Web page, one method of getting the link's path into the **Address** box is to select **Browsed Pages**, and then look for the Web address you need. This method, however, only works if you have visited the Web site previously and the address is still in your temporary Internet files. A more reliable (and usually faster) way of getting a Web address into the **Address** box is to visit the Web site in a browser, copy the Web address that appears in the browser's address box, and then paste that path into the **Insert Hyperlink** dialog box's **Address** box.

3 **Recent Files** is used even less than **Browsed Pages** because you must have previously opened the desired file in order for its path to show up here. Browsing for the file directly is

normally better unless you happen to know that the file was opened earlier.

4 Clicking the drop-down arrow in the box next to **Look in** allows you to select a level as a starting place for browsing. Unless you store all your files in My Documents (not a good idea), start by clicking your computer's C drive, and then work down by double clicking through folders in the dialog box's main window.

5 As an alternative to item 4, you can use the **Up One Folder** button to move upward through folder levels to find a file.

6 The **Browse the Web** button is a direct connection to the Internet and opens your default home page in a browser window. When linking to a Web site, we use this button to access the Web, browse for the desired Web page, copy the page's path, and then paste this path into the **Insert Hyperlink** dialog box's **Address** box.

7 Using the **Browse for File** button is another way of searching your hard drive for a file. In this case, you browse for the desired file within the window that pops up rather than directly in the **Insert Hyperlink** dialog box's main window.

8 The **ScreenTip** button gives you the option of changing the default ScreenTip that displays in Slide Show Mode when the cursor is held over an active link. Normally, we would have no reason to recommend this feature, but it is very useful for getting rid of a displayed path.

9 By default, a hyperlink that opens another slide show starts the new show at Slide 1. If you want it to start at Slide 5, for example, use the **Bookmark** button. To link to a specific slide in another show, browse in the normal manner to find the show you want and click once on the file name. Then click the **Bookmark** button to open the **Select Place in Document** dialog box. Double click the displayed slide that is to be the starting point. The dialog box disappears, setting the link.

Think twice before taking advantage of this feature because it has an unfortunate drawback. On the surface, bookmarking seems to offer a convenient way of accessing a specific slide in another show when needed. And the method actually does work quite well—as long as you don't change the slide order in the bookmarked show.

Therein lies the problem. A PowerPoint bookmark is an absolute link, meaning if you point it at Slide 10, it will always point to the Slide 10 *position*, regardless of what content appears there. Let's say you decide to move Slide 10 to the Slide 5 slot and want the link to point to the new location. Unfortunately, the bookmark will not readjust to the move. It will still point to the Slide 10 position, even though that spot now contains different content. In other words, if you make changes to a bookmarked show, you are likely to mess up the bookmarked links so that they no longer point to correct content.

10 The **Address** box shows the link's path. PowerPoint fills in this path sequentially as you browse to find a file and records the electronic directions needed. You can enter the path directly, but allowing PowerPoint to do it for you is recommended.

7.9 Linking to a Web Page

When accessing a Web site from a slide show, PowerPoint opens the browser window on top of the current show. Thus, returning to the slide show is as easy as closing the browser window. But what if you want to leave the browser window open while returning to the slide show? Unless the Web site has a way that allows you to move back and forth without losing your place, your best bet is to use the **Alt Tab** key combination: Hold down the **Alt** key while pressing the **Tab** key. Each press of the **Tab** key cycles through the currently open windows and makes it possible to select either a PowerPoint slide show window or the browser window. Pressing **Shift Alt Tab** cycles in the opposite direction.

When including Web links in the network, we recommend building slide shows that contain categorical collections, clusters of related links. That way finding a specific link is easier, in a way similar to looking for links in the *Favorites* section of your Web browser. Typically, such collections exist in a special area of the network called a *Resources Section.*

7.10 External Linking and Memory

Using PowerPoint presentations to open other presentations via hyperlinks produces seamless transitions between groups of content. The presenter never leaves Slide Show Mode while accessing a practically unlimited number of available shows. It's this process that gives Relational Presentation its true power and value. Everything needed is instantly viewable by click.

At the same time, keep in mind that each open slide show window requires computer memory equal to the size of that show. Clicking link after link opens window after window on top of each other, all of which require space while open. It's not uncommon during a long, involved presentation or teaching session to have 50 to 100, or more, windows open at the same time!

Generally, this is not a problem. Most modern computers have plenty of memory to handle such demands. Even if they don't, and PowerPoint runs out of actual memory to use, it creates what is known as *Virtual Memory*. The software temporarily allocates necessary space on your hard drive and calls it *memory*. This course of action is quite efficient and you probably won't notice the difference in performance. Your network will seem to function as normal, with only a slight decrease in speed.

So, unless you are using a very old computer with little memory, don't worry about having a lot of slide show windows open. Just make sure to leave plenty of space available—at least 3 gigabytes—on your hard drive.

By the way, if your network seems to be operating slowly—for example, external shows take a long time to open—it may not be a problem with memory or even the speed of your computer. Make sure your virus protection software is not automatically scanning all Microsoft Office files that open.

7.11 Closing Slide Show Windows

If, for some reason, you can't leave 3 gigabytes of free space on your hard drive and there is concern that both memory and hard drive space will run out at some point, then you must occasionally close the extra open windows. Theoretically, you can right click and select **End Show** repeatedly to close one window at a time, or hit the **Esc** key repeatedly. A more efficient way of closing windows is to run a small module of Visual Basic code (a macro). This code closes all the windows with a single click. We discuss its use while exploring Presentation Network structure because it also comes in handy for closing all your shows after the audience has left and it's time to shut down the network.

7.12 Getting Rid of the Link Path Display

When linking to an external destination, such as another slide show somewhere on your computer, PowerPoint records the path to that object. In other words, it maps out the digital steps necessary to find the show, as though recording street names necessary to move from one side of a city to the other. A path might look something like this:

C:\ASPIRE\ASPIRE RELATIONAL NETWORK\Relational Presentation Shows\Relational Presentation Cover.ppt

This path appears in the **Insert Hyperlink** dialog box's **Address** box.

Much to the dismay of relational presenters, this path also displays when holding the mouse over an external link while running a slide show. The result is an unacceptably distracting ScreenTip that constantly pops up every time the presenter moves to click the link. In a perfect world, one would expect this functionality could be turned off—but it cannot.

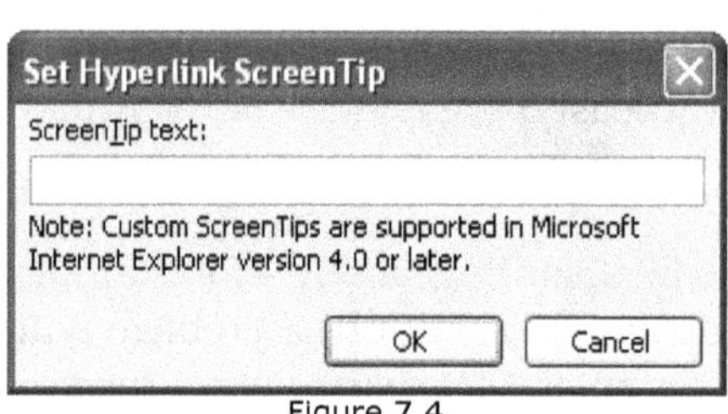

Figure 7.4

The only way to almost get rid of this path display is to override it by creating a custom ScreenTip using the **ScreenTip** button in the **Insert Hyperlink** dialog box. Our standard practice is to place a single space in the custom ScreenTip box. Such action overrides the link path and results in only a tiny rectangle displaying when the cursor rests over the link. Minimization of the link path in this way is the best you can do. We tell relational designers to just get in the habit of adding a single-space ScreenTip to all external links. It's annoying but important.

NOTE: You DO NOT need to add this space for internal links because internal links never display a path.

You can, if desired, label your links with a meaningful ScreenTip. However, we do not recommend doing so for the following reasons: If your source is an AutoShape, you can give the shape a meaningful name directly by typing text. If the source is a picture (or thumbnail), the picture should give enough of a clue to indicate where the link leads. Thus, a custom ScreenTip is normally unnecessary. In reality, ANY ScreenTip only adds unnecessary flashes on the screen that may distract viewers.

7.13 Hyperlinks and Stacking Order

Hyperlink availability is affected by stacking order rules associated with AutoShapes and pictures. If, for instance, you place a hyperlink on a shape, and then cover that shape with another shape or picture, the original hyperlink will no longer be accessible until uncovered. That is, the shape or picture on top masks the hyperlinked shape. Similarly, if you place a link on a shape or picture, and then cover that shape or picture with another linked shape or picture, the link on top always takes precedence. Sending a linked shape behind another shape sends the link back as well. These rules are quite logical and become important when building various forms of navigation. Be careful to always have your linked objects on top of other decorative elements, or those links will not be available when needed.

7.14 Hyperlinks and the Slide Master

Placing Navigation Elements on the Slide Master is a smart idea in general. Hyperlinks on the Slide Master work beautifully. For example, you can place a small AutoShape in the bottom right corner of the Slide Master, link it to Slide 1, and then start the show. That linked shape will appear on all slides in the show and will function as if the shape really existed on all the slides. We call navigation components placed on the Master *Virtual Navigation* because the sources seem to exist on the slides.

Master-controlled navigation is very efficient and easy to maintain. It exists in only one location and yet spans any number of slides. Making modifications is easy.

On the other hand, placing hyperlinks on the Master is not always the best strategy. You will notice in upcoming chapters that numerous navigation models require placing hyperlinks on actual slides, rather than on the Master. This is true because of a limitation in PowerPoint's design scope. Namely, anything placed on actual slides appears higher in the stacking order than items on the Master—and you cannot bring Master items to the top of the stacking order above slide components. As a result, if links are on the Master and you then cover a slide with a full-screen picture, the links will be covered and there is nothing you can do about it. The only way the links can be brought on top of the picture is to have the links on the slide itself.

7.15 Hyperlinks with Invisible Sources

Several navigation techniques explored in later chapters make use of invisible sources. An AutoShape need not be visible to contain a hyperlink. Indeed, invisible Navigation Elements allow the presenter to have secret options available for choosing appropriate content. They also enable a designer to use a slide's background as a visual guide to finding such invisible links. Hidden navigation can be used to foster audience intrigue, the "How did you do that?" effect, and to boost presenter confidence by being in total control of message selection—even when dealing with confidential information. Invisible hyperlinks take interactive presentation to its highest plateau, where a speaker can continually shape visual dialogue, without the audience knowing what is happening or why.

The expression *Referential Integrity* refers to whether or not a hyperlink continues to work properly after making a change to either its source or destination. It's an immensely important issue to relational presenters.

Maybe you decide to change the order of slides, rename a slide show, or move a show to a different location on your computer. Will the links inside of, and between, these shows automatically reconfigure themselves to reflect the changes? When software has perfect Referential Integrity, the answer is yes; ideally, PowerPoint should notice any changes you make and restructure links accordingly by rewriting their paths.

So how good is PowerPoint's Referential Integrity? The news is both good and bad. In some instances, PowerPoint handles change very well. In others, links break. In general, PowerPoint's link management is not very good, and there are numerous ways to inadvertently break links. On the other hand, its Referential Integrity has become better and better over the years with each successive version. That's why you should be using the most recent PowerPoint version and upgrade when a newer version becomes available.

WHAT BREAKS LINKS

Here are a few situations that definitely (or probably) WILL cause links to break. Keep in mind if you are using a version of PowerPoint older than 2003, a few additional situations might lead to broken links as well.

- **Deleting a slide that is the destination of a link:** If a source on Slide 1 links to Slide 2 and you delete Slide 2, the link no longer has a valid destination, and PowerPoint does not know where you want the link to point. In this case, the link on the source will appear to be still in place and active, but clicking the link does nothing. To fix the problem, you must manually remove or redo the link.

- **Moving a slide containing a source to another show, or moving a destination slide to another show:** Moving a linked slide to another show basically means you are copying and pasting it into the new show, and then deleting the original slide from the first show. From a linking standpoint then, moving a slide has the same effect as deleting it from the first show. The link will continue to look for the original slide in its initial location.

- **Deleting a slide show, deleting a file, or taking a Web site offline—when any is the destination of a link:** Obviously, removing an external destination results in the link pointing to blank space, so to speak, and, therefore, the link will break.

- **Moving a slide show from one folder to another folder, especially if the new folder is a parent folder (in other words, the slide show is moved up a level):** In some cases you can get away with moving linked shows between folders. For example, you normally can move the show to another folder at the same level—move the show to another folder within the same parent folder. Unfortunately, if you move the show up a level or down a level, PowerPoint does not always appropriately rewrite the path, and the link normally breaks. Similarly, moving audio or video clips to a different folder has detrimental results. To be safe, always check links after moving ANYTHING to a different folder.

- **Renaming a linked slide show:** If you rename either a source file or a destination file, the link's path does not update to recognize the new name. The broken link will display an error message saying that it can't find the specified slide show. The solution is to manually redo the link to the renamed slide show.

- **Renaming a folder containing a destination file:** As in the case above, the link does not recognize the folder's new name and, thus, can't find the desired destination.

- **Changing slide order or adding/deleting slides in a show that is the destination of a bookmarked link:** A bookmarked link always points to the same place in the external slide show, regardless of what content happens to be in that location. Any changes made to the external show typically have unintended consequences with bookmarked links pointing to it. For this reason, we rarely use bookmarked links.

Considering all of the above scenarios that potentially can have detrimental effects on links, be careful when making changes and always error check your materials before show time. Planning ahead when building out the network is critical as well.

In our experience, the link issues mentioned can result in serious problems and annoyances for relational presenters. A better solution is needed and hopefully will be forthcoming in PowerPoint 2007. We also are working on a solution through the creation of software that augments PowerPoint 2007. See the last chapter of this book for more details.

WHAT DOES NOT BREAK LINKS

- **Moving slides within a show:** When using internal links (links within the same show), you can move slides around as desired and the link paths adjust as expected. Moving Slide 2 to the Slide 10 position modifies the link so that it points to the correct slide.

- **Copying sources and pasting them onto other slides in the same show, or even onto slides in other shows:** Most designers place a navigation button on every slide throughout the network that points back to the Main Switchboard, the top (home page) of the network. Usually, you can get away with creating such a button once, adding the hyperlink, and then pasting the button onto other slides in the same show or onto slides in other shows. The pasted link normally works perfectly, even if placed in shows at different folder levels. We don't understand why this works, whereas moving shows to other folders often does not. It's a good idea to always check pasted links before using or duplicating them, especially when target shows are in different folders.

7.17 Editing Hyperlinks

Needing to move, add, delete, and edit components of the network is inevitable. So, too, is fixing broken links and otherwise editing their destinations.

1. To edit a link, right click the source and choose **Edit Hyperlink**.
2. Browse to find the new destination, as when initially creating the link.

To minimize the number of broken links in the remodeling process, we strongly recommend mapping out network development in advance. Predicting all future presentation needs and development is impossible, but you certainly can design the initial network structure to be as flexible as possible, accommodating probable scenarios. Doing so may greatly reduce the amount of link restructuring required later.

"I am intrigued by the possibility of creating a Presentation Network to facilitate taking requests for songs folks want to sing during worship. The liberation a Network would offer is obvious. It seems to me that the concept of Presentation Networks blows the future of PowerPoint wide open. Such a radical re-thinking!! You are a truly gifted visionary."

D. McCoy
Church Admin. Assistant, USA

Chapter 8

Working with Custom Shows

2
1
3
2
4
5
3
1
1
2
3
4
2
3
1

We have a like-dislike attitude toward PowerPoint's Custom Show feature. Certainly, in some circumstances, it can be helpful to relational presenters, and in this chapter we look at the benefits. Interestingly enough, if it hadn't been for the limitations of Custom Shows, Relational Presentation might not have come about at all. In the past, we used Custom Shows a lot, and yet constantly wished they could do more. Frustration eventually led to new methods that worked around the drawbacks and established the full Relational Presentation process.

You may, or may not, end up using Custom Shows yourself, depending on the design strategies guiding your network's logic. We still find them helpful sometimes. So give them a look. Knowing they are available at least provides more design options.

Think of a Custom Show as a *show within the show*. Take, for instance, a presentation that has 20 slides. In one situation we may wish to show all 20 slides in their regular order. But what if at another time we only need to display Slides 3, 14, 5, and 10, in that order and we don't want to build a separate slide show for the purpose?

Setting up a Custom Show lets us leave the original show intact and simultaneously tell PowerPoint how to display subsets of slides from that show, in a custom order. In fact, we can set up any number of such Custom Shows, displaying various slides in different orders. The advantage of doing so is that we avoid the problem of having multiple copies of the same slides scattered across several presentations.

The main disadvantage of Custom Shows is that they still lock a presenter into a set sequence of slides. Without internal navigation to jump around within the show, or external navigation to jump outside the show, delivering a Custom Show in its purest form is little different from trudging through a standard presentation, albeit shorter perhaps.

Therefore, we approach the use of Custom Shows in much the same way as with Picture Stories; they are kept short and have a tight focus. Indeed, Custom Shows can be Picture Stories. One of the advantages of such a strategy is that all of the stories then are in a single show, and, in that case, the entire presentation full of stories can be e-mailed or easily transferred if desired. The ***Show and Return*** aspect of Custom Shows is especially useful in this regard. When that option is checked, and shows open from a switchboard, users automatically return to the switchboard when the show is complete.

8.2 Creating a Custom Show

To create a Custom Show, start with a regular slide show that contains multiple slides. Create as many Custom Shows as desired. Custom Show slide sequences are stored *per show*. Unfortunately, you cannot transfer a Custom Show to another presentation or access a Custom Show outside its presentation. Each new Custom Show appears listed below previous shows.

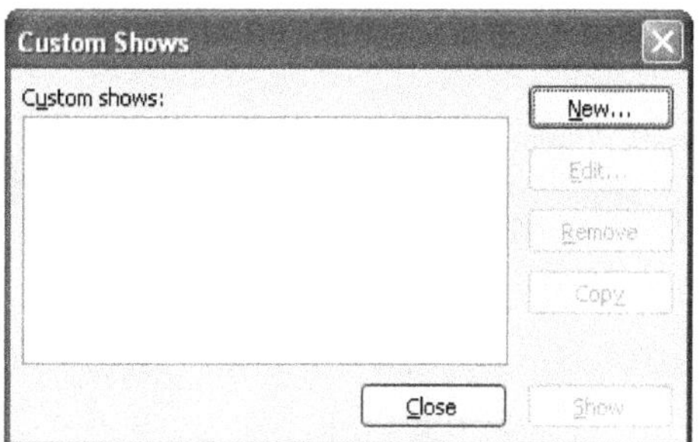

Figure 8.1

1. Open an existing slide show.
2. Click **Slide Show** on PowerPoint's main menu and select **Custom Show** at the bottom. The **Custom Shows** dialog box opens, revealing all existing Custom Shows in this presentation. Unless you have previously created Custom Shows in this show, the window will be blank.
3. Click the **New** button. The **Define Custom Show** dialog box appears. Here you can type a name for the Custom Show, select the slides it will display, and determine their order.
4. To add slides to the Custom Show, either click the slide name once and click the **Add** button, or double click the slide name. Note also you can select more than one slide name at a time, and then click the **Add** button. Holding down the **Shift** key and clicking two different slide names selects all slides in between. Holding down the **Ctrl** key and clicking slide names allows noncontiguous selection.

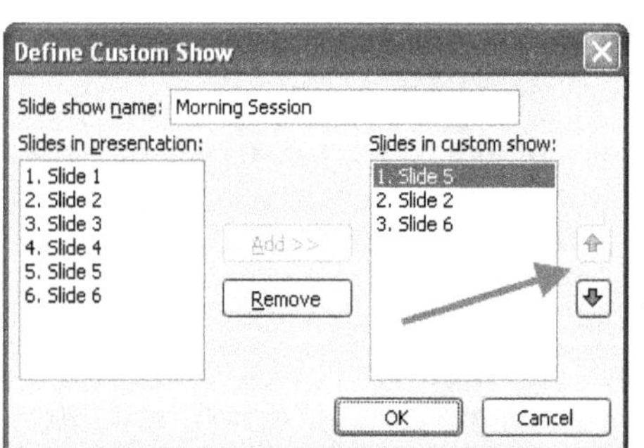

Figure 8.2

5. Once slides are added, you can change their display order by using the arrow keys on the right. Remember

that changing this order, as well as adding or removing slides, does not actually change slide order in the underlying slide show—changes affect only this Custom Show.

6. Click OK to complete the show.

8.3 Using a Custom Show

Creating a Custom Show is the first step, but then what do you do with one once it's created? The best way to access a Custom Show while presenting is to open it by hyperlink. Linking to a Custom Show, therefore, requires an internal hyperlink. Use an AutoShape or picture as the source (as usual) and make the Custom Show the destination. Custom Show names appear in the **Insert Hyperlink** dialog box when **Place in This Document** is selected.

1. If you haven't already done so, click the **Close** button when finished creating Custom Shows.
2. Choose a source for your hyperlink, such as an AutoShape or picture, right click it, and select **Hyperlink** from the shortcut menu.
3. Make sure **Place in This Document** is selected. Notice your new Custom Show is now available for hyperlinking (below the slide titles).

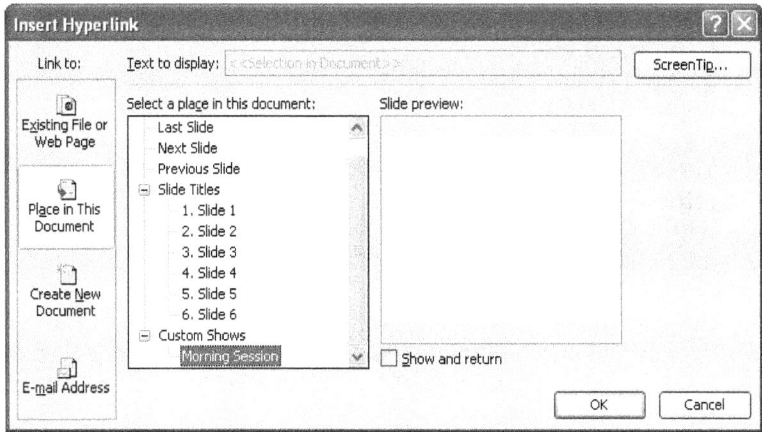

Figure 8.3

4. Click the Custom Show name to select it. The **Show and Return** box to the right of the show names becomes active.
5. Click this box to select it. Check marking the **Show and Return** box means PowerPoint will display the slides in your Custom Show in prescribed order and, after the last slide, return to the slide where the hyperlink originated.
6. Click **OK** to close the dialog box. Your source now contains a link that, when clicked, starts the Custom Show.
7. Start the slide show and test that the link and Custom Show work properly.

8.4 Pros and Cons of Custom Shows

Custom Shows certainly expand a presenter's options for varying how content is delivered, but they also are quite primitive compared with other visually interactive strategies. Before moving on to those strategies in succeeding chapters, let's review a summary of the advantages and disadvantages of Custom Shows.

PROS

- The primary reason Custom Shows might be used, as opposed to other Relational Presentation strategies, is so that the original show can remain in linear form. When first adopting a relational approach, for example, you might wish to leave a long, theme-based show just as it is, and add Custom Shows to enable random selection of individual content pieces. This strategy makes possible both standard linear delivery and random selection of content, without a lot of obvious navigation mechanisms.
- Custom Shows are compact and easy to keep track of.
- The Show and Return option works very well for automatically returning a speaker to the presentation's switchboard when done with a Custom Show.

CONS

- BIG DISADVANTAGE: Custom Shows are not accessible outside the current show. There is no such thing as book marking a Custom Show, and you cannot link to one in any other way except within the same show.

- When inside a Custom Show, you are almost as restricted as being in a standard linear presentation. If the Custom Show is 10 slides long, you will be stuck with those slides until the show ends. This is not a major issue if Custom Shows are short. Long Custom Shows, on the other hand, offer little advantage over standard delivery. As relational presenters, we need more options and flexibility—to break out of the slide-to-slide mentality.
- The fact that Custom Shows are programmed in advance, with exact slide selection and order, means a presenter solely using these devices cannot be truly relational or visually responsive to an audience. The goal of Relational Presentation is to place the presenter in total control of all content, at all times, anywhere, and in any order. Custom Shows allow a small degree of choice but are of limited value in a truly interactive context.
- In theory, one could try to use Custom Shows to mimic the Presentation Network mechanisms featured throughout the remainder of this book. The attempt soon would become hopelessly time-consuming and convoluted. We tried. We experimented with taking a large, 200-slide show and carving it up into many Custom Shows. It can be done but rearranging slides within a large Custom Show is laborious to say the least because the format does not support drag-and-drop positioning. Using the positioning arrows is the only option. Plus, slides are not displayed as thumbnails. So there is no way of telling visually based slides apart, to know which ones should go in which order, as is possible in Slide Sorter View.
- Custom Show stability is (or at least was) somewhat questionable. When we first began experimenting with visually interactive design and delivery, as mentioned, we used Custom Shows on a regular basis, not yet knowing other options were possible. Then we upgraded from version 2000 to XP. For some reason, XP corrupted most of our Custom Show names, which then, of course, meant that their associated links no longer worked. Our glorious and burgeoning network at the time came to a humble demise when all of a sudden half of the links broke. We had to spend who knows how many hours redoing the network. It was right about then we began looking for better ways—and have seldom used Custom Shows ever since.

Custom Shows seem to have been an early attempt by PowerPoint designers to break free from the restrictive, linear paradigm that came to symbolize digital presentation. Unfortunately, they stopped short of further developing the concept into a fully nonlinear platform, and Custom Shows never really gained popular use.

"I'm often in a room with a couple of our sales managers, the owner of the company (that we are calling on), and a couple of his people. Our role is to say, 'This is where we were and here's where we are now. Let's figure out where we can take the business in the future.' Having flexibility with my slide shows has completely changed the way I approach the customer."

Paul Kinney, National Accounts Manager
National Gypsum Company

Chapter 9

Navigation Elements and Styles

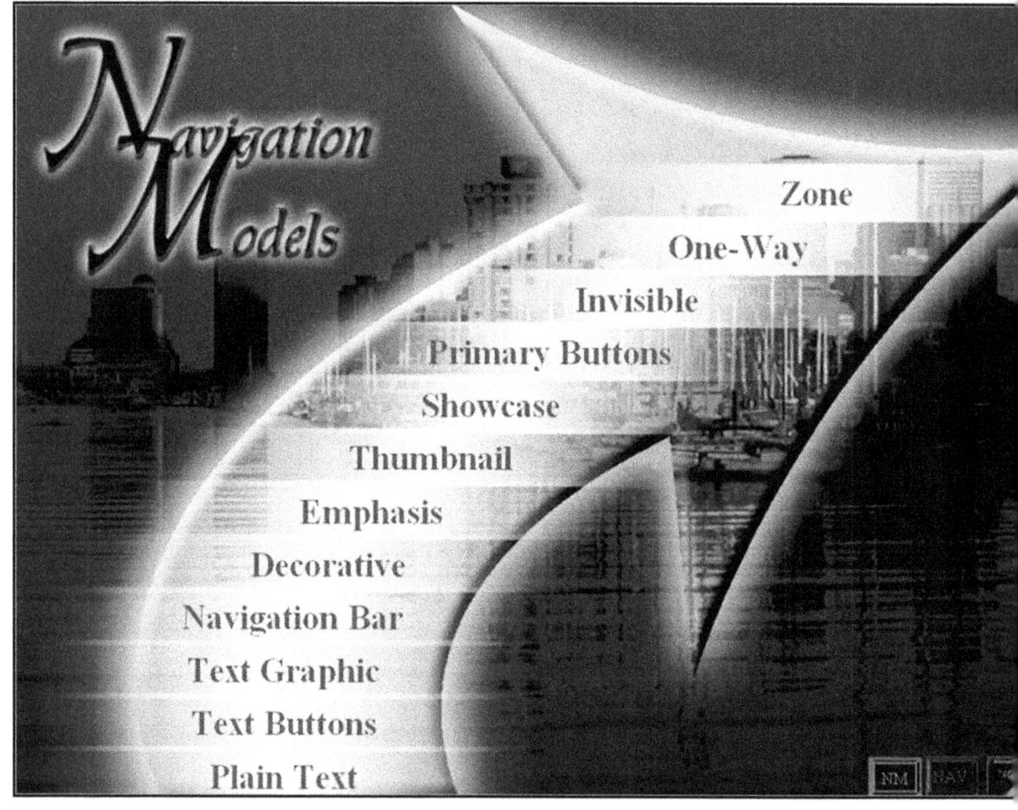
Navigation
Models
Zone
One-Way
Invisible
Primary Buttons
Showcase
Thumbnail
Emphasis
Decorative
Navigation Bar
Text Graphic
Text Buttons
Plain Text
NM
NAV

9.1 What Is Navigation?

The term *navigation* appears frequently in this book. Considering we use the word rather broadly, definitions probably are in order. Technically, any movement from one place to another, even if it involves nothing more than scrolling to the next slide, is navigation. For us, it normally involves hyperlink-based movement, when the presenter clicks something on the slide to execute an action, such as jumping to another slide or slide show. We also apply the term generically in reference to hyperlink-based objects. A phrase such as "The navigation on this slide allows the presenter to ..." may refer to any mechanism or strategy that facilitates movement or actions, such as a particular arrangement of AutoShapes.

The ultimate goal of navigation, regardless of form, is to give the presenter freedom of expression. Well-designed navigation components enable quick access to any slide, even if thousands of choices exist. Being able to tailor content on demand allows a speaker to focus on the true needs, interests, and pre-existing knowledge of viewers, immediately and continually.

And there's more. Navigation-based presentation has fascinating positive side effects as well. It can act as a prompt to remind the presenter of what content is available and where to find it. It can give the impression your network is larger (more complete) than it actually is. In many situations, navigation components enhance audience perception of a speaker's expertise, which, in turn, tends to boost his or her confidence and enjoyment while on stage. Hierarchical navigation structures provide a form of content management, adding to display professionalism.

Sometimes navigation roles are hidden to facilitate subtle or secretive selection of sensitive information. In other words, the orator has complete control of the message at all times, whether or not that control is apparent. In other cases, navigation components actually are woven into a slide's design and provide an intentional decorative flair. While presenters, in general, tend to regard navigation components as *plumbing* that should be covered over as much as possible, such need not always be the case.

Clearly, understanding navigation's role in Relational Presentation extends far beyond the mechanics of attaching hyperlinks to AutoShapes or pictures. Psychology is involved, as well as artistry, strategy, and a host of other considerations. Flexible delivery transforms plodding, monotonous PowerPoint monologues into what we call *digital conversation.* As a relational presenter, your performances likely will become much more interactive—and there is a good chance you will find this process richly rewarding.

9.2 Navigation Design Logic

We begin by exploring the three major categories of design logic underlying most forms of relational navigation: *linear, hierarchical,* and *interconnected.*

Linear Logic: Scrolling from one slide to another, within a single show, is certainly a part of Relational Presentation. Just because we frequently use hyperlinks to move around does not at all imply the abandonment of linear delivery. On the contrary, linear display is often quite appropriate within an interactive context. The distinction, of course, is that relational presenters are never trapped by sequential slides. At any time, they have options for nonlinear movement, either within the current show, within the network as a whole, or both.

It's important to consider that linear delivery takes on somewhat of a different meaning here. Traditional presentations often contain 30 to 60, or more, slides. Linear delivery using relational methods often entails moving through multiple short sequences of slides, rather than one long show.

Figure 9.1

Notice that having such modular linear components does not restrict you from displaying the entire message in traditional linear fashion, if desired. One could divide a 50-slide show into 10 five-slide shows, and then each of the 10 shows could be selected in order (by hyperlink). The effect would look similar to normal sequential progression and almost identical to using Custom Shows.

Here's an example of how we use linear delivery: While giving an overview of the main ideas behind Relational Presentation, we typically start with the slide shown in Figure 9.1 and scroll sequentially through the remaining 11 slides in this presentation. However, if someone asks a question, or if we think of a related topic that would be helpful, many options are available. All slides in this show, along with hundreds of supporting visuals (also in linear but separate shows), are immediately available from the menus and/or thumbnails on the left side of the slide.

Hierarchical Logic: Think back to the earlier example of the grocery store. The reason finding one piece of information out of 10,000 choices seemed quick and easy was because of hierarchical design. With this approach, information is clustered in meaningful ways, and then lumped under progressively higher (broader) categories. Eventually, a structure emerges that resembles the roots of a tree. Starting with the trunk of the tree, one can proceed down any major branch of the root structure until eventually reaching a tip, which in our case represents a target slide or individual small slide show. At any point along the way, one can return to previous junctures, or jump all the way to the top and proceed down another branch.

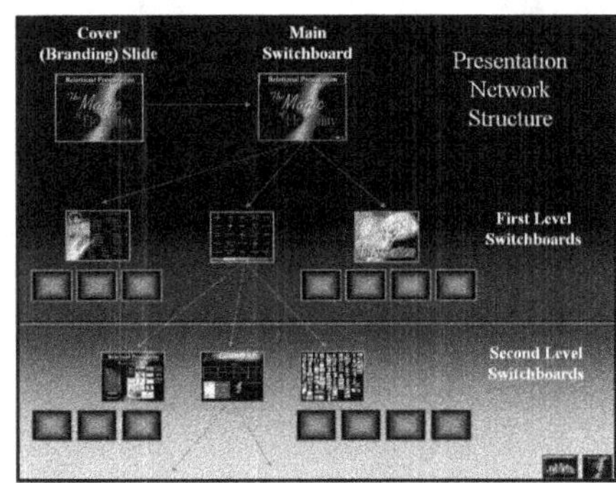

Figure 9.2

A nice feature of hierarchical design is its scalability. Because the process normally is built upon separate slide shows, you can apply it to either a small amount of information, or just as easily organize a massive collection of material. In the latter case, the result can be thought of as a type of *visual database*, constructed solely with PowerPoint.

Interconnected Logic: The third design strategy is based upon internal navigation and, therefore, applies to slides within a single show. The idea is that all slides within the show link to all the other slides in the show. As a result, every slide is constantly available from every other slide. Figure 9.3 provides an example.

Clicking any thumbnail transports the user immediately to the slide represented by that thumbnail. Upon reaching that slide, the exact same menu is available for accessing the other slides. A presenter can quickly choose any needed slides, and only those slides, in any order. As we will see, when exploring a style of navigation called *Inline Navigation*, the effect is made possible by building the navigation strip once, and then copying and pasting it onto all remaining slides—or, alternatively, placing it on the Slide Master if appropriate.

Figure 9.3

Interconnected navigation can also reach beyond single slide shows. It has a more complex parallel form we will analyze at length while learning about the *Nested Navigation Style*. In this powerful hybrid approach, internal and external navigation work together seamlessly, so that all slides in the current show AND those in related shows are available.

9.3 Navigation Elements

Navigation techniques make use of devices we call *Navigation Elements*. Navigation Elements normally are collections of AutoShapes or pictures, each of which contains a hyperlink. The slide on the next page displays the four most common Navigation Elements: *button, bar, panel,* and *block*.

Button: A single picture or AutoShape containing a hyperlink and used for navigation is called a ***button***. Buttons are the building blocks for the other three Navigation Elements.

Bar: When buttons are arranged horizontally in a single row on a slide, they are called a ***bar***. Bar elements most frequently appear at the very bottom of a slide, although some presenters prefer bars at the top to mimic common Web design styles.

Panel: Buttons stacked vertically are called a *panel*. Some people argue, from a cognitive science perspective, that panel elements should be located on the right side of the slide. Their reasoning is that (in Western cultures at least) the eye scans from left to right, and we should not force people to scan over the Navigation Elements every time they view content on a new slide. This may be a legitimate point. However, we tend to place panels on the left because this positioning continues to be common in Web design. And we're not really convinced that one side or the other makes much difference anyway, especially when using the Nested style of navigation.

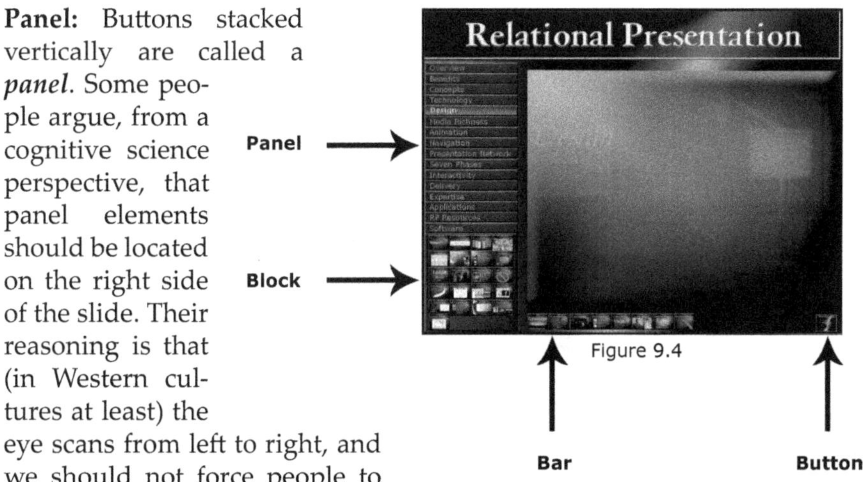

Figure 9.4

Block: When buttons are arranged in a combination of rows and columns, they are referred to as a ***block***. Block elements are usually composed of thumbnails because these buttons require less space.

When links are text-based (text inside AutoShapes) panel elements generally are preferred because more links can be stacked on top of each other, compared with being spread horizontally as bar elements. On the other hand, panel elements take up more usable space on the slide. So choosing one or the other is normally a tradeoff. Whichever kind of element you ultimately select, consider the following rules of thumb: Thumbnails often are the most space efficient whereas text-filled AutoShapes are the most descriptive, for cases when the audience needs to use the navigation for interaction.

9.4 Navigation Styles: SHOWCASE

Navigation Elements, coupled with design logic, produce what we call *Navigation Styles*. Throughout the rest of this chapter, we analyze several important Navigation Styles that together probably will form the bulk of your network's structure. We start with a simple yet highly effective style known as *Showcase*.

Figure 9.5

Showcase Navigation Style works especially well for categorical collections of content such as pictures, graphs, Web links, quotes, and so forth, where selection of individual items from a larger group is useful. The process is a back-and-forth movement between a switchboard slide that contains the main Navigation Element (normally a block—and usually a thumbnail-based block as shown here) and the content slides. In most cases, Showcase Navigation uses internal hyperlinks, so all associated links are within a single show.

The logic behind Showcase Navigation is very simple. First you build a standard linear slide show filled with content slides (each slide contains its own picture, graph, and so forth). Then you add one additional slide at the beginning of the show to hold the main navigation (switchboard). Each link on the navigation slide accesses a respective content slide and each content slide, in turn, links back to the navigation slide. That is, you create a loop. Clicking a link on the switchboard takes the presenter to content. Clicking the content transports the presenter back to the switchboard. The loop can be cycled through as many times as desired, viewing any content slide in any order.

The slide pictured in the top portion of Figure 9.5 contains 49 thumbnail images. Each thumbnail represents a slide. Therefore, this Showcase presentation contains 50 slides. The first slide holds the thumbnails, and each of the remaining 49 slides features a full-screen picture.

Showcase Style need not be restricted to internal navigation. Our *Navigation Switchboard* links to numerous short, separate shows. As each show concludes, the presenter is returned to the switchboard for more options.

Exercise—SHOWCASE Navigation

Building Showcase Navigation is easy. We will now create a simple Showcase Style presentation using four pictures. Use any pictures you may have on your computer. The show you are about to make will have five slides total (one switchboard slide and four content slides).

Figure 9.6

1. Create a new slide show.
2. Add four new slides. You want five slides total.
3. Remove the default text boxes on all the slides by clicking the first slide thumbnail, holding down the **Ctrl** key while pressing the letter **A** to select all slide thumbnails, and then clicking the **blank** option on the **Slide Layout** task pane. (Review Chapter 4 if necessary.)
4. Ignore Slide 1 for the moment. We will come back to it shortly.
5. Click the Slide 2 thumbnail to activate Slide 2.
6. Insert the first picture (green ferns in this example).
7. Click the Slide 3 thumbnail to activate Slide 3.
8. Insert the second picture (blue flowers in this example).
9. Repeat this process for the remaining two slides. You should end up with one picture per slide on Slides 2 through 5.
10. Now return to Slide 1 by clicking the Slide 1 thumbnail.
11. Insert all four pictures at once onto this slide. To do so, make sure to select all four pictures in the **Insert Picture** dialog box before clicking the **Insert** button.
12. After all four pictures are inserted onto Slide 1, downsize the images to 4 inches wide and arrange them as shown above.
13. Right click your first picture (green fern - now essentially a thumbnail) on Slide 1 and hyperlink it to Slide 2 (the full-size picture).
14. Hyperlink the remaining picture thumbnails to their respective slides.
15. The final step is to hyperlink each full-size picture on Slides 2 through 5 back to Slide 1, completing the loop.
16. When finished linking, start the slide show and test links. You should be able to move back and forth between thumbnails and slides.

9.5 Navigation Styles: IN-LINE

In-line Navigation Style accomplishes the same goal of allowing a presenter to randomly select individual slides, but the mechanism is different. Instead of a back-and-forth movement between a switchboard and content, all of the content slides are, in effect, their own switchboards. That is to say, the Elements used for In-line Navigation remain always visible, regardless of which slide happens to be displayed at the moment. There is no switchboard slide. The presenter at any time can immediately select another option from the available links. In fact, the links appear to remain fixed in place even while content on slides changes with each transition to another slide.

Figure 9.7

As with Showcase, the In-line Style typically ties together slides within a single show. Again, this show is linear and generally each slide in the show hosts one piece of content, such as a full-screen picture. The Navigation Element can be either a bar, panel, or block—and be text or thumbnail-based.

In-line Navigation takes advantage of a delightful optical illusion that has profound implications for relational presenters. Here's how the illusion works: If you place the same picture in exactly the same location on two different slides, and then transition between those slides during a presentation (assuming no slide transition effect), there will be absolutely no visual change during the transition. Because the second slide looks exactly like the first slide, PowerPoint does not modify the display between the two slides. In other words, it's impossible for the audience to tell that there is more than one slide, or notice the transition between the two.

Consequently, if we place the exact same Navigation Element on every slide in a show, that Element will appear to remain stationary and available, even though everything on the slide is really changing with each transition. The following exercise demonstrates this effect and its application. You will need four pictures again, as was the case with the Showcase exercise.

Exercise—IN-LINE Navigation

1. Create a new slide show.
2. Add three new slides (you need a total of four slides). The reason we need only four slides this time instead of five is because In-line Navigation does not require a switchboard slide.

Figure 9.8

Figure 9.9

3. Remove default text boxes. (Click first slide thumbnail, press **Ctrl A**, and click **blank** option in task pane.)
4. Insert one picture per slide. When finished, your four-slide presentation should contain a different full-screen picture on each slide.
5. Now click the Slide 1 thumbnail to make the first slide active.
6. Our goal is to build thumbnail navigation on one slide, in this case a bar, and then paste that Element onto every slide in this show (in the exact same position). Start by creating a navigation strip on Slide 1. Note that we do not have to start on the first slide, but always starting with Slide 1 is a good habit to develop. Click the **Insert Picture** icon on the **Picture** toolbar to open the **Insert Picture** dialog box.
7. Select all four pictures and insert them onto Slide 1. There should be five pictures on this slide—the original (green fern in the example shown) picture and the four new pictures on top of it (one of them being a second copy of the green fern picture).
8. Downsize these four new pictures on Slide 1 to be 0.5 inch wide. Notice that they may already be selected immediately after the

insert operation. If so, double click the top picture to open the **Format Picture** dialog box. If the four newly inserted pictures are NOT currently selected, select them first, and then double click the top picture. After downsizing, you should end up with small cascaded thumbnails in the upper left corner of the slide. SPECIAL NOTE: A common error is to also have the original picture (green fern in our example) selected along with the other pictures when downsizing, resulting in five small pictures and a white background. This is not what you want. Be careful that only the four pictures on top are selected before downsizing. Otherwise, step backwards (**Ctrl Z**) and redo the downsizing operation.

Figure 9.10

9. Because these thumbnails will be difficult to see against the picture backgrounds, add a colored border using the **Format Picture** dialog box.
10. Arrange the thumbnails along the bottom of the first slide, toward its center. **Important: Keep the thumbnails in the same order as the slides in the show.** Although doing so makes absolutely no difference to PowerPoint, it will simplify the forthcoming linking procedure and expedite future editing. Remember too that so far we are working on Slide 1 only.
11. To speed up the arrangement process, you may want to try the **Align and Distribute** functions on the **Drawing** toolbar.
12. Right click the first thumbnail and link it to Slide 1. That is, link the green fern thumbnail to the slide it's on.
13. Link the remaining thumbnails to their respective slides.
14. After links are in place, and thumbnails are positioned as desired, copy the entire group of thumbnails and paste them onto remaining slides using the scroll-paste (**Ctrl V**) procedure described earlier.

15. As you probably have noticed, our strategy here was to build one master set of navigation on Slide 1 first, and then copy and paste that set onto remaining slides, rather than starting from scratch each time. The copy-paste approach is much more efficient, especially with large slide shows.
16. Return to Slide 1, start the show, and test the links. You should be able to click any link and be transported to the appropriate slide—where, of course, the exact same navigation awaits. Notice the navigation appears to remain stationary, even though you know in reality that each set is unique to the slide it's on.
17. Editing: If you need to make changes to the navigation later, BE VERY SYSTEMATIC and always start again with Slide 1. Work your way down from there. Try the following scenario:
    a. Delete Slide 4.
    b. Now your navigation bar needs to be changed. Return to Slide 1 and delete the Slide 4 thumbnail.
    c. Copy the new bar, scroll to the next slide, select and delete the old bar, paste the new bar, and so forth.

9.6 Navigation Styles: ZONE

Zone Navigation Style offers a wealth of creative options for accessing subject detail or otherwise customizing messages. With Zone Navigation, a slide seems to have very few (if any) obvious Navigation Elements, and yet at the same time may be a full-scale and complex switchboard. The slide design itself enables the presenter to easily locate hidden links, what we refer to as *Zones*. In a sense, graphical components on the slide take the place of Navigation Elements, or seem to at least. They help a speaker know where to click and are another example of using Visual Clues. An audience member looking at a Zone Switchboard sees content, and nothing else. The presenter, on the other hand, has a different perspective.

A common example of Zone Navigation is a slide containing a bar graph, where invisible rectangular AutoShapes lie on top of each data bar. These shapes, in turn, are hyperlinked to related slides that show more in-depth information about the data in those bars. Clicking a data bar has the effect of *drilling down* into the numbers behind the numbers.

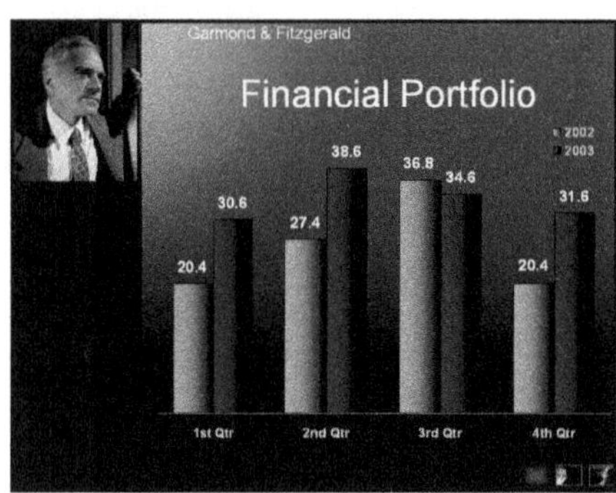

Figure 9.11

The slide in Figure 9.11, for example, might be the first in a show that holds 20 or 30 additional slides, each helping to explain the original graph. The speaker chooses either to show the initial numbers only or to customize the discussion, at any time, with additional facts perhaps two or three levels deep.

Ironically, one of the most important characteristics of Zone Navigation is that **it may not be needed at all**. The initial switchboard, in many situations, offers sufficient detail; there is no point in dragging viewers through additional information that might be boring or confusing at their level of understanding. Because the graph looks like any other static bar graph, an audience never thinks twice about more content being available. Even so, it is there, if and when needed.

As a presenter, you are constantly thinking to yourself, "I know there is more information here. Is it relevant? Is it needed? Is there time to show it? Is it too sophisticated or perhaps inappropriate for the current audience?" These questions are asked both before the event (during preparations) and on the spot (while interacting with viewers). Notice that slides in this way integrate smoothly with your thought processes. After all, during a normal conversation over dinner, we constantly ask ourselves questions similar to those above. We wonder if a topic is appropriate, if more detail is needed, or if we should change the subject altogether. Navigation, and especially Zone Navigation, brings this natural decision-making process into digital presentation. Now we are simply deciding, "Should I bring up AND show this particular topic or not?"

Zone strategy works exceptionally well in sales contexts, when featuring products or service details. Ken Dion, with the Power Tan Company, created a "products" switchboard (Figure 9.12) where each product group is a navigation zone. Clicking a product group gives more detail about that group, such as appropriate display details and marketing facts. These subslides, themselves, feature additional Zone Navigation that can be clicked to highlight individual product details, such as ingredients or usage directions. In some cases he includes even deeper content levels that may be applicable to any of several groups (vendors, customers, retailers, or sales staff).

Figure 9.12 Courtesy Power Tan, Inc.

Zones also work well for diagrams, maps, tables, and other kinds of descriptive display. Anytime a slide displays complex ideas or multiple objects, think about making it the basis for Zones.

The two most common uses of Zone strategy during interaction are: (1) to visually customize an answer to a question, such as showing phases of a project, on demand; and (2) to give examples or demonstrations, such as showing a product from different angles or magnifications, or displaying it in motion via video clip or animation.

As a general caution, be careful about the level of detail you build into Zone components. It's very tempting to want to include EVERYTHING right away that might be needed. In an ideal world, your network eventually will hold this level of detail. But for now, some priorities inevitably are higher than others. Focus on the highest priorities first. If a new line of products is coming out and people will be likely more interested in those products, build that section first. You may never have time or money enough to fill in all desired Zone components. Focus on the most important aspects first and add the others over time.

Example—ZONE Navigation

There are five slides in the example shown here. Slide 1 (Figure 9.13) is a Zone Switchboard. AutoShapes on top of four pieces of chocolate in this slide link to four corresponding content slides. The intent is for a presenter to pull up more information about chocolate, without using an obviously visible switchboard. Said another way, the presenter clearly knows Slide 1 is a switchboard but the audience has no idea, at least not at first.

This example calls for a little-known style of AutoShape that enables freeform construction. Freeform AutoShapes are perfectly suited for Zone Navigation because you can draw any design. Notice the shapes in the picture below. A light color was added to the normally invisible shapes on the four pieces of chocolate, showing their positioning.

Figure 9.13

To make freeform AutoShapes, use the **Scribble** tool that is categorized as an AutoShape **Line**. The Scribble tool lets you draw a shape with the mouse, as if using a pencil—tracing whatever shape is needed. It quickly fashions irregular navigation zones, such as areas that cover products, states or countries on a map, pieces of a diagram, and other complex areas.

9.7 Navigation Styles: INVISIBLE

Invisible Navigation Style bears a strong resemblance to Zone Navigation in some respects but there is a critical difference. With Zone Navigation, design elements on the slide act as visual guides to reveal link locations. The bars on the graph, the product displays, and the pieces of chocolate are all aspects of a slide's imagery that indicate where it makes sense for links to be. With Zone Navigation, the links are *hidden* in the sense that they are not immediately obvious. However, a viewer can quickly catch on that more links are (or should be) available, based on the slide's background.

Invisible Navigation is even more subtle. In fact, it is intended to be secretive. The slide design does not necessarily reveal in any way that a slide includes hyperlinks. When using truly Invisible strategy, there are no Visual Clues per se to guide finding links, or that might inadvertently give away the existence of hidden links.

Obviously, we are talking here about techniques intended for experienced relational presenters. Invisible links without Visual Clues can be confusing or even harmful if not handled correctly. And they can be easily overlooked. Even so, in the hands of an experienced user, these techniques are valuable.

A presenter might turn to this strategy when dealing with sensitive information that is not intended for all eyes, but that nonetheless should be available and customizable as usual. Objection handling comes to mind or creating audience intrigue—causing something to happen the audience doesn't expect. Think about the following examples:

Perhaps you are a consultant and have several clients with similar, or even competing, interests. Undoubtedly, some material in your network will be inappropriate for certain groups to know about, much less ever see. Having secret navigation in the right places protects confidential information, while simultaneously leaving it available when needed.

When working with government institutions and agencies, such as the Department of Defense or Federal Drug Administration, a successful contract bid or drug approval can hinge upon a single eight-hour final presentation. During this time, applicants are expected to successfully field questions related to the bid. Having the ability to visually and randomly answer questions is extremely important in this situation. However, using a normal (visual) switchboard may not be a good idea.

Let's say you know the panel will likely ask about certain concerns that have arisen in the past. So you prepare materials to address those matters on demand. Do you want to use an obvious switchboard that lists all the problems, 1 through 25, your interrogators can see as you navigate? Probably not. They may look at your navigation and think, "Oh yeah. We forgot about that issue. Let's go into more detail there." Hundreds of millions of dollars may hinge upon this single presentation, and you certainly do not want to offer any opportunity for unintentionally *opening the proverbial can of worms*. Still, that information must be available when questions are asked. Invisible Navigation puts the presenter in control of what is shown, with minimal risk of revealing too much.

Similarly, in more general objection-handling situations, you don't want viewers to see anything obvious that implies "Hey, look. This is where I go to handle any objection you can throw at me." Instead, augment relevant slides with invisible links that anticipate predictable resistance. If the issue comes up, deal with it on the spot. If it doesn't, the link remains hidden. A salesperson might say, "That's a really good point. Our competition does have a cheaper model that performs a similar task. But let me show you something about that product you may not be aware of."

Another way we employ Invisible Navigation is in the secret selection of parallel presentation tracks. We might have parallel presentations available that communicate approximately the same message, yet have different graphics, emphases, or examples. A group of engineers might relate to a particular style of presentation differently than a group of artists, and vice versa. Parallel ways of explaining the same topic can help you tailor a message. Invisible links allow this process to occur in secret. Key examples can be given with a sports theme, a family theme, an environmental theme, cats or dogs, red or blue, or whatever. The speaker gets to choose which variation is most helpful at the moment, and viewers do not even know a selection was made.

Figure 9.14

The slide at left looks innocent enough. One might correctly guess it introduces the concept of Relational Presentation. But this slide is far more powerful than might be obvious at first. It is, as previously mentioned, our Main Switchboard and links us to thousands of available slides. Is there any way to really guess, by simply looking at the slide, what potential waits? Not really. It would be impossible for someone looking at this slide to know it holds numerous animated menus, multiple parallel tracks, and a host of other link devices. That's exactly the effect we want. The audience doesn't have to know what is available. That's our job, as trainers and presenters. We just have to remember where to click.

What actually exists on the Main Switchboard slide appears here. This is the view one would really see if all the invisible Navigation Elements were made semitransparent. Yes, we could have accomplished the same navigation goals by using visible elements, but one of our purposes with this slide is to create intrigue.

Figure 9.15

Because the Relational Presentation concept is relatively new to most people, we typically approach audiences by starting with the slide in Figure 9.14 (our version of an Invisible Switchboard) and scrolling to succeeding slides in the show, just like everyone else. Later, we come back to the Invisible Switchboard and show viewers what they didn't see before, what they never would have guessed was there. Generally, we are greeted at that point by stunned looks of disbelief or amazement and the fun begins.

You may or may not apply the Invisible Navigation concept this same way, but surprising audiences with hidden flexibility and expertise is a potent technique. People are not expecting it and you can use such intrigue to your advantage. Until visually interactive presentation becomes more widespread, play it for all it's worth.

So how does a presenter find these invisible links or know they are there? For the most part, the process relies on some form of spatial logic, coupled with what we call *indirect* Visual Clues. Perhaps you mentally divide the slide into four quadrants. Clicking an invisible AutoShape in the upper left quadrant does something different from clicking one in the lower right quadrant. Or, maybe separate links exist in the four corners of the slide. Links might be placed on one side of a slide or the other, with a top, middle, and bottom option. Similarly, links might exist along the top or bottom.

As long as the presenter knows where to find the links when needed, the specific logic used is not important. In our case, we know there are six links along the top. The first link is to the left of the words and the last link to the right. The other four links exist on respective halves of the two words. Taking advantage of this kind of spatial-visual logic, we know exactly where to click.

9.8 Navigation Styles: NESTED

A while ago we had amassed about 200 digital video clips and were wondering how to organize them efficiently in the network. None of the existing Navigation Styles seemed adequate to handle the needed level of organization. Two years before that, we had decided to take up the challenge of inventing a new form of relational navigation. Eventually, that effort resulted in a primitive form of what we analyze next: **Nested Navigation Style**. At the time, the strategy seemed interesting but we could not imagine how it would ever have practical applications. So the concept was stored away in the recesses of thought and practically forgotten. Later, while thinking about these video organization tasks, it became obvious that the time for Nested Navigation's debut had come.

Figure 9.16

A newfound realization of what this Navigation Style might accomplish inspired experimentation. A few tweaks here and there eventually led to more than we bargained for. It transformed the entire Relational Presentation approach. Nested Navigation is now seen as a fundamentally important Relational Presentation navigation style.

No doubt you have noticed that a majority of the screenshots in this book resemble Figure 9.16. That's because Nested Navigation now serves as the backbone for our training materials. After finally realizing the potential it offers, we made the decision to convert almost all of our primary presentation content into this format. Doing so was a big task, but well worth the effort.

Nested Navigation essentially is a hybrid of all the styles you have learned so far. It is a rather involved idea, but don't let that be a concern. The methods to be mastered here are just complementary ways of looking at the skills and techniques you already know.

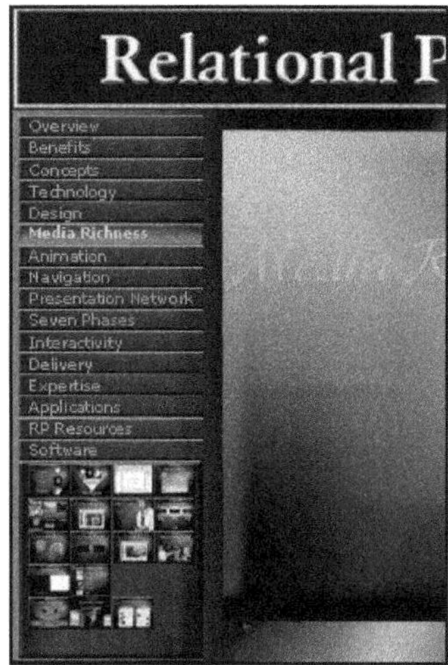

Figure 9.17

Nested Navigation, as the name implies, is based upon having menus within menus—menus that expand into more options. That is, clicking a menu item does more than just reveal another slide or open a slide show. It also exposes a submenu full of additional navigation options that are context-specific to the item clicked. On the screenshots shown here, notice that clicking the *Media Richness* link reveals a group of thumbnail links below. Clicking the *Concepts* link reveals a different set of thumbnails in the same area. As might be anticipated, all the links at the top activate a different set of options at the bottom.

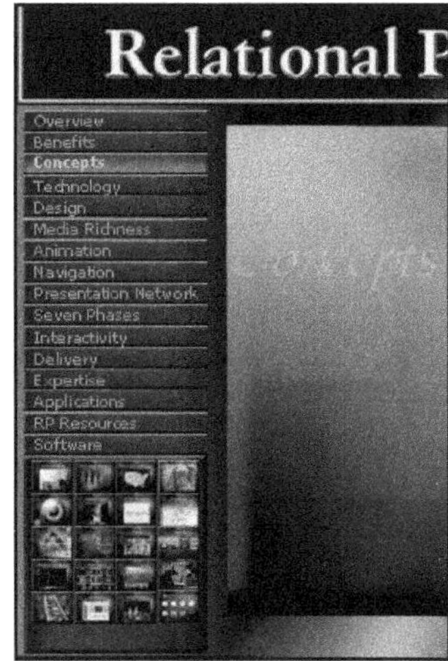

Figure 9.18

The effect is like standing before your kitchen cabinets. If you open the cabinet holding dishes, those items are available and nothing else. If you open the cabinet for pots and pans, you won't see dishes, cooking utensils, spices, or anything else. Nested Navigation offers this same kind of practical organizational logic for finding content in your network, where everything is conveniently clumped together and accessible, yet only visible when needed.

Let's examine the illustrations a little more closely. Each of the upper 16 AutoShapes in the panel links to a separate slide show. There is a show called *Overview*, a show called *Benefits*, a show called *Concepts*, and so forth—16 separate slide shows in all. Every time one of the upper links is clicked, the respective show opens. Now it just so happens that all 16 of these separate shows contain exactly the same 16 panel links (think back to In-line Navigation) on the upper left side. As a result, any show can open any other show, at any time. And, no matter which show is open, the main panel will look the same, as though we were in the same show all along.

And what about the bottom links? The thumbnail blocks or text links you see at the bottom represent the actual slides available within whatever show happens to be open at the moment. Thus in Figure 9.17, the *Media Richness* show is open and the thumbnails accordingly access its 17 slides. Figure 9.18 represents the *Concepts* show when it is open, with the thumbnails linking to its 20 slides.

Take a moment to think about this logic. The upper links are external because they are opening separate shows. The bottom links are internal because they are jumping to slides within the show that is open at the moment. Therefore, Nested Navigation is a mix of the two link types and uses both **Place in This Document** and **Existing File or Web Page** in the **Insert Hyperlink** dialog box. Furthermore, note that the panel element we are using here is really nothing more than a fancier version of In-line Navigation. The upper part of the panel, instead of appearing across all slides in a show, appears across multiple slide shows. It's exactly the same idea, just applied on a larger scale. The thumbnail links at the bottom are the same In-line Navigation you already know, applying across all slides in the show.

For many people, Nested Navigation is a difficult concept to grasp at first. Rest assured that everything we are accomplishing here is 100 percent standard PowerPoint. This same navigation strategy theoretically could have been put in place 10 years ago, in PowerPoint 97. Apparently, no one thought of it back then, and the adventurous are beginning to explore it now. Give it a try and see what you think. Once familiar with the Nested Navigation concept, we suspect you will find it irresistible.

There is one other critical aspect of Nested Navigation you should think about. All of the Navigation Elements are located on the Slide Master. Taking this approach is essential due to the linking complexity involved.

It also results in efficient editing strategy, should links need to be modified in the future. So plan on working with the Slide Master often from now on. Also remember, as mentioned previously, that when navigation appears on the Master, content cannot cover the entire slide because it would hide the navigation.

To our delight, the Nested design has turned out to be so user-friendly and intuitive that we now recommend it for all relational presenters, especially those working within a teaching or training environment. A huge advantage of Nested Navigation is that it constantly provides an outline of all available content. Presenting this way is like having a map in front of your eyes at all times. The presenter can progress through content and yet be subtly scanning available options as a guide for where to go next.

What makes the Nested approach even more powerful is that navigation need not be restricted to the obvious menus on the left side of the slide. Sometimes we take advantage of the content area to hold links as well. For example, during a discussion of Visual Clues we might discuss the overall topic using the slide shown here. To no one's surprise, though, all the thumbnails below the text labels are active links also—external links, in fact. Our content in this case has a dual purpose: It serves as both information and navigation. The thumbnails link to short, supporting slide shows and, therefore, give us a way around the partial screen restriction. It's not a big deal to open a two- or three-slide, full-screen presentation on top of our Nested platform (hiding menus) because as soon as we scroll through those two or three slides, that show will end and we will be automatically transported back to our Nested Navigation.

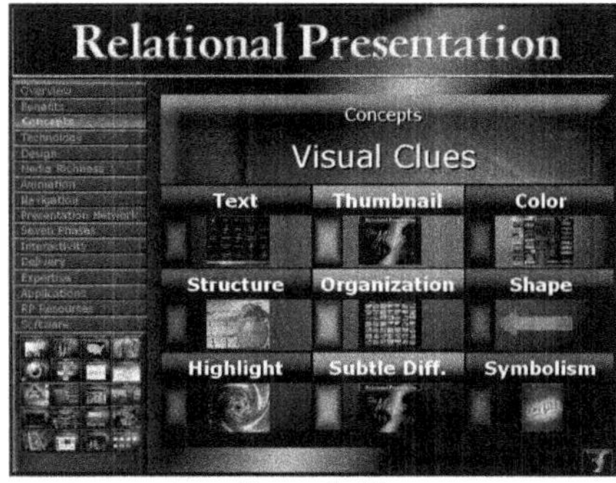

Figure 9.19

An observation some people make about Nested Navigation Style is that the panel element noticeably reduces the amount of usable space on the slide. This is true. However, you may be surprised to discover that using this extra space might not be necessary. If adhering to the one-idea-per-slide principle, the space available for content using Nested design is large enough for just about any idea. Even so, if you do need more space, it's OK to modify the Nested design as needed. Perhaps your menus will appear at the bottom or top instead.

Because Nested strategy enables you to organize a large amount of related content, the overall structure typically has a unifying theme. For example, the Nested slides pictured throughout this book are all related to the Relational Presentation training process. It's even common for Presentation Networks to contain more than one Nested platform, each with its own focus.

A classic example might be a professor who teaches three classes. The presentation materials for each class might appear as separate Nested elements within the larger network framework. Information within the Nested components then breaks down by class period, and finally by individual slides needed during those class periods. Such a highly organized approach would allow the professor to say, "Ah, that's a good question. Remember when we talked about that a couple of weeks ago and I showed you this?" There would be freedom to move around at will, within all levels of the Nested material. Or, just as easily he or she could access content from one of the other Nested areas, along with any other relevant slides in the network.

When a Presentation Network's Nested sections are organized around themes as described above, these sections are called *Core Networks*. Each Core Network literally is a small network within the larger network and is relatively independent. Think of the analogy of a Web site that ties together several smaller sites. Each small site has its own purpose and mechanisms, but the larger (enveloping) site unifies the individual pieces and enables easy navigation between them. In a large relational network, such Core Networks can be, in effect, *plug and play*. You might decide to drop a new Core into the existing structure, and then access all that material with a single hyperlink.

9.9 Navigation Styles: ANIMATED

Navigation Styles continue to evolve and emerge. This book cannot possibly cover all the creative mechanisms relational presenters are discovering. We do, however, want to touch on one more fascinating style that is beyond the scope of this book and will be covered in a companion book. This style, called **Animated Navigation**, gives a highly professional, impressive, and useful flair to your network. It is a must-have for experienced relational presenters.

Animated Navigation, as one might guess, uses PowerPoint's animation functionality to create motion-based Navigation Elements. That is, menus need not be static, or even take up space, on a slide. They can be totally hidden from view in their normal state, and then animated into view when needed—and, naturally, hidden again.

We use this style on our Main Switchboard, as shown in Figure 9.20. In fact, almost all of the navigation on our Main Switchboard is animated. You can't see the various Elements but there are four other menus here that can appear in the same space as the displayed menu, all available on demand. When we don't need a particular menu, it is invisible. Any menu then requested fades into view in 0.02 second and is ready for clicking. If we don't click an option within 4 seconds, the block of thumbnails begins to gradually fade back to invisibility.

Figure 9.20

There are practically endless ways of creatively applying animation to accentuate and improve static navigation. In a sense, we are mimicking some of the fancier menus found in advanced Web sites, such as drop-down and context-based menus.

Animated Navigation is certainly impressive and unusual. At the same time, to be candid, it's not necessarily for everyone, nor appropriate for all situations. It takes extra time to create and is a little more work to edit. We are not bashful in saying that, often, good old-fashioned static links are the best way to go for standard network operations.

"I created an index page for my principal and assistant principals to use for the numerous PowerPoint presentations they share at the beginning of school. It worked great! They were very impressed and the transition from one presentation to the next was seamless. Thank you."

Shelly Flowers
Technology Instructional Specialist, USA

Chapter 10

Navigation Strategies and Concepts

Choice

10.1 Navigation Best Practices

The idea of spontaneously moving within and between slide shows is, to say the least, an unusual concept for most presenters. Don't be surprised if the process you are learning takes time to get used to and perfect. Early attempts at building Navigation Elements, laying out attractive designs, and formulating organizational logic will be experimental at first—perhaps even somewhat crude. This is a normal part of seeing your message from a different perspective. A year from now you might even look back and ask, "Why did I do it that way?" All of us go through the same transition.

What is important at this stage is experimentation. Expand upon the knowledge you have learned so far and begin integrating navigation into your existing shows. There are many important topics yet to come in this book, but you have enough knowledge at this point to start. Begin testing these concepts in your actual speaking activities. That's the only way to really know which Navigation Styles and strategies work best in your circumstances.

Fortunately, thousands of people have gone before and have beaten down well-defined paths of best practices that can help guide decision making. This chapter outlines some of these guidelines. We'll look at additional navigation-related issues, along with tips for easier implementation. Suggestions offered here are merely that—suggestions. Your presentation environments and subject matter may necessitate alternative perspectives and approaches.

10.2 Navigation Element Aesthetics

A question we frequently encounter in one form or another is "What should my navigation look like?" Without a doubt, there are practically infinite answers to that question. A given look and feel might be appropriate in one context and not work well in another. Additionally, what might look good to you may be perceived differently by others.

Here are our opinions: We often see novice relational designers adding extra large, showy Navigation Elements, similar to those pictured on the next page, that serve no purpose being so big. We're not sure why this phenomenon occurs, but the frequency is high enough to warrant mention. Although occasionally you may want large and readable navigation

Figure 10.1

buttons—to encourage audience participation in subject matter—navigation normally should be as subtle and out of the way as possible. In other words, unless the audience really needs to see the options available, try blending navigation components into the slide background and make them relatively small. Our general preference is for subtle panels or bars made of small, invisible, text-filled AutoShapes that are located along the side, or at the very bottom of the slide. Designing discreet navigation should be your preferred practice because, after all, navigation generally exists for the sole benefit of the presenter; there is no need to draw undue attention to it.

Figure 10.2

Keeping navigation small and unobtrusive is not a problem (visually) for the presenter either. Almost invariably, he or she is closer to the screen or can look at a computer monitor. In both cases, blended navigation that is too small or obscure for the audience to clearly distinguish is readily visible to the presenter. Button design generally can be very subtle. Do be careful, though, if there is a chance ambient light may be cast across the screen during a performance and you have no access to a computer monitor. In this case, subtle navigation can become TOO subtle and disappear into the background, causing the presenter difficulties. Furthermore, most relational presenters do not want to be tied to their computer and loath being dependent upon looking at a computer monitor while presenting. Navigation design, therefore, should be a balance between subtlety and readability when projected.

A VERY STRONG recommendation is to never mix two brightly contrasting colors. Doing so draws undue attention to the buttons and gives presentation materials an amateurish feel—unless, of course, you are designing presentations for a circus or a football team! Especially avoid red and blue combinations and red and green combinations.

10.3 Encouraging Interactivity

Sometimes a presenter really does need big and bold navigation so that the audience can easily see available options. In this situation, navigation components serve a dual purpose. They provide access to content and are themselves content. A presenter typically uses such links as a springboard for audience engagement.

Lisa Koss, a consultant on cross-cultural issues within multinational corporations, applies this approach during half- and full-day seminars. She allows participants to choose areas of interest and relevance. Lisa spends most of the agenda covering core topics, but along the way weaves in opportunities for participants to choose topics out of potentially hundreds of hours of additional material. Her techniques not only help solidify audience interest, they give her valuable feedback on viewer experiences that helps dynamically shape the regular agenda. In Lisa's case, the buttons must be easily readable from anywhere in the room. The navigation is intended to be the focus of the slide.

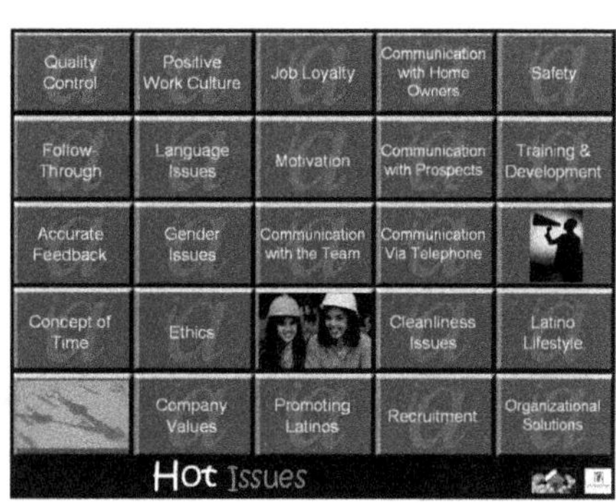

Figure 10.3 Courtesy Lisa Koss, International Advantage

When setting up navigation to promote dynamic exchange, don't assume the audience will automatically jump at the opportunity to interact with you. Many people have never seen this form of presentation before and will remain passive. In most cases, you will need to *prime* their interest by showing navigation potential, and then directly soliciting participation.

10.4 Promoting Presenter Expertise

Lisa's slide also has a third, unspoken purpose—to communicate presenter expertise. A fascinating aspect of visual expression is that it often has both obvious and not-so-obvious consequences. Said another way, a savvy presenter can structure slide layout, pictures, and graphics to casually *say* far more indirect information than dare be spoken by actual words. Lisa's switchboard, for example, along with her other carefully designed slide displays, implies she as a trainer and consultant really knows what she is talking about. She has a great deal of valuable information available on demand, and this fact increases viewer perception of her expertise and right to be in the spotlight.

It's imperative you think about this issue very carefully. Anytime a speaker addresses an audience, there is some degree of acknowledgement the person has a good reason to be in that position, that he or she is an expert on the topic at hand and worthy of attention. However, this attitude is tenuous at best. You can easily lose onlookers' initial respect based upon your subsequent performance. Effective public speaking is a delicate mix of ability, artistry, and psychology. The latter component should not be taken for granted. Speaking, in any capacity, involves selling yourself to viewers. You are competing for their attention and asking for their valuable time. Do you have something valuable to share with them? Are you worth listening to? Are your materials worth watching? Hopefully so because if not, there's always the football game, the hot date, or the new car to think about. Like it or not, every speaker is a salesperson—and you are the product being sold.

As a result, strategically crafting your presentation materials to accentuate positive audience perception is very important. If your displays give the impression you have a great deal of valuable information to share—more than possibly could be covered in the allotted time—there will be a subconscious sense of "Wow. I guess he is the authority." When we have people's respect, we have their attention. With attention, their minds are open to our message.

10.5 Obscuring Information

Speaking of psychology and artistry, in certain cases you may wish to craft navigation components that discourage interactivity. That is, the elements are designed to intentionally obscure or hide available information. We introduced this concept while analyzing Invisible Navigation in Chapter 9, but keep in mind that slide components need not be invisible to obscure a presenter's interactive options. Design can effectively mask or redirect meaning.

Think back to our former Invisible Navigation examples, where delicate situations demanded secretive selection of visuals. Invisible strategy is powerful but should be used only sparingly because it can backfire. If viewers catch on to your techniques because of overuse, they may take offense at the *cleverness* of hiding information. An alternative and innocuous approach is to keep links visible, yet set them up so that only the presenter understands their meaning or potential.

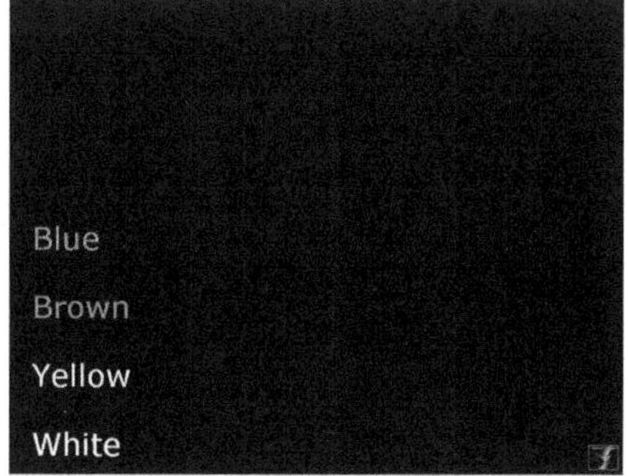

Figure 10.4

The example shown in Figure 10.4 demonstrates this idea. The *Blue* link could signify just about anything—a blue car, the code name for a company division, a line of products. The presenter knows what the link signifies within the context of its use and perhaps because of other Visual Clues on the slide. Viewers cannot possibly know what that link will open.

Figure 10.5

In this example, the *Blue* link displays a blue butterfly. What does the *Brown* link do? Does it access a brown butterfly on another slide in this show? Does it perhaps open an entirely different slide show or run a movie? There is no way for sure to tell—and that's the desired effect.

Picture thumbnails, and especially screenshots, offer a perfect way of obscuring link content, while giving presenters strong visual meaning. Observe the thumbnail links on the left in Figure 10.6; they exist in one of our animated menus. What do they mean? If you knew nothing about

Figure 10.6

Relational Presentation techniques, would you have even the slightest idea of what this menu accomplishes? Would you know, in fact, that these links help us handle common audience objections? We certainly know exactly what these links do.

10.6 Link Consistency

When identical links exist across multiple slides within a show, and especially when such links appear across multiple slide shows, consistency of placement and look are critical. For example, if you have a link back to the Main Switchboard from every slide in your network, make sure this link ALWAYS appears in the same location and has the same appearance.

Consistency of both navigation appearance and placement helps a speaker find frequently used links without having to search for, or remember, their location. Think of main navigation components, such as the link pointing back to the Main Switchboard, as similar to the brake and accelerator of a car. During a high-stress driving situation, you don't want to have to think about where to find the brake. It's in the same place, no matter what kind of car you drive. The consistency of positioning makes switching between different car models relatively easy. Now imagine yourself as a nervous presenter. The main navigation links should always be in the same location on slides, to provide assurance and control.

We prefer the bottom right corner for main navigation buttons because it is the least important area of the slide (from a viewer's perspective). Keep in mind that these buttons are used a lot during a typical performance. If they are at the top of slides, viewers are more likely to be distracted by your cursor movements. It's a good idea to keep cursor activity as inconspicuous as possible.

The placement of other linked objects is not as critical. Even so, from an aesthetics perspective, consistency of Navigation Elements is recommended. Having panels on opposite sides of different slides, for example, might result in navigation appearing to jump back and forth during transitions.

10.7 Link Redundancy

Have you ever been in a situation where you performed a Web search using a search engine, found an interesting Web page, and then could not find additional links on the page to access other pages at that site? A similar situation could happen with your network if you do not use a fundamental principle called *link redundancy*. Link redundancy means you always have multiple links to somewhere in the network on every slide. In practice, every slide should contain a link back to the Main Switchboard and at least one other link pointing somewhere.

Occasional broken links are just a fact of life. Even those of us who have been presenting this way for years get lazy sometimes and forget to thoroughly check our materials before a performance. What is NEVER acceptable is to be stuck on a slide without access to other slides in the current show, or at least to other areas of your extended network.

To avoid being trapped, always have several links on slides. That way, if one link happens to be broken, it's unlikely all links on that slide will be in a similar state. For example, we have a link to our Resources Section on every slide. If the link to the Main Switchboard doesn't work, we at least can navigate to the Resources Section, and then get back to the Main Switchboard from there. Making sure link redundancy is part of your design thinking from the beginning gives you a fallback plan just in case something goes wrong, which is the biggest fear of most people starting out with these techniques. Having alternative navigation options is very comforting.

It is possible for novice (or careless) designers to break all external links in a show in one fell swoop. Normally this happens when a show is moved to an entirely different branch of the network, at a different folder level. In this case, the best redundancy strategy of all is for all slides to include the *Magic Back Button* mentioned earlier (and to be discussed soon).

10.8 The Illusion of Completion

Sooner or later it will happen, if it hasn't already. While continuing to read this book and experiment with your own materials, questions will start floating around in your brain, such as "Gosh, how am I ever going to have resources to create all of this stuff? How will I find the time, money, and talent to fill out all the branches of what I want in my network?" The answer is simple: You won't—not this week, not next month, and probably not next year. Maybe by the time you are 95 and squeezing out your last breath, you may have come close to finally completing all the content that *would be nice to have* in your materials.

The point is, what you have begun here will never be finished, not really. There will always be something that can be improved upon or augmented. That's OK. You don't have to have it all right now. The good news is that your network does not need to be finished or perfect to be highly useful. A recommended strategy is to build the most crucial pieces first and make the rest of the network look like it's there.

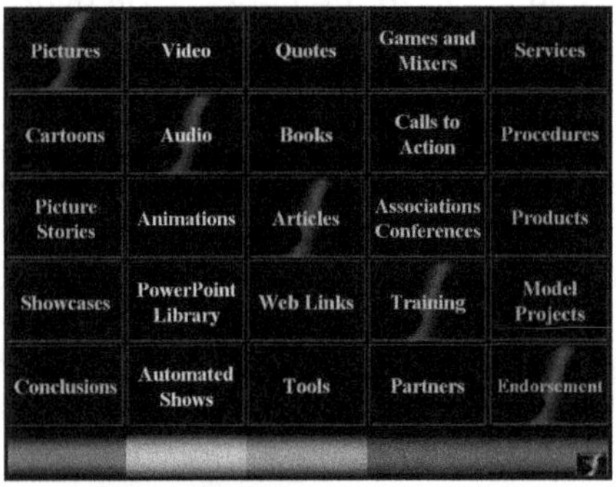

Figure 10.7

Most of us have encountered Web sites where some links are *under construction*. This technique of building an initial shell and filling in detail gradually, according to priorities, is common among media designers. The same approach is perfectly acceptable for your content branches as well.

Look at our Resources Switchboard in Figure 10.7. In theory, all of these categories link to other switchboards that in turn potentially link to other switchboards, and so forth. Here sits a massive, hierarchically arranged collection of everything we could ever imagine needing while presenting. Well, that is true in our wildest dreams, anyway. The reality, though, is that we are just like you. There are only 24 hours in a day.

Many of the links pictured here go only to placeholder slide shows. The audience doesn't know the difference. The material looks like it's there. It will be ... someday.

Navigation, by its very nature, means you have a choice of whether or not to use it. Learners, when first approaching Relational Presentation methods, often develop a misconception that becoming *relational* means giving up linear (slide-by-slide) delivery. This cannot be further from the truth. Almost all relational presenters leave substantial portions of their materials linear to some degree. That is, interactive speakers do not constantly click links and move about randomly.

Most presenters deliver key messages in linear shows and augment slides within those shows using internal navigation. That way they can deliver a message in the traditional fashion and still jump around occasionally. We strongly encourage beginners to stay mostly linear at first and gradually experiment with more and more sophisticated nonlinearity. Those who try to change established patterns too quickly sometimes become overwhelmed with the shift.

Again, it's imperative to begin integrating simple navigation ideas into your existing shows and try these ideas. Gradually work toward more sophistication. When trying Nested Navigation, you will discover another reason why we like it so much. All of the shows represented by the upper links are just linear shows. They can be delivered in traditional style if preferred, or you can access specific slides or any of the other shows available at any time. This organization seems to represent the ideal union between linear and nonlinear delivery.

It is true, though, that linearity in a relational network tends to have different characteristics. Linear shows normally are shorter and, therefore, more modular in nature. A sequence containing 50 slides might be divided into five 10-slide shows that are then arranged for selection by switchboard. Doing so offers the significant advantage of being able to select pieces in different orders or to leave out pieces. At the same time, the original linear sequencing can be simulated by simply showing each of the five shows in progressive order. A modular approach to linearity offers more flexibility without giving up the original sequencing.

Remember that navigation is there to aid your communication style, not dictate it. A certain amount of linear delivery is perfectly acceptable, especially when used in short bursts.

10.10 Navigation Building Strategies

As a final comment on navigation, let's take a closer look at an issue mentioned previously. When building or modifying Navigation Elements, it's very important to be rigidly systematic with the steps followed. Developing good, methodical habits at the beginning of your journey not only helps preserve your sanity, it greatly improves efficiency. The more efficient you become in your design activities, the more time you will have for perfecting other skills. Even more critical, methodical building habits translate into less (and generally zero) errors at show time. The best way to guarantee your network structure will work as expected on stage is to discipline the design process.

When creating any form of navigation, try to follow the formula in Figure 10.8 as much as possible. Let's say you are building a panel Navigation Element. Create one button first, with all aspects of the desired look and feel. Copy and paste that button as many times as necessary. Then add your links. Finally, copy and paste your completed panel onto other slides if necessary. When making In-line Navigation, first build one strip on one slide. Next add your links. Then copy and paste the strip. Always complete these processes starting on Slide 1 and work your way down.

When editing navigation components, DO NOT change the individual links on all the slides. Change the links on Slide 1 only, and then copy this master set, delete the old navigation, and paste the new set throughout. If you are placing or editing navigation that spans multiple shows, first open all the shows at the same time. Place (edit) the navigation in one show only. Copy this navigation. Save and close the show. Go to the next show. Paste the new navigation. Save and close that show. Go to the next.

These procedures may seem tedious but they minimize the chances of your making a mistake, such as forgetting to change a link in the middle of a show. Don't take that chance. Discipline your design habits or spend a lot more time later fixing mistakes. Can you tell we learned these lessons by hard experience?

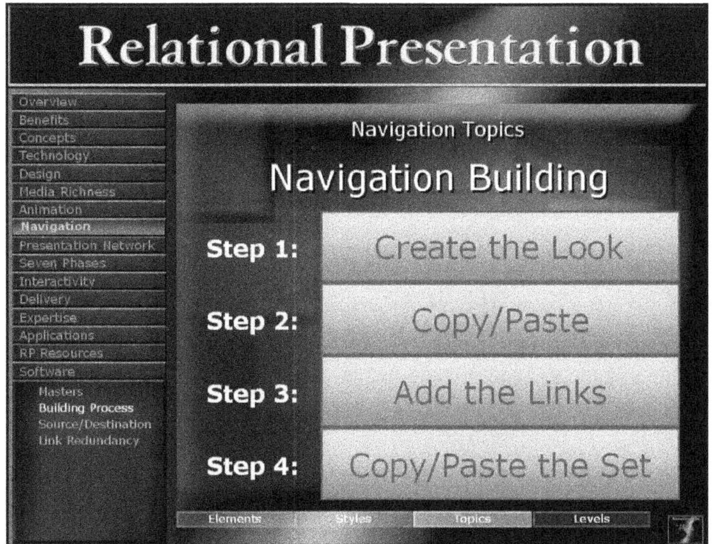
Relational Presentation
Overview
Benefits
Concepts
Technology
Design
Media Richness
Animation
Navigation
Presentation Network
Seven Phases
Interactivity
Delivery
Expertise
Applications
RP Resources
Software
Masters
Building Process
Source/Destination
Link Redundancy
Navigation Topics
Navigation Building
Step 1:
Create the Look
Step 2:
Copy/Paste
Step 3:
Add the Links
Step 4:
Copy/Paste the Set
Elements
Styles
Topics
Levels

Figure 10.8

"It was the funniest thing. The other day I was presenting at a conference and displaying (interactively) various home healthcare technologies that are available. My switchboard contained thumbnail images of products from several companies. The problem was that one company hadn't provided me with images of their products despite several requests, and I'd forgotten to edit out their blank line of image placeholders in the switchboard. As it turned out, one of their representatives was in the audience. When he saw the potential of this kind of visual display—and that his company wasn't represented—he raced up afterwards to make sure I had images for next time."

Steve Hards, Independent Consultant
TelecareAware

Chapter 11

Components of a Presentation Network

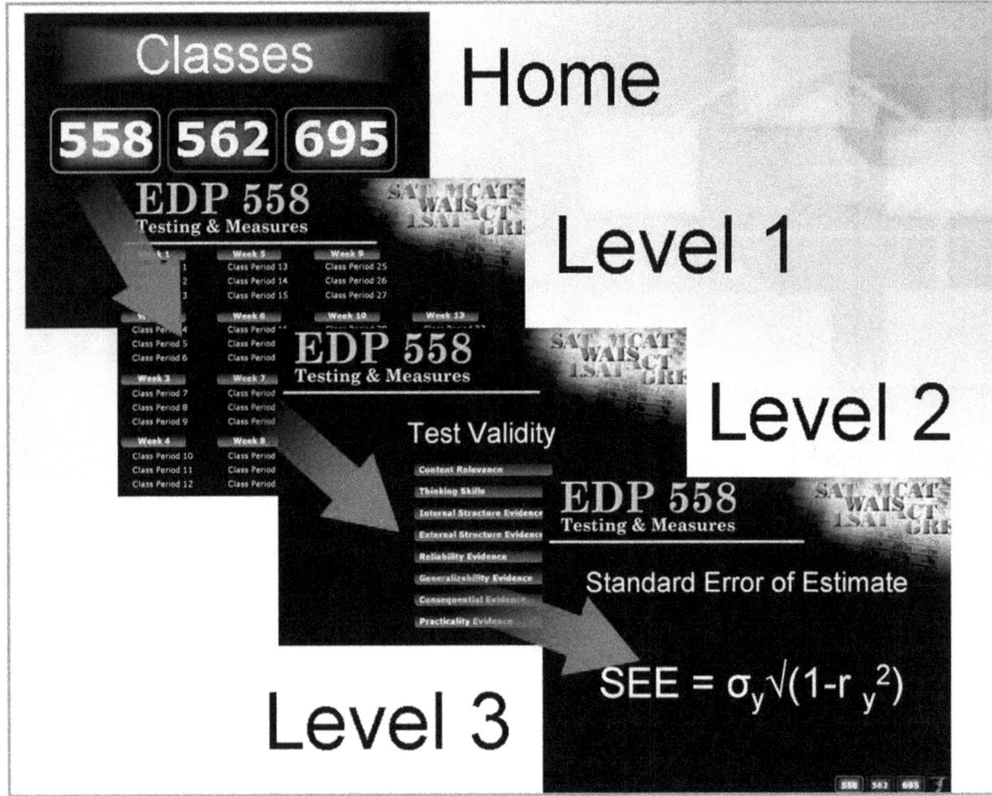

Classes
558
562
695
Home
EDP 558
Testing & Measures
Level 1
Level 2
Test Validity
Content Relevance
Thinking Skills
Internal Structure Evidence
External Structure Evidence
Reliability Evidence
Generalizability Evidence
Consequential Evidence
Practicality Evidence
Standard Error of Estimate
SEE = σy√(1-r y²)
Level 3

11.1 About Presentation Networks

Up to this point we have used the term *Presentation Network* frequently and compared this presentation structure to a Web site. It is similar to a Web site but is based entirely on PowerPoint rather than built with an html editor. In this chapter, we explore the components that go into fashioning a Presentation Network and explain how to get the most out of this essential tool. As we explore the individual components, keep in mind your network does not need to contain all of them. Your design preferences and priorities may vary from ours, or you simply may not need this full array of options. There are no set rules on how a network should look or work. So feel free to experiment with any or all of these ideas, on any scale.

It's quite possible you will even develop alternative methods that better suit your situation. In that case, we would love to hear about them. Many of the ideas in this book have come from a workshop attendee or former graduate saying, "Hey, did you know you can do this?" Every now and then, we didn't know.

When building a network, know it will be an ongoing process. Most relational designers never really reach a point where they call their structure *finished*. It may be very powerful and functional, yet a Presentation Network is a living entity of sorts that continues to grow and evolve over time, along with your increasing knowledge, experience, interests, needs, and circumstances. The major components may be reasonably complete, but there will always be something else that would be great to have or some new technique that performs tasks better and easier.

We have also found—almost without exception—that people end up remodeling their network's design logic from time to time. It's impossible to know at the moment exactly what your needs will be months or years from now. You may look back and ask, "What was I thinking?" That is a normal part of the learning and growth process.

That said, our goal is to give you a wealth of recommendations that will make design decisions more efficient and hopefully shortcut the need for future revisions. Suggestions in this chapter are based upon our years of experience, making both successful decisions and mistakes you will want to avoid. We'll get you started in the right direction, and then let you experiment with finding the strategies that ultimately make the most sense in your presentation environments.

Expect initial attempts at organizing and building to be somewhat crude. Some decisions you make today will remain unchanged months from now, while others will be discarded. The only way to know for sure is to make decisions and experiment with the results. Experience is the best determinant.

Finally, realize that the expression *Presentation Network* can be interpreted broadly. A network initially might be little more than a small number of slides and/or slide shows—or it might eventually grow to hold tens of thousands of either. For our purposes here, think small. When first experimenting, put together a small network to gain experience and the satisfaction of success. You can always expand this effort later. As a matter of fact, probably the best approach you can take starting out is to build a medium-size nested section (Core Network) and then tie it together with a Cover Show, a Main Switchboard, and perhaps a Resources Section, all of which are profiled here.

Other than a few exceptions, the rest of this book contains little additional material regarding PowerPoint skills. You already know all the technical wizardry needed for creating elaborate networks. Now it's just a matter of applying those skills in both practical and creative ways.

11.2 Network Components

A very small network, in theory, could be based on a single slide show only. In this case the presentation might have a combination of internal navigation styles and perhaps a collection of Custom Shows. This actually is a good strategy if you are sure the network will stay around 100 or less slides. Such a scenario might work well if the network is being created for a single event.

For larger content collections (almost all normal networks), you definitely want to base the structural logic on multiple shows, instead of just one. Most networks have a combination of both internal and external navigation.

The following components may be found in a typical full-scale Presentation Network, as explained throughout the rest of this chapter. Keep in mind these definitions are not meant to be distinct or fixed. Sometimes lines between the category definitions are very blurry. Use these categories as suggestions for structural ideas. Components may be:

- Cover Show (also known as a Branding Show)
- Main Switchboard
- Seed Presentation (or more than one Seed Presentation)
- Subswitchboards
- Core Networks (such as one or more nested sections)
- Primary shows and collections
- Picture/video stories
- Conclusions Section
- Resources Section

11.3 Cover (Branding) Show

A *Cover Show* serves a purpose similar to the cover of a book. It is the beginning and ending of all performances. A presenter opens this show as the starting point of an event and eventually returns here to provide a closing backdrop and shut everything down at the end, after attendees have left. In some respects it resembles the idea of a title slide (used by many presenters) except that a Cover typically is more generic—spanning all performances rather than being specific to one. A Cover Show also resembles a Web site splash page. Regardless of analogy, the Cover Show is always the first and last slide the audience sees. It is the ONLY show a relational speaker ever manually opens during (actually, before) a performance. All other shows in the network open via hyperlinks.

Here's how it works: The image in Figure 11.1 is the Aspire Cover Show, displayed full-screen. When preparing for a live speaking event, we open the Cover and leave it displayed on screen for the half hour or so before the presentation, seminar, or training starts. Audience members see it when first filing into the room. For all they know, this is the first slide of a typical linear

Figure 11.1

slide show. In reality, this Cover Show has only one slide. We use it as a basis for introductory remarks and as a launching point into the rest of the network.

A Cover Show has three main purposes:

- **Branding:** Because this slide is the first image viewers see, it provides an excellent opportunity for displaying powerful branding elements. Many presenters who design a network for their own teaching activities or nonwork-related presentations initially think, "Well, I don't have a company per se. Why do I need this slide to be branded?" Possibly you don't, but remember that this network, this collection of content, will become a representation of your knowledge, skills, and value to clients, trainees, or students. It sets the stage for what you have to offer. In the very least it should be visually attractive and professional. A Cover's imagery doesn't have to be complex. The image in Figure 11.2 is the Cover Show for a University of Arizona research project called the *DISCOVER Projects*. This same imagery appears across their Web site, brochures, letterhead, and so forth.

Figure 11.2 Courtesy DISCOVER Projects, University of Arizona

The graphic in Figure 11.3 was created for the University of North Texas Health Sciences Center demonstration project as their prototype Cover. That same graphic, by the way, doubles well as a background for their nested template.

Figure 11.3

- **Link to the Main Switchboard:** Usually the entire Cover Show graphic links directly to the Main Switchboard. Clicking this link in Slide Show mode opens the Main Switchboard in a new window on top of the Cover Show. From the Main Switchboard, the presenter accesses the rest of the network. This is why the Cover is the only show ever opened manually during a performance.

- **Shutdown Macro:** In the bottom right corner of a Cover Show (that's our preferred position) is an invisible AutoShape that runs a Visual Basic macro. The purpose of this macro is to close all your network components after the performance is finished and return you to PowerPoint's Edit mode, where you can close the program. As explained before, external links open a slide show as a new window on top of the existing window and, therefore, slide shows stack up as if pancakes on top of each other. The macro functionality simply closes all these windows automatically when your performance is over. Shutdown macro explanations are covered in our workshop sessions and in the full-version textbook. Nevertheless, we'll be happy to send you a blank Cover Show with the macro already embedded. Request this slide show (shutdown macro) by e-mailing us at: info@aspirecommunications.

11.4 Main Switchboard

Presentation Networks contain a show called a *Main Switchboard* that—like the Cover Show—has only one slide. This show sits at the top of the network's hierarchy and serves a purpose similar to a Web site home page. The Cover Show links directly to the Main Switchboard, which holds links that access the network's major switchboards (content branches). Needless to say, the Main Switchboard typically is the most frequently visited slide.

Figure 11.4

Main Switchboards can have a very complex, all-purpose design. Our Main Switchboard incorporates very advanced features such as hidden tracks and animated menus, but such sophistication is not necessary. A text-based menu works fine. We presented that way for years, happily using nothing but static text-based links. You can always add the fancier components later when your network is better formed and stabilized.

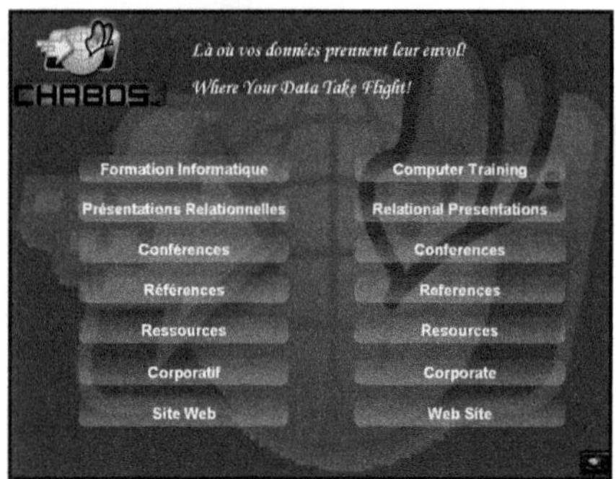

Figure 11.5 Courtesy Chantal Bossé, CHABOS

Main Switchboard designs can have attractive imagery in the background to reinforce branding. A watermark of branding imagery can appear behind the Navigation Elements in the Main Switchboard, as in Chantal's example (Figure 11.5). Also notice that her switchboard is bilingual. She is a presentation consultant in the French-speaking region of Canada and, therefore, has parallel networks accessible from a single Main Switchboard.

Unless using an all-purpose design that displays categories of links, Main Switchboard navigation typically has somewhere between 4 and 12 links. Each of these links represents the network's *top-level categories.* Top-level categories are the major content branches that fan out into more detail (subcategories) as the presenter searches for specific slides or slide shows.

11.5 Seed Presentation

Many relational presenters incorporate an interesting tactic in their networks called a *Seed Presentation.* A Seed Presentation is a quick, linear introduction to a performance that is otherwise fully interactive. Sometimes, in fact, speakers have several Seed Presentations (or parallel Seed tracks) available, allowing them to choose an appropriate introductory segment on demand.

A Seed Presentation is a summary of upcoming topics that will be discussed and is usually somewhere between 5 to 10 minutes long. In effect, it sets the stage for the navigation and interaction that follows shortly thereafter. We use a Seed Presentation at the beginning of all introductory talks discussing Relational Presentation.

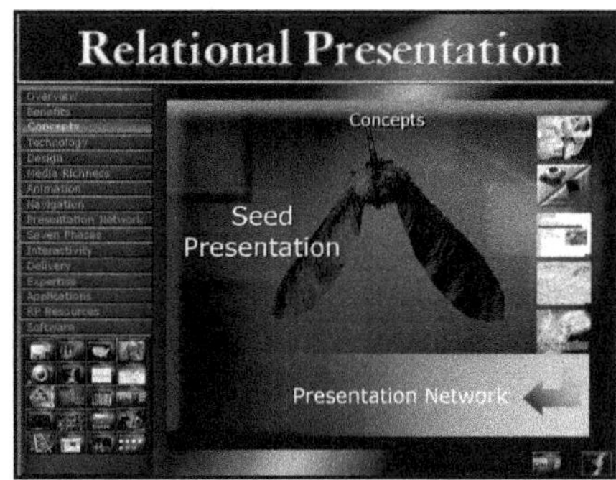

Figure 11.6

Keep in mind that audiences are not used to experiencing interaction during a PowerPoint performance. Springing a relational network on viewers can lead to a certain amount of surprise and disorientation at first. It's better to ease them into the process. A Seed Presentation gives viewers a preview, a taste of coming content, so that they are better prepared later when giving input back to the speaker. Think of it as *priming the pump.*

A Seed Presentation usually has these characteristics:

- It is a strictly linear slide show with little or no obvious navigation. The presenter moves through the slides in linear order, as would be typical of a normal PowerPoint performance.
- It is relatively short in duration, less then 10 minutes long as a general rule.
- Its slides are a quick and powerful summary of the main ideas you want to get across to the viewers. Consider it a visual elevator speech. In a way, it is like your conclusion materials, but given at the beginning instead of at the end.

The goal of this strategy is to let audiences see the big picture of what you have to offer. They are more inclined and prepared then, during interactive portions of the message, to ask for detail on individual topics. The speaker starts with the Seed, and then branches into the larger network.

In a sales context, this presentation might be something to the effect of, "Here's my current understanding of your situation and what you might want to think about." After the Seed, an appropriate segue might be something like, "Now let's look at your situation in more detail and see what areas of our expertise might be relevant to your needs." Again, the

Seed Presentation gives them a taste of the issues at hand, and then leads into active participation. It communicates a quick and focused message and also lets you clarify that this summary will be followed by a more flexible, customizable message. The priority of the presentation shifts to determining their needs and dynamically matching up what you have to offer for those needs—as opposed to a rambling sales spiel that may not best suit their interests. Basically, you introduce yourself and then say, "OK. Where should we go from here?"

In a teaching or training context, a Seed Presentation might be an extended picture story or a fast overview of what will be covered in the current class period. In an executive presentation situation, it might be a brief look at the data being presented to the board, with subsequently open opportunity for exploration.

You might choose to deliver a Seed Presentation without the audience knowing that most of the session to follow will be interactive. In general, however, we recommend educating the audience up front on how your performance will work. In this case, simply let them know you will give a 5-minute summary of the most important topics, and then they will be free to ask questions and explore topics with you in more detail. You might even show some of your navigation components and demonstrate the ability to access categories on demand. That gives viewers a chance to mentally adjust. It also usually catches audiences off guard and creates intrigue. Use such moments to your advantage. You now have their attention.

11.6 Subswitchboards

Subswitchboards perform basically the same tasks as the Main Switchboard, except that they are further down in the hierarchy. They help a presenter find and access information within each of the network's content branches.

Each of the major links on a Main Switchboard normally opens one of these subswitchboards. For example, a Main Switchboard link might be called PRODUCTS. This link would open a slide show (containing one slide) called *PRODUCTS Switchboard*. Here the speaker finds additional links that open slides and/or linear slide shows, or perhaps open other switchboards at the next level down. A company might have three different categories of products, and each category has its own corresponding subswitchboard, all accessible from the PRODUCTS Switchboard.

There are no rules, per se, on how many levels down you can go. However, each level represents an additional mouse click, and we try to minimize the number of clicks overall. Rarely do we go more than two subswitchboards below the Main Switchboard. Moving two subswitchboards down generally translates into three clicks to get from the Main Switchboard to a content slide. This level of depth, for most people, is more than ample. As demonstrated in the grocery store example, three clicks allowed us to find a single variety of apple out of 10,000 products in the store—and this demonstration used only one of the network's potentially many major content branches!

Figure 11.7

One of our top-level Main Switchboard links is called Navigation. It opens the slide show represented in Figure 11.7, our Navigation Switchboard. All of these links open their own slide shows, giving examples of various navigation styles and strategies.

Notice an important technique here, what we call *spreading laterally*. We theoretically could have built another level down, a switchboard each for *bars*, *panels*, *buttons*, and so forth. Instead, we grouped relevant links on the same higher-level switchboard. Doing so allowed us to avoid a click, and finding information is still just as easy and fast.

11.7 Core Networks

Because the Relational Presentation approach is based upon modules of content, such as a group of slides that naturally belong together, it makes sense for the entire Presentation Network to be modular from top to bottom. That is, the overall network can be composed of several smaller, relatively independent networks that are tied together by hyperlinks.

Approaching the larger network as a combination of Cores is a very useful strategy for large companies, organizations, and institutions.

Think of it this way: A hospital might commission a systemwide Presentation Network platform that potentially includes all the presentation topics relevant to its digital communication activities. This large platform is then divided into more manageable core components such as pediatrics, neurosurgery, nutrition, and so forth. That way each doctor or administrator can have his or her own version of the network and add or subtract Core Networks as desired. Adding a Core is as simple as copying that material into the main network folder and placing a link on the Main Switchboard to the new Core material. Each smaller network just plugs into the larger structure and all of that material is ready to use immediately.

Actual logistics are slightly more complicated than that, to make sure links work properly, but a plug-and-play approach can greatly expand the amount of material available to numerous presenters, with little effort on his or her part. Perhaps a pathologist wishes to add a large collection of tissue sample pictures showing various stages of disease progression, or emergency personnel might want categorical collections of x-rays. Any group can have any collection that has been built. The possibilities are endless.

Of course, the utility of Core components is not limited to hospitals or universities. A company's human resources department might use a similar approach to organize training activities. A charitable organization might organize donor campaigns, and a pastor might arrange sermon topics.

11.8 Primary Shows and Collections

Topically arranged components of your network are, as the name implies, arranged according to topics. In all likelihood, most if not all of your current linear slide shows are topically organized. That is, a single show contains all the ingredients needed to cover a particular subject or theme.

When slide shows are arranged by category, they no longer work well for linear display. They do, on the contrary, work exceptionally well for quickly finding individual pieces of information. Shows in this case hold slides that are related to categories, regardless of the overall topic. Categorically arranged slide shows are called *collections*.

Topical Organization

Drug A	Drug B	Drug C
How It Works	How It Works	How It Works
Side Effects	Side Effects	Side Effects
Cost	Cost	Cost

Categorical Organization

How It Works	Side Effects	Cost
Drug A	Drug A	Drug A
Drug B	Drug B	Drug B
Drug C	Drug C	Drug C

Figure 11.8

Here's an example contrasting the two organizational strategies: Pretend you are a medical researcher reporting on various allergy medications. If your presentation materials are topically arranged, you might have three linear shows, each focusing on one drug at a time and describing perhaps how that drug works, its side effects, and its cost. Show 1, therefore, covers all subtopics directly relevant to Drug A only—and the other shows, their respective drugs.

Categorical arrangement, on the other hand, highlights one subtopic at a time, across all three drugs. In this case, Show 1 might contain modules describing how each drug works, allowing the researcher to say, "That's how Drug A works; now let's look at how Drug B works." This approach better facilitates comparison and contrast, or selection of individual characteristics from a larger group.

Most Presentation Networks, not surprisingly, are a combination of the two strategies. Sometimes it makes sense to progress from subtopic to subtopic in a linear presentation, within the larger network framework. There is absolutely nothing wrong with linear delivery, even in a Relational Presentation context, as long as you are never trapped by it. At other times, it makes far more sense to access individual slides from a collection.

Interestingly enough, you probably will use both strategies in combination with each other. A realtor might set up categories such as two bedrooms, three bedrooms, and so forth, and then within these categories have topical shows, perhaps each containing inside and outside pictures of featured properties.

Deciding between topical and categorical organization (primary shows and collections) will be one of the greatest challenges you face from here on. You MUST decide one way or the other. In Relational Presentation, we never duplicate slides. You cannot have the same slide in a categorical collection here and also in primary shows over there and there. Recall that the term *relational,* in part, references the logic of a relational database. Duplicating a slide in your network is a violation that will come back to haunt you later. Don't do it, no matter how tempting it may seem. Discipline yourself to having a slide in only one location—then go get it when needed, from wherever you happen to be.

Sometimes making the decision on which way to go is very difficult because there is no obvious answer. Keep in mind that topical organization works best when you almost always deliver certain slides in a set sequence (such as in a picture story or to demonstrate a fixed process). Categorical organization works best for randomly selecting components during interactions, or to highlight individual pieces of larger topics. What if you use a particular slide as part of a sequence on a regular basis, but also need occasional or frequent random access? That's when the decision becomes challenging. Often it could go either way—and you have to make a choice.

11.9 Picture/Video Stories

Picture and *video stories* should make up a sizeable portion of your network. Picture and video stories by nature are topical, yet normally are organized by category to enable quick access. They are tiny modules of linear content, organized within collections. Some people place these devices in categories within the Resources Section (described later), while others give them a top-level category of their own on the Main Switchboard; others still weave them throughout the network, linked to slides where they are most applicable. Those decisions will be up to you.

11.10 Conclusions Section

If you use conclusion slides, adding a *Conclusions Section* to the network is a good idea. A Conclusions Section is a special categorical collection of all your conclusion slides. Such a section might feature different kinds of conclusions, for different audiences, venues, clients, and so forth. It might also include an option for concluding in a lighthearted manner, with a more serious call to action, or some other variation.

Some presenters like their Conclusions Section to hold multiple forms of the same conclusion slides, giving them options similar to having multiple parallel presentation tracks available. That way they can subtly adjust final remarks according to preceding audience interactions or how much time is left. For example, a speaker might have detailed conclusion slides and also shortened versions of those same slides.

Lest there be confusion, the above phrase, "multiple forms of the same conclusion slides" is not a contradiction of the former mandate that slides should never be duplicated. In this case, the *duplication* is intentional. Variations are placed side-by-side in the same area. So they really are separate, unique slides, with similar but alternative intents. There is less danger a designer will make changes to one, and not change the others, considering this section was created especially for derivations. Even so, DO be careful to make changes to all the variations.

A link to a Conclusions Section normally exists on every slide in the network and, therefore, is accessible through its Primary Navigation (topic 11.12). Having a Conclusions Section allows a presenter to gracefully end at any time, regardless of prevailing circumstances. It is a form of safety net.

Nevertheless, as your familiarity with Relational Presentation techniques increases, you may sense a decreasing need for conclusion materials. In effect, your entire network is a conclusion area, where anything and everything is available for review or highlight. We long ago abandoned altogether having a formal Conclusions Section. Now we review dynamically, if necessary.

11.11 Resources Section

Having a *Resources Section,* on the other hand, is imperative beyond words. This section, for all practical purposes, is a catchall region in your network. It generally holds everything that is not part of your regular presentation materials, but that nonetheless might be useful and important at any moment. A Resources Section can be quite large and varied, meaning it definitely should be one of your top-level categories on the Main Switchboard and should have its own folder. Most networks feature a link directly to the Resources Switchboard from every slide, so that these items are always available. By default, this section is highly categorical in form because you normally use it to select individual items at a time. Following are some of the categories it might feature: pictures and picture stories; showcases (products, area of expertise, contact information, etc.); conclusions; audio; video; books, articles, and tools that you recommend; partners; services; procedures; and whatever suits your needs.

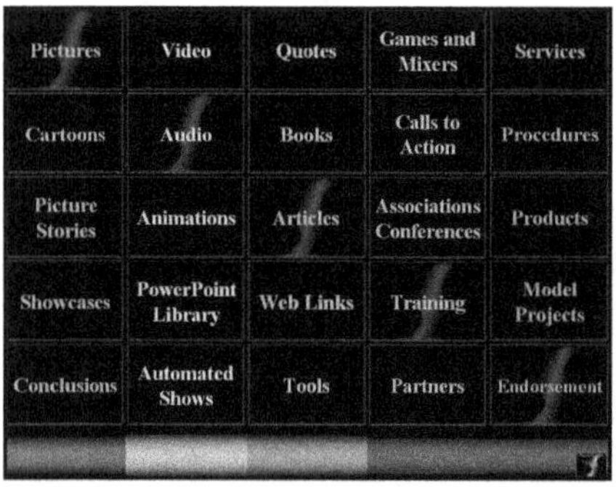

Figure 11.9

Any or all of these categories might have their own switchboard, accessible from the Resources Switchboard. Showcase and Nested Navigation styles work well for this purpose, considering the categorical logic involved.

Because of the staggering amount of information this section might eventually hold, or can potentially hold, you ABSOLUTELY MUST determine development priorities before construction begins. Do not fall into the trap of adding content to categories just to feel as though you are accomplishing something. A Resources Section may take years to adequately fill. Be sure to decide up front what will be added first, and to what depth. Build only the most critical categories and leave the rest as a shell for now. As a guide for determining priorities, think about the items you have needed to show in the past, such as Web links, contact information, or perhaps even personal profile items such as pictures of family members or pets. This section should contain everything you might spontaneously need on a regular or occasional basis.

What makes a Presentation Network so useful during speaking engagements is the ability to go anywhere at any time. So far we have discussed moving from the Cover to the Main Switchboard, and then down through subswitchboards to eventually reach content shows or individual slides within those shows. Now we need to look at moving in the opposite direction—accessing previous-level switchboards and cycling all the way back to the Main Switchboard or Cover Show. That is, we need to be able to complete loops, just as with Showcase Navigation but on a much grander scale.

The Navigation Elements we use for this backward navigation are called *primary buttons*. A group of primary buttons as a whole is called *Primary Navigation*. Keeping primary buttons bunched together as a group is a good idea. The word primary, as with primary shows, indicates the importance of these buttons. They are the network's central nervous system. Being able to access content via switchboards, and then complete the loop back to those switchboards, is critically important.

Where you decide to place your Primary Navigation on slides is a matter of personal preference. As mentioned previously, the actual location is not nearly as important as the consistency of that placement across slides. Our personal preference is to locate primary buttons in the bottom right corner of EVERY slide. In doing so, we guarantee access to important network hubs, while at the same time posing little risk of the buttons interfering with regular slide content. In other words, if placing buttons in the bottom right corner were to cover something important on the slide, it almost certainly means we have way too much information on that slide anyway and should redesign it.

Why don't we put the Primary Navigation on the Slide Master? Sometimes we do, especially when using Nested Navigation. In general, however, it's a good idea to have primary buttons on actual slides so that you can bring them on top of any content that covers the entire slide. Primary Navigation must always be accessible. Never allow it to be accidentally covered by a picture or AutoShape.

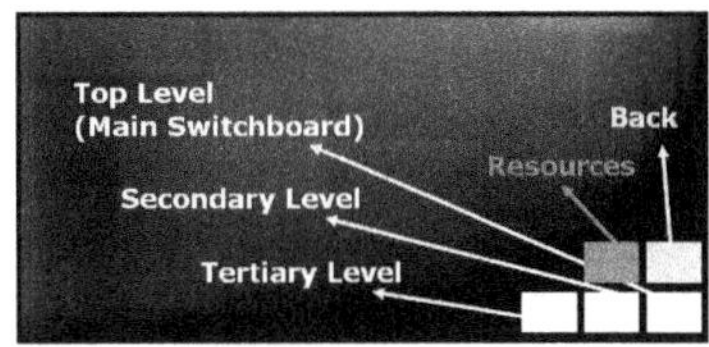

Figure 11.10

Figure 11.10 shows the placement logic we use. It's fine if you choose a completely different approach or configuration. The button to the furthest right and bottom always points back to the Main Switchboard. The button to its immediate left returns the user to the first subswitchboard down from the Main Switchboard. The button to its immediate left returns the user to the second subswitchboard down, and so forth. Realize that this bottom row of buttons will vary in number for any given slide, depending on how many levels down you are in the network. In the grocery store example, the first button points back to *walking in the door*. The second button points back to the produce section, and the third button points back to the apples section. Thus, if we decided we were not hungry for a green apple after all, we could select another variety of apple, a different kind of produce, or go to any other section of the store, depending on which button was clicked.

Immediately above the second button from the right, we place one that accesses the Resources Switchboard. Remember: The buttons discussed here appear ON EVERY SLIDE. We always want to have access to the network's resources, regardless of which slide we happen to be on. In the Aspire network, the Resources link source is an invisible AutoShape so that the audience can't tell it's there. Making this link invisible is not necessary, but it's fun to watch audience reaction when they realize we have access to vast amounts of material on demand by clicking what appears to be nothing but thin air. The concept of having a Resources Section available while presenting with PowerPoint is such a novelty that we like to keep the link invisible for the purpose of creating intrigue. You might want it visible, especially if designing for other presenters who may not be familiar with these mechanics.

The last primary button, immediately above the Main Switchboard link, is a very special button. We call it the *magic back button* because of what it does, or appears to do.

This button allows a presenter to jump away from the current show—that is, open another slide show using an external hyperlink—and then come right back to the original show. One might think PowerPoint would have such functionality built in. Surely PowerPoint has a back button just like Web browsers, right? With a Web site, one can click a link that goes to another site and then click the back button to return to the previous site.

Alas, PowerPoint does not have a back button. Once you use a hyperlink to jump to another presentation, there is no obvious way of returning to the starting point. Consider this scenario: Let's say you have 1,000 slide shows. Right at the moment you are in show 436 and click a link to open show 798. How would PowerPoint know how to get you back to the starting show? We tried finding an answer using computer code and finally decided it couldn't be done, not at our knowledge level anyway. Fortunately, such complexity is not necessary at all. A very simple optical illusion accomplishes the same feat and essentially takes you back to the starting place, in a nonobvious way.

Think back to previous revelations of how external links work. A link from one PowerPoint show to another opens the new show as a window on top of the current slide show window. The new show's window completely covers the underlying show. That means the show containing the link is still there and is still open, but is merely hidden for the moment. What would happen if you were to simply close the top show? Precisely. The show you linked from seems to magically reappear. In reality it was there all along, and removing the top show just makes it visible again. This ultra-simple illusion enables you to access another show, and then seem to return to the previous show with a single click. It's a methodology that, once discovered, completely changed our relational delivery style. It's beautiful and oh so elegant. All we need our ***magic*** button to do is close the show on top. Fortunately, PowerPoint makes this process very easy, without requiring Visual Basic code or any other fancy techniques. To close the show, you must have an AutoShape (by our preference, invisible) and an Action Setting. The needed Action Setting is located in the **Hyperlink To** category.

1. Select an AutoShape or picture thumbnail as usual that will be the source of the link.
2. Right click this source, choose **Action Settings** from the options, and make sure you are on the **Mouse Click** tab.
3. In the **Hyperlink To** box, select **End Show**.
4. Click **OK**.

While running the slide show, this shape or picture will appear to be a regular hyperlink—the cursor changes to a pointing hand when held over the source. However, clicking the link closes the current slide show window, revealing the next window below.

As simple as this process is to set up and use, it's easy to underestimate its importance. From our experience, there's a good chance this single technique will completely change the way you present. It will reshape your thinking. You now can be in the middle of any bullet point list, jump out spontaneously to any other show in your network—even if there are thousands—and then come right back and pick up where you left off with the bullet points. Never again are you restricted by bullet lists, linear slide shows, animation sequences, or anything else. At the risk of sounding trite, this humble button symbolizes speaker freedom. Rather than the computer controlling your delivery, you now have the reigns.

Keep in mind that because the magic back button closes only one show at a time, you may need to use it more than once when returning to a previous show. If, for instance, you click a link that opens a show, and then from there click a link that opens another show, two windows now sit on top of your original show. If the button is in exactly the same place on every slide (as it should be), you can rapidly walk backward through your previously viewed shows by clicking multiple times in the same spot.

11.13 The Virtual Switchboard Illusion

Here is another marvelously useful illusion that is closely related to the magic back button, an effect we call a *virtual switchboard*. This technique allows a presenter to jump to an external linear show, walk through that show's slides, and then seemingly return to the original switchboard automatically when the show ends, as if using a Custom Show.

Years ago we were wrestling with the idea of how to make the Relational Presentation process easier for presenters. We really liked the **Show and Return** option of PowerPoint's **Custom Shows** feature. Remember that the Custom Show feature allows you to create a *virtual* slide show within a slide show. If the overall show contains five slides, we can make a Custom Show that displays, say, slides 4, 2, and 3 in that order. Then if the **Show and Return** box is checked, scrolling past the last slide in the Custom Show (in this case, Slide 3) returns the presenter to the starting slide (the switchboard used to start the Custom Show).

This functionality was attractive because it allowed us to build a Custom Show-based switchboard. We could access any number of Custom Shows from a central slide, show the contents, and then return automatically to the switchboard after each Custom Show ended. What that REALLY meant to a speaker was that she didn't have to remember how many slides were in any given Custom Show. If she scrolled past the last slide, the original switchboard *magically* appeared, without needing a return link.

We wanted to create the same effect with external shows so that the presenter could open an external show from a switchboard, scroll past the last slide in the show, and then return to the switchboard automatically. Unfortunately, this idea did not seem possible because scrolling past the last slide displayed what we called the *black slide of death (BSD)*, the **End of slide show. Click to Exit** black slide PowerPoint presenters know so well.

Switchboard-based navigation tended to result in this slide being displayed continually, an unacceptable situation. To make matters worse, we used to tell presenters (and still do), DO NOT EVER show this black slide. It's as if you are showing your underwear. It's telling the audience, "Oops. I guess that was my last slide after all." In other words, it's unprofessional. Avoid it.

How did we end up solving the problem? Few people know that this black slide can be turned off, so it doesn't display at the end of shows at all. In that case, scrolling past the last slide simply ends the show. And you know what happens when the show ends with the former show beneath it.

If you uncheck the **End with Black Slide** setting in **Tools/Options** (**View** tab) and then scroll past the last content slide, PowerPoint ends the show and the effect is exactly like clicking the magic back button or using the **Show and Return** feature. The real switchboard once again appears. The presenter can now click a link on a switchboard to open an external show, scroll through the slides in the show and past the last slide, and be returned seamlessly to the original switchboard.

Note that when unchecking the **End with Black Slide** option, this change need be made only once per computer. It then applies universally to all slide shows. Keep in mind that if using someone else's computer, you need to change this setting (once) on their computer as well, or the BSD will appear while using your network. While here, also uncheck the **Show Popup Toolbar**. Doing so removes the semitransparent navigation bar that appears in the bottom left corner of PowerPoint slides during a slide show. This built-in navigation mechanism just gets in the way of your custom-made navigation devices.

"I'm taking your suggestion to stay linear at first with my sermons—still working towards picture stories and switchboards. I'll tell you what, though. You have already transformed my slide-making techniques. There are a lot fewer bullet point lists. Instead I'm using more illustrations and large, simple text to create series of compelling graphic slides. People are noticing and responding."

Pastor Will Nelken, Trinity Community Church, San Rafael, California

Chapter 12

Communicating with Visuals

Growing
Harvesting
Aging
Touring
Enjoying

12.1 The Current Mindset

While discussing slide content with a graphic designer recently, we heard an all-too-familiar lament. "No matter what I do to add visual interest to our slides, our presenters just want to face the screen and read their bullet points. I don't know how to get them out of that habit."

That reminded us of another discussion with a consultant who had worked in a large governmental agency that shall go unnamed. She expressed her vehement disgust with PowerPoint and told how engineers in this agency were forced to sit for mind-numbing hours on end, watching black and white slides full of bullet points and line diagrams. Her solution was to remove all the chairs from the room so that viewers would be much less patient in tolerating such a visual assault on their senses.

We never heard if her strategy worked, but hopefully we can find alternative ways of weaning speakers from addiction to text-based presentation. This chapter explores the importance of adding visual media and high-quality design to your Relational Presentation activities. We look at a wealth of ideas for helping presenters forsake the traditional bullet list and find other, perhaps better, means of expression.

12.2 Moving Beyond Bullets

Moving away from text-based presentation may be one of the most important steps you can take for enhancing message effectiveness. While research on the subject is admittedly spotty, and essentially nonexistent in a direct PowerPoint context, some studies are pointing in that direction. One experiment in particular found detrimental effects when two redundant forms of text (written and auditory) were presented simultaneously in a training environment.

Their results call into question whether written text is treated by the brain as visual information after all. Perhaps when we *see* text, our cognitive capacities really *hear* it and encode the information in verbal channels. Have you ever noticed when reading to yourself from a book that you hear the words being read? It's quite possible that inundating our audiences with text may provide little, if any, meaningful visual stimulation.

At any rate, if bullet points are all we have to offer onlookers, we may be better off NOT displaying any slides at all and giving people information in purely auditory form, rather than presenting the same information in both auditory and written form. Fortunately, there are better uses of the projector, and we need not turn it off.

Instead, you have the opportunity to learn a new language—a visual, media-based language. Mastering a visually interactive style of communication is remarkably similar in many ways to enrolling in a foreign language class and discovering how to express thoughts using an alternative coding system. You must ponder how to get your meaning across when the alphabet, words, and syntax take on unfamiliar forms.

Learning this visual language, you will be happy to know, is reasonably easy because both you and your viewers already intrinsically know most of the rules, whether realized or not. We just need to tap into real life experiences and show people what we see in our thoughts. Think about what those words on the slides are saying, and then find a way to bring those expressions to life in a practical, visual way.

One of the most frequent and important questions students ask during training sessions is, "How do I translate my bullet points into pictures (or graphics, or video, or animations)?" The remaining segments of this chapter explore this question and offer numerous constructive suggestions that help you on your way and start creative energies flowing.

Consider the suggestions here, and then expand upon them. Experiment and share your findings with us. Your insights may one day help someone else who is struggling to understand what it means to be visually expressive.

12.3 Think Picture Stories

We dedicated a lot of space earlier in this book to introducing picture stories precisely for the discussion here. Using picture stories is one of the most useful strategies you can implement in the quest for effective visual communication. Additionally, such stories generally are quite easy to make and express.

Here is a quick review: Picture stories are very short, linear, picture/graphic-based presentations that sequentially help you tell a story or demonstrate a process. It's important to note that pictures used in these stories are not random or purely decorative in nature; they must contribute some kind of relevant meaning on their own, especially if the presenter complements them with very few spoken words. They should add depth or detail in some way, even if only providing emotional *punch*. Ideally, an audience should be able to view the images and understand the gist of the story, even if no words at all are added.

On the other hand, realize that picture stories do not necessarily have to directly and literally represent actual content under discussion. They can be ancillary and simply supply context.

Think about this example: Fred Barbee is a professor at the University of Alaska. He teaches several courses on accounting methods. One might presume his presentation materials contain a lot of numbers and formulas, along with a few spreadsheets and balance sheets no doubt. During a workshop session, Fred discussed this idea of picture stories with us. The thought of including such stories along with course topics, in Fred's case, seemed rather remote. After all, it's not as though the accounting profession is known for its artistic expression—Fred being a notable exception, of course.

We told Fred, "You know what you should do? You should scan some old newspaper clippings and even keep an ongoing file of such clippings. That way when you are ready to approach a certain subject you can pull up a picture story and say, 'OK folks, let me show you why today's subject is so important. You see this guy? He's in the fourth year of a 10-year prison term for violating the rules we're going to look at today. You NEED to know this stuff.' " Certainly, the class period could do without that little one- or two-slide interlude, but including it makes the formulas all of a sudden jump to life and seem a little more worthy of notice.

The only caveat that applies here is to make sure your visuals are directly relevant to the prevailing message goals. Stories that are interesting but off the topic might merely distract.

12.4 Include Real Experiences

Whether creating picture stories or otherwise integrating visuals into your content, constantly ask yourself, "What am I seeing in my mind when I think about this topic?" If there is some kind of tangible image you see, try to find relevant physical imagery to display that mental picture. Ask yourself whether there is anything in your real-life experiences, or those of others, that can bring this topic to life in some way. Is there an allegory, maybe something they might see on TV or have experienced while growing up? Can you relate your topic to events, objects, natural phenomenon, or human characteristics that might help people better grasp a concept?

When we are subject experts, there is a natural assumption that what we are talking about is so *obvious*. But others do not have your experiences or perspectives, your collage of memories or visual references. They cannot see inside your brain. You must show your thoughts, in a tangible, visual way.

Figure 12.1

Here is an allegory taken from our experience that we use to illustrate an abstract concept: One of Relational Presentation's most fundamental and defining characteristics is its use of illusion. You already have seen several visual examples, such as obscured navigation and the magic back button that appears to step users backward though previously viewed shows.

Figure 12.2

We use this allegory to explain the importance of illusion: There is a large, beautiful, black and yellow butterfly in Arizona called a Giant Swallowtail (Figure 12.1). The butterfly lays its eggs on citrus trees, and the caterpillars then eat the leaves. These little caterpillars are fascinating in that, while growing up, they look for all the world like a bird dropping (Figure 12.2). You can stare at them six inches away and the illusion created is phenomenal. What self-respecting hungry bird would want to eat THAT?

This amazing visual trick probably gives this species of insect special control over its own survival, especially considering how many of these butterflies are floating around the yard on any given day. You can use this same kind of visual redirection to your advantage in PowerPoint. Use of illusion gives you enormous control as a speaker, staging events that happen without the audience even noticing—and they don't need to notice.

In this case, we took an example from personal experience, created a two-slide picture story, and used it to explain an abstract concept. With a little creativity, you can produce illustrations for just about any concept imaginable. People will never see what you see unless you show them.

12.5 Augment Graphic Arts Skills

Must you be a graphic artist to be a relational designer? No. Will it greatly benefit your presentation activities to gain some graphic design skills? Absolutely. Creating digital graphics may not be your primary calling in life, but that doesn't mean you should always leave the job to someone else. Give serious thought to expanding your abilities in this area.

Consider that the definition of *communication* is changing. Because of the ever increasing influence of digital media in our lives, everyday communication (not to mention presentation) is becoming more media-based. This shift means our interactions are coming to include more visual elements. Old communication skill sets that used to consist mainly of talking, writing, and typing are being supplemented, and sometimes replaced, by media creation skills. If you don't believe that, look at the way our kids are interacting today. Video exchange platforms such as *YouTube* are rivaling television in terms of viewing influence. Anyone with a cell phone can capture video clips of all imaginable events, and then the clip circulates around the world within hours on the Web.

Now granted, you may not have aspirations of turning into a digital videographer, but gaining some media skills, especially graphics skills, is up there with knowing how to type. If you don't have these basic skills that even grade school kids are learning today, your influence in coming years will be negatively affected. As forms of visual/media language become more commonplace, you don't want to be left behind. Adobe Photoshop is the professional standard for working with digital imagery, but numerous other options are available as well. If nothing else, learn how to downsize images (reduce the dpi), add bevel and glow to text and shapes, crop and erase portions of images, and combine different pieces of images together in aesthetically pleasing ways to create collage graphics.

12.6 Look for Visual Inspiration

Another related issue designers sometimes struggle with is not feeling confident in their creative abilities. They wonder, "How do I know what kind of content to design? What should it look like and what are the standards? Where can I find practical ideas and how do I adapt them to my message?"

Years ago a speaker addressing this very issue said one of the best things we can do to increase creativity and inspiration while designing is to *feed the brain* long before. In other words, devote regular time to gazing at graphically rich magazines, news programs, Web sites, and other sources of rich visual content. He said to do this for no other purpose than to absorb the imagery and let it be stored somewhere up there in our subconscious. Someday, somewhere, that raw material will be tapped and out of nowhere the inspiration and ideas you need will be available.

This is another way of saying that we have the capacity to augment our own natural abilities. Our talents are not static. To a large extent, we get out what we put in. The more exposure you have to other people's ideas, as well as the wealth of design ideas available in nature, the more likely you will produce creative, attractive, professional content for your network.

Honest and constructive feedback from others can be helpful as well, especially from people who clearly are skilled and talented in design matters. Outside perspectives can point out issues you never would have seen and generate ideas you would not have thought of on your own.

All of the above is to say that you will determine your own creativity. Never underestimate latent potential. Use it and it will grow.

Finally, as a last tip for converting text-based messages into visual display, be sure to include the obvious and the mundane in your displays. This may sound like strange advice but here's what we mean: Undoubtedly, you ARE an expert (or are on your way to being one) in your subject matter, or you wouldn't be in front of people teaching, training, selling, or speaking in the first place. As experts we tend to overlook the small, personal, seemingly trivial components of our message in favor of those impressive facts or complex results we think will so impress our viewers. Remember that ultimately your connection with people is as important, or more important, than any facts given. You put the human face on the mechanical and the abstract alike.

Making a connection, in part, involves showing people your world—your lab, your team, examples of projects that are ongoing, and the seemingly trivial pieces of the larger ideas. People are curious about who you are, along with the facts you bring. If you neglect the personal and human aspect of your topics, you are throwing away both understanding and interest.

We are fascinated with television shows and books that depict the lives of rich and famous people because we are curious who they really are, what life is like for them. We use our familiar understandings and compare them with what we see, as a way of trying to understand an unknown lifestyle.

The same process occurs between speaker and audience. You are part of the message system. Viewers are curious about you and issues that are going on behind the scenes, the human interest side of your job or hobby. Be diligent to include those kinds of visuals as well. Ultimately all of us, when taking in information, are asking, "Is this relevant to me? How does this relate to what I know and understand already?" Building in the common and human elements will help people relate better to your communication goals.

Here is where a digital camera or video recorder can really come in handy. If you really want to give people a feel for where you are coming from, show them details of your world. That kind of behind-the-scenes glimpse makes you approachable and real. It's a concept that is especially important in a teaching context. Isolated knowledge without real-life context tends to be discarded. Anticipate that need and address it with practical, down-to-earth displays people can relate to.

"I first did a little "beta" presentation, just to see if I could get the links to work. Once I got my test run to work I started linking in my new project. It's working terrifically! I'm very excited about this technique."

Susan Cedar
Social Worker , USA

Chapter 13

Design Strategies

Colors

Consistency

Aesthetics

Lighting

13.1 The Importance of Quality Design

Years ago, when the Relational Presentation model was still in its infant stage, we focused mostly on helping speakers develop more flexible delivery styles. The idea of navigating to content on demand seemed so novel and desperately needed that we didn't think much about also assisting with design—the look and feel of content. Over time, this situation changed. We realized that interactive delivery alone is not enough. A presenter also needs to have visual content that is *worth showing* in a flexible way.

Learning effective design strategies is vital to your full development as a relational designer/presenter. PowerPoint users, in our experience (and for whatever reasons), tend to have very little knowledge of design issues. They frequently are unfamiliar with fundamental layout and aesthetics principles and don't have a good grasp on what the expression *quality content* means. That is to say, there are a great deal of very UGLY PowerPoint slides in existence. We hope to change that fact.

The lessons in this chapter have been garnered through hard experience, with years of observation, classes, advice from designers, and exploration of other media forms. By distilling our perspectives here, we hope to save you similar effort. It's a good practice, even so, to continually pursue new ideas for making your content more appealing and visually appropriate to audiences. There is much we do not cover here as well.

We also recognize that what looks attractive or professional to one individual might not to another. Aesthetics sometimes are quite subjective and your perspectives may differ from ours. That's OK. Consider our recommendations as suggestions, and then compare them with your own sense of appropriate visual appeal. It's quite likely, moreover, that your organization or institution has set standards that will guide and determine your design parameters. Unfortunately, these standards can be unnecessarily restrictive in some cases. You may need to use your creativity to bend the rules if necessary.

Our focus here centers on two critical aspects of design that should constantly influence your network's construction activities: aesthetics and functionality.

13.2 A Quick Summary of Design Principles

Topics in this chapter approach design from a nontechnical perspective. You don't need to be a graphic artist to appreciate and implement the principles discussed. Most of the techniques are easily doable in PowerPoint alone.

On the other hand, if you already have—or plan to gain—graphic design skills, the principles here will take on even more meaning. We encourage you to move in this direction as your experience with Visual Interactivity increases.

Numerous important design issues have been mentioned in this book already. Here's a review and summary of these topics before continuing with additional techniques and strategies:

Text:

- Large, simple text on slides helps viewers quickly grasp the main point and doesn't distract them from your verbal embellishments.
- Add shadow to text appearing on top of colorful backgrounds such as pictures. Remember that the most versatile method for doing so is to add shadow to the AutoShape, and then remove its fill.

Pictures:

- Whenever possible, use large pictures that cover the entire slide pane to create a more dramatic impact. In many cases there is no need for text to accompany these pictures.
- Use sequential pictures to help gradually show your message (picture stories).
- When pictures do not cover the entire slide pane, consider having a dark or pure black background behind them, so that the background does not distract from the picture.
- Use real pictures rather than clip art whenever possible, and never use animated GIFs that endlessly repeat.
- When using stock photos, change the images in various ways so that they are less recognizable. Flip the images horizontally, crop them, or combine several images via graphics editing software.
- For picture transparency, add the picture as a fill effect inside an AutoShape. Then increase the transparency of the AutoShape.

- When a slide contains more than one picture, try to keep the lighting angles consistent. If necessary (and possible), flip one or more of the pictures horizontally.

Navigation:

- Place navigation bars (horizontal strips) at the very bottom of slides as a general rule, to be less distracting.
- When Navigation Elements are transparent, it's a good idea to have the slide's design provide Visual Clues for finding links. The only exception is when the presenter is very experienced and there is a need to use truly Invisible Navigation.
- Make Navigation Elements as small and nondistracting as possible, normally. The primary exception to this rule is when navigation is specifically designed to encourage audience participation, in which case it should be large for easy viewing.

General:

- A principle related to the *simple* text concept is to have only one main idea per slide so that audience members do not become lost in the complexity of information presented.
- Consider dividing long slide shows and video clips into short shows and clips so that individual content pieces are randomly accessible.
- With complex graphs, tables, diagrams, or charts, add mechanisms for zooming in on, or highlighting, specific segments.
- Devote design resources to the most important (showy) parts of your network first. The Cover, Main Switchboard, top-level switchboards, and most frequently used content slides are the top candidates.

13.3 Use of Colors

The color combinations you place on slides significantly affect their visual impact and appeal. Keep in mind the following characteristics: Reds, oranges, and yellows are referred to as *warm* colors. They tend to pop out and attract attention, especially red. Greens, blues, and purples are

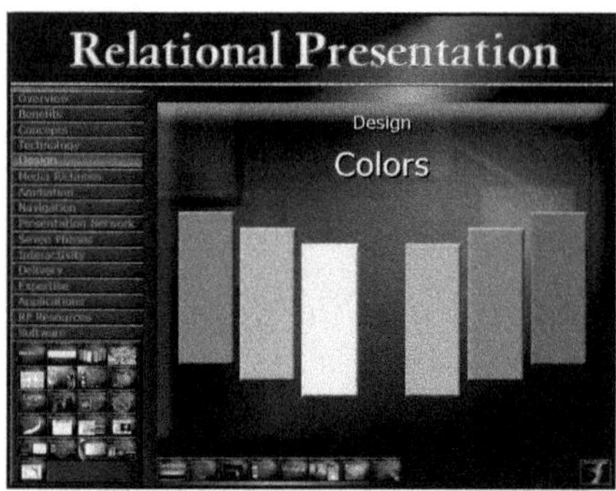

Figure 13.1

cool colors. These colors recede into the background and draw less attention. White and very light colors also catch the eye, whereas black and very dark colors generally are less noticeable.

Interestingly, the above effects are not absolutely fixed. They can flip, depending upon the quantity of one color present compared with another. For example, if you were to place a small black shape on a solid white slide background, the *black* shape would pop out as more noticeable than the *white* background. In this case, the brain is looking for meaning in the display rather than simply reacting to color characteristics. Not surprisingly, some optical illusions take advantage of this phenomenon. Realize, therefore, that the *quantity* and *contrast* of colors can be important to slide designs. This issue is most critical in a PowerPoint sense regarding text usage. Use opposite extremes of light verses dark between text and backgrounds. If the slide background is light, use black or very dark text for best results—unless, of course, you are intentionally creating some form of subtle effect, such as making Navigation Elements less distracting.

There is an interesting and complex interplay between color characteristics, contrast, and quantity. We'll look more at contrast later. For the moment our focus will be color characteristics and interactions. How you combine colors definitely affects a design's overall desirability.

Mixing bright blues and reds is a terrible practice to inflict upon an audience, and unfortunately it happens more often than one would hope. If you stare at such slides for very long, your eyes begin screaming. The same goes with mixing reds and greens. The color interactions are very harsh and fatiguing to the eyes.

A red and green combination also brings up the issue of color blindness, which apparently affects somewhere around 7 percent of men and less than 1 percent of women. Difficulty distinguishing between red and green is the most common form of color blindness. If you place green text on a red background, and there is not a lot of contrast between the colors, some viewers will not be able to read the text. Avoid such problems across the board by never mixing these two colors, especially in a text-background combination.

When it comes to mixing colors, here are broad guidelines:

- As a rule, mixing warm colors with each other or mixing cool colors with each other is safe. Aspire's color scheme stays with warm colors. Most companies prefer a cool combination, especially blues, grays, teals, and black.

- Black and white work fine in combination with all other colors, as does beige, surprisingly. For example, you can get away with having light beige text on a dark blue background equally with placing it on a dark red background. Browns, however, are best combined with warm colors. Grays fit better with cool colors.

- Mixing warm and cool colors is risky and is best left to graphic design contexts. Such color combinations can look fine in graphics (Figure 13.2) because graphics often use complex gradations and mixtures of colors. Without such subtleties, mixed warm-cool colors on slides tend to portray the gaudiness of sports uniforms.

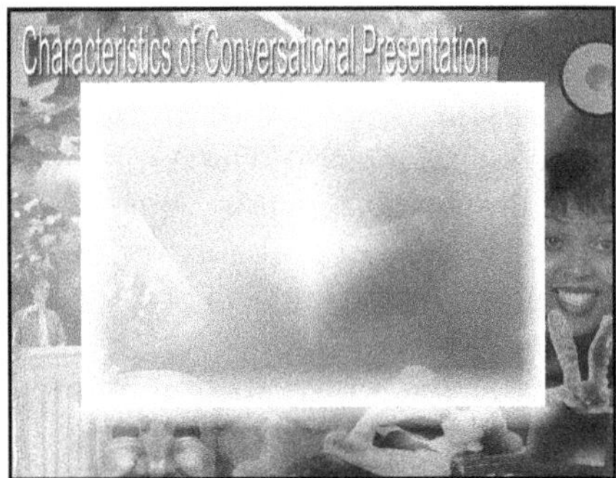

Figure 13.2

With text, the same mixing guidelines apply. For text used as content, we almost always use white or beige on a dark background, or black on a light background. Above all else, you want observers to be able to read the text easily. When text is graphical in nature, such as a label or title that is part of a picture, just about anything goes. Again, such text should be easily readable, but color and design can vary considerably.

13.4 Consistency

Consistency of design, inside and across slide shows, is a well-established mantra of digital presentation. We certainly recognize and value this tradition. Design consistency is important in numerous aspects of Relational Presentation as well.

In our opinion, however, PowerPoint designers often go overboard with this subject, resulting in mind-numbingly boring performances (at least visually). PowerPoint Slide Masters and templates ensure all slides in a show look monotonously alike. Company policies often take this practice a step further and guarantee all separate *shows* look monotonously alike also.

Design consistency need not be so absolute. Rigid template use, for instance, is not a good idea because it ignores the way people normally see media. Think about your experiences surfing the Web. When moving around between multiple Web sites, do you really care if they all look alike? Probably not. Of more interest is whether the information found is relevant to your needs.

To a large degree, the same is true with a Presentation Network. A certain amount of visual and functional consistency is helpful, to both the presenter and audience. Absolute uniformity, on the other hand, is not. Allow slide appearance and navigation structures to vary, to provide more visual interest. The Aspire network is a case in point. Every screenshot illustration in this book is taken from a slide somewhere in our network. As you probably have noticed, many of the slides have similar characteristics. Many do not.

With the above caveats in mind, let's explore design consistency and its appropriate applications:

1) Consistency of Branding: This type of consistency is critical if your presentation activities represent branded activities or products. You may want to have brand symbolism appear somewhere, perhaps in a corner, on all or most of the slides. A very easy and logical way of accomplishing this feat is to use your logo as the primary button that accesses the Main Switchboard. That way, by default, your logo appears in the exact same position on every slide, and it has a logical reason for being there. Note, however, that branding consistency does not necessarily imply the rest of your slides all have the same appearance. A show might contain full-screen pictures, yet still have small logos on top of those pictures.

2) Consistency of Colors: Uniformity of color scheme is a good idea. Notice we did not say uniformity of *color* but of *color scheme*. In other words, choosing from an array of related colors, perhaps in an established color palette, is fine, but that doesn't mean all slides have the exact same colors. Use common sense here. Having customers associate particular colors with your activities or image (dark blue for one discount store, red for another) reinforces branding elements. That's good. Too much color consistency becomes tedious. Note that one way of adding variety and visual interest, without constantly worrying about color consistency, is to rely upon pictures as content, especially full-screen pictures. No one expects meaningful pictures to necessarily match company colors. Graphics on the other hand—because they are crafted for specific purposes—should incorporate colors of your overall color palette.

3) Consistency of Positioning: Placement consistency in Relational Presentation often is extremely important, both for professionalism of slide appearance and as an aid to a presenter's navigation activities.

- **Navigation:** We mentioned previously how important it is for Primary Navigation buttons to ALWAYS be in the same place on every single slide in the network. Don't make exceptions here. If something goes wrong with the network, such as a broken link, the presenter must know for certain (if all else fails) that the primary buttons are available and where to find them. She should not have to think at all about this issue. When speakers are already nervous, and something unexpected happens, logic and memory sometimes disappear. Finding primary buttons should be as automatic as pressing the brake pedal in congested traffic. Consistency of positioning with other types of navigation is not as critical, but a certain amount of uniformity is comforting and makes a presenter's job easier. For example, we almost always place navigation panels on the left side of the slide and bars at the very bottom (as opposed to the right side or the top). Technically such positioning doesn't really matter, but it aids flow and visual consistency when moving both between slides and between shows.

- **Content:** When several content pieces are the same size and each piece exists on its own slide (such as video clips included as part of a Video Switchboard—see Figure 13.3), we like to keep the positioning of each piece, on each slide, exactly the same. That way

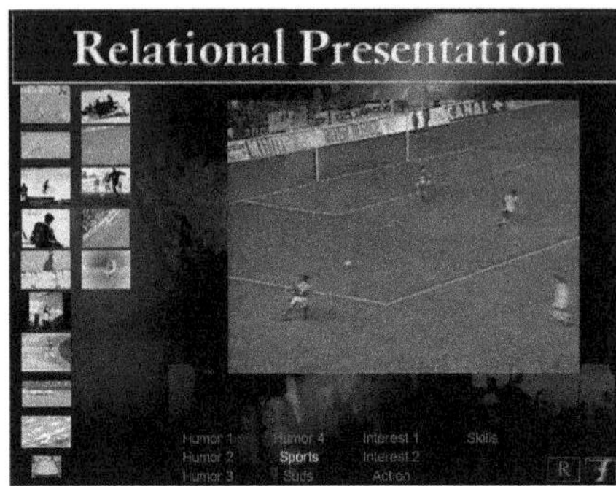

Figure 13.3

moving between the slides creates an illusion that one piece of content simply replaces the other. Furthermore, if the backgrounds of all these slides are exactly alike, the content is the ONLY noticeable change. That is, the resulting transition is very smooth. You can improve this transition effect even more by adding a **Fade Smoothly** slide transition. Then one piece of content seems to fade gracefully into the other. If, on the other hand, content positioning is not consistent across slides, it appears to jump sideways or up-down with each transition.

- **Text:** If you use AutoShapes as text boxes, be aware that text, by default, is aligned at the middle of the shape. This can cause a problem from an aesthetic standpoint. Let's say there are several slides in a row and each contains similar text boxes. What happens during transitions is that text seems to jump up and down when there is more or less text on subsequent slides. It's a good idea, therefore, to change the vertical alignment of the text so that it is anchored at the top of the shape. Then at least the upper position of the text stays stationary with each slide transition. In other words, there is less distracting movement.

1. To change the text anchor point, double click the AutoShape to open the **Format AutoShape** dialog box.
2. Click the **Text Box** tab and, under **Text anchor point**, change the **Vertical alignment** to **Top**.
3. Click **OK**.

4) Consistency of Lighting: We discussed this issue before. When multiple pictures appear on a slide, flip them if necessary (and possible) to match lighting angles.

5) Consistency of Font: Although not a major issue, using the same font consistently throughout the network contributes a sense of professionalism to its general appearance. Whether an audience actually notices or cares about this kind of consistency is questionable. Across all of our thousands of slides we probably have several fonts scattered here and there. We doubt anyone has ever made note of it. As a normal practice, however, we do stay with a generic and multipurpose font such as **Verdana** for most purposes. There is another reason for maintaining a consistent and generic font: If we switch between computers (perhaps ours has a technical problem), or other people transfer our network to their computers, we don't have to worry about the other computers not having the correct font. All computers have Verdana installed.

6) Consistency of Overall Design: We recommend Nested Navigation as an easy way to add overall consistency to large network sections. At the same time, with a large network it's ridiculous to have the same template design throughout. Use your best judgment. Having several Nested sections, each with different but similar design characteristics, is fine.

13.5 Off-center Placement

A design technique that works as well in Relational Presentation as it does in painting, floral arranging, and every other form of visually artistic expression is *off-center placement*. Off-center strategy with slide content causes the eye to be pulled in different directions simultaneously, potentially leading to a more interesting visual display. That's not to say centered, symmetrical arrangements are bad. Ideally, designs in your network should contain both kinds of placement.

In Figure 13.4, the bold mountain draws your gaze upward and to the left, whereas the hiker's image draws it down and to the right. This is called creating *visual tension* because your eyes are drawn in two directions at the same time.

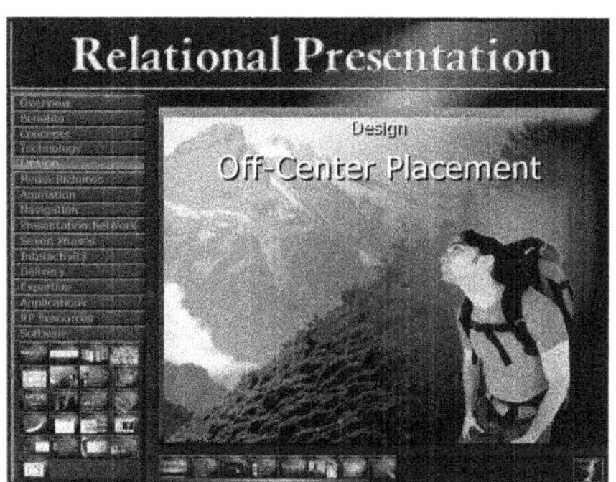

Figure 13.4

There is one more interesting fact to point out about off-center design. Even though the slide's design components are askew in various ways, they normally still contribute to an overall sense of balance across the slide; tension pulls in at least two directions.

13.6 More Lighting Effects

Simulating glows and shadows in PowerPoint is relatively easy, does not require any graphic design knowledge, and can significantly enhance the aesthetic appeal of your network's design features. Many varied effects are possible. In this segment we look at several common examples. All effects use AutoShapes that have been given a **Two-Color Fill Effect**, with one of the fill colors increased to **100% Transparency**. As a clarification of terms, *glow effects* generally are placed on top of dark slide backgrounds or pictures (to lighten certain areas), whereas *shadow effects* normally sit atop light backgrounds (to darken certain areas). Both are referred to collectively as *lighting effects* and use identical procedures, except for color choice.

Radial Glow: To form a soft radial glow on a slide, typically from one or more of its corners, use a very large oval AutoShape that has been rotated to approximately a 45-degree angle. Allow at least half of the shape to hang off into the gray area outside the slide pane. Fine tuning of positioning usually occurs after the transparency is added.

Format the shape with a **Two-Color Fill Effect**. One of the colors doesn't matter, considering it will be invisible. Slide the transparency bar for one of the two fills to **100%**. Change the other color bar to the desired shade. We often use white or a very light yellow to simulate natural lighting, but other bolder colors can create a nice effect, too, especially when two or more such shapes overlap and have different colors.

Figure 13.5

Make sure the **Shading style** is **From center** and the nontransparent color is in the center radiating out. Remove the shape's line (border) also. After closing the **Format AutoShape** dialog box, you should obtain an effect similar to Figure 13.5.

You may wish to increase the transparency somewhat for the center color, if a less-intense glow is desired. Another option is to move the oval further into the gray area and increase its size. This dilutes the glow over a larger area. In Slide Show mode you see only the portion of the oval that overlaps the slide pane. Make adjustments to the shape's angle or positioning as desired.

Rectangular Glow: A similar effect, composed with slightly different methods, can be produced by starting with a large rectangle instead of an oval. This results in a glow with a radiating beam at its center projecting onto the slide. In this case, as before, most of the AutoShape is left hanging off the slide pane, in the gray area.

As before, give the shape a **Two-Color Fill Effect** and take one color up to **100%** transparency. Select a color option for the other color, and adjust its transparency level as desired. Sometimes it's better to increase the size and position of the rectangle rather than change the transparency of the second color. We usually make such a rectangle quite large and leave most of it outside the slide pane. Be sure to remove the line.

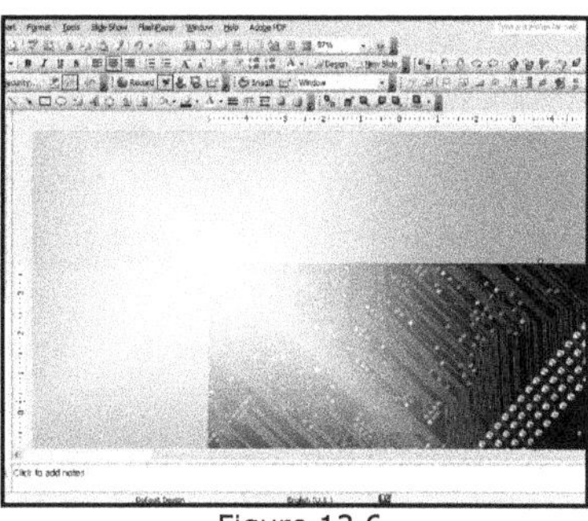
Figure 13.6

A square shape makes a uniform star pattern, and a more elongated rectangle produces a distorted pattern where beams on one side are shorter than beams in the other direction. Experiment with different designs and choose the preferred look. If desired, rotate the shape.

With this technique you are simulating natural glare, as if taking a picture in bright sunlight, resulting in a camera lens flare. Try experimenting with other AutoShapes, too. The hexagon shape, for example, produces an attractive six-beamed star. These more complex shapes tend to not work well for lighting effects, per se, but can provide attractive emphasis effects when overlaid on top of pictures.

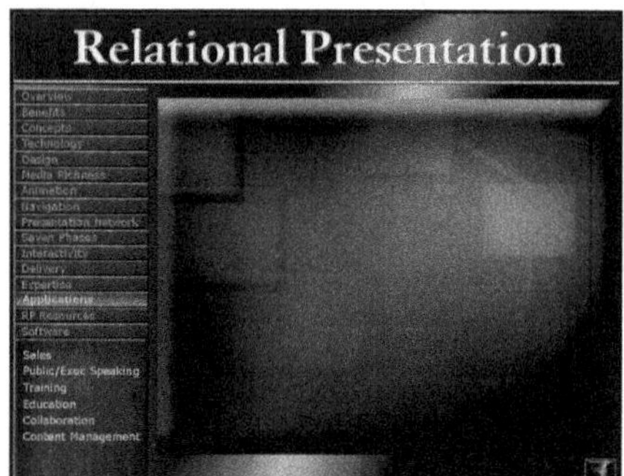

Figure 13.7

Corner Glow: A variation of the rectangular glow that works well with Nested Navigation is to place a rectangle on the slide pane, exactly in the corner of the defined content area. Then apply a **From corner** fill effect instead of **From center**.

Figure 13.7 shows our Nested Navigation template with its standard dark red graphical rectangle, representing the content boundaries. As shown here, this slide does not yet have an AutoShape lighting effect on the content area. It is essentially a blank slide waiting for content (or in this case, a lighting effect).

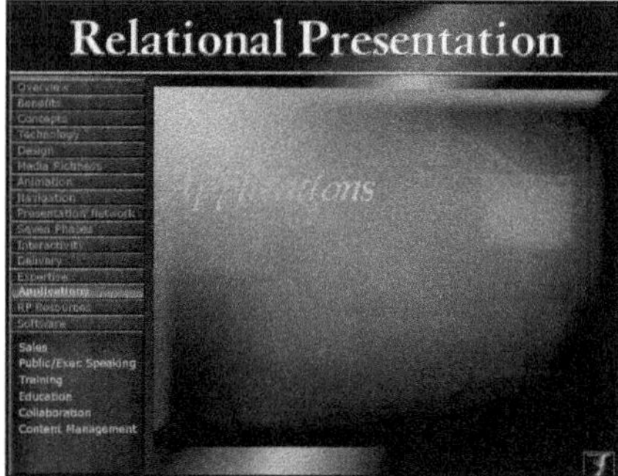

Figure 13.8

Now notice the glow in the upper left corner of the content area in Figure 13.8. It's the same slide with a two-color lighting effect added.

Figure 13.9

This particular effect is built by first laying a large rectangular shape on top of the entire content area (Figure 13.9) that fades from red (in Aspire's case) out to nothing. Then a second smaller rectangle fading from orange (again in Aspire's case) out to nothing is placed on top of the red rectangle. Note that the example here shows the two rectangles offset, but this positioning is only for your reference so that you can see both of them. In practice, the two rectangles are exactly aligned with each other.

When two or more shapes containing transparency are overlaid on top of each other, the gradients fade together, producing an attractive and smooth blending. Basically, we are faking more robust gradient techniques available through the use of graphics editing software.

When the two gradients are placed on top of a white text label, the gradients partially obscure the stark whiteness of the letters and give a subtle, softer feel.

13.7 Backlighting

The process of creating backlighting involves having distinct, dark objects (normally AutoShapes or pictures) sitting on top of a similarly dark background. Then lighting-effect AutoShapes are placed between the objects and the background, to create the impression the shapes or pictures are suspended in mid-air. We want to simulate a situation where the objects literally would have a light behind them, shining on a wall.

The slide in Figure 13.10 features backlighting as a decorative element. There are three lighting-effect AutoShapes behind the three content AutoShapes. The shape in the middle is a square, and the shapes on either side are rectangles. All three have a two-color fill, from center, with one of the colors made transparent—as usual. Although not evident in this black and white book, a light yellow was chosen as the interior color to produce a light orange blending with the Aspire red slide background.

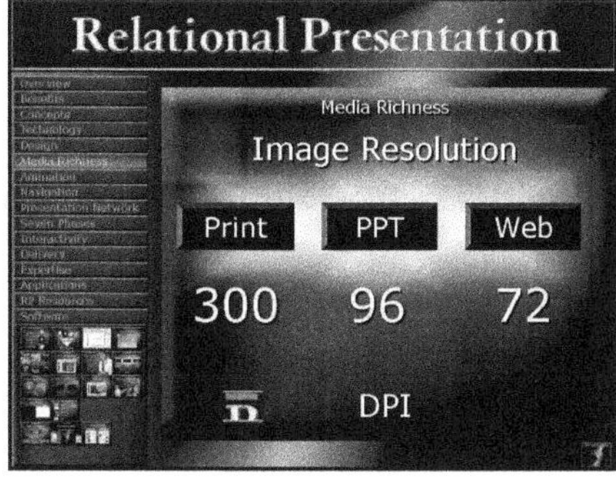

Figure 13.10

13.8 Design Coordination

Often, individuals or institutions creating a Presentation Network also have a Web site and perhaps a database, marketing materials, a book, and/or other promotional materials. Be sure to coordinate the network with these other forms of media and materials. Customers may come in contact with different forms of your marketing activities and outreach. They should see the same look and feel in your network as they would everywhere else.

In other words, your Presentation Network is part of your larger messaging system. It does not exist in isolation. Coordinate it with all external activities, trade shows and conferences, training materials, intranets, and other forms of organizational communication.

13.9 Unnecessary Labeling

Relational designers, when first starting out, tend to label everything. We did, too. Certainly labels on slides can be helpful, particularly when they are for the audience's benefit. Before adding a label to a slide, however, think about whether it is truly needed. If labeling accomplishes no useful purpose for the audience, don't include it.

Switchboards are the most common example where slides often receive a label when one is not needed. Many designers label their Main Switchboard, not surprisingly, *Main Switchboard* or a Video Switchboard, *Video Switchboard*. If you think about it, such titles are unnecessary. The presenter, by glancing at a switchboard, had better know what that switchboard does. If he doesn't, he is grossly unprepared or the switchboard is poorly designed. The audience doesn't need to know what a switchboard does because such slides exist purely to help the presenter jump from point A to point B. With a Video Switchboard, for example, the audience doesn't care about your network's mechanisms or the purpose of slides, as long as the video plays when needed.

Your goal as a designer is to minimize clutter on slides in every way possible. If a label serves no useful purpose, remove it so that the text doesn't compete for attention. Summary labels, on the contrary, should stay.

Understanding the use of *Visual Clues*, and including them throughout your network, is a relational designer's most critical mission. Visual Clues make or break a presenter's ability to smoothly and immediately find needed content. Without these devices, all of the other lessons in this book fall apart. Here is a comprehensive summary of Visual Clues, to clarify what they are and how they work.

By definition, a Visual Clue is any visual element on a slide that gives a presenter some kind of feedback about what content is available, where to find it, and what functionality exists for doing so. Visual Clues are, in effect, the presenter's cheat sheet. They visually guide the process of dynamically locating needed slides or slide shows. They also help a speaker stay oriented within the network's potentially daunting complexity. Without Visual Clues, he or she could easily become lost or disoriented.

Text: Simple text, whether in the form of navigation, slide labels, or content, help a presenter immediately grasp the intent of slides and know where he is in the overall structure. Text-based navigation, in particular, enables a speaker to casually scan available options; he then can pursue needed content immediately or mentally prepare for upcoming topics. A relational presenter on one level is constantly talking to, and interacting with, the audience. Simultaneously on another level, she is looking for Visual Clues on the slides and asking herself, "OK. Where to next? What are the highest priority topics to cover in the remaining time?"

Picture Thumbnails: Whether photos, graphics, or screenshots, thumbnails used for navigation provide highly effective previews of available options. Thumbnails are remarkably useful on the Main Switchboard and as primary buttons on slides. Choose this kind of Visual Clue when the slides being represented have clearly identifiable visual content. In other words, if you make a screenshot thumbnail, be sure the content depicted in the screenshot is easily identifiable in the small image.

Color: Color can communicate valuable information to a presenter, without viewers being the wiser. Dark gray buttons might have a particular purpose and blue buttons have a different purpose. White text on a slide might indicate that a word represents an active link, whereas beige text is not yet linked. Navigation Elements located in a red zone on a slide may have a different function from those in an orange zone.

Structure: Remember the apple example in Chapter 2? We have fun with trainees using this process. We start with the red apple slide and say something like, "OK, we don't want a red apple after all. We want some other color instead." Then we have trainees pick a color (yellow, green, blue, or purple), and as they choose a color (in whatever order) we *magically* change the apple's color in front of their eyes. They are asked to explain how we made the changes.

Figure 13.11

Most pick up on the fact that we are clicking the slide for each color shift, but very few grasp the logic of our actions. As mentioned previously, we are using the basket in the background as a structural Visual Clue so that we know where to click. In essence, the navigation method being used is an invisible version of Inline Navigation.

Zone Navigation, of course, is completely dependent upon this form of Visual Clue. Without the slide indicating where to click, the presenter would have a difficult time finding meaningful links. Which elements on slides you choose to make into clues is irrelevant, as long as the presenter has clear guidance. Ideally he or she should have input into which structures ultimately are chosen.

Organization: Organizational strategies might guide a speaker to individual categories of links on complex switchboards. An organizational Visual Clue refers to the process of grouping links according to similarity of purpose or content. In Figure 13.12, notice that the thumbnails are arranged in meaningful groups. If we are looking for a building, as opposed to scenery or a nature slide, we can ignore the five left-most columns (eliminating 35 links from focus) and look at the two right-most columns (the 14 remaining links).

Organizational logic is even more important when a switchboard contains a complex array of text-based links. Clustering in this case is needed for fast selection. Ideally, such clusters should contain less than 12

Figure 13.12

items, but larger groups are possible as well. It depends a lot on the kind of content being represented. Placing colors behind the different groups might also speed up selection. By the way, selection speed (finding relevant content quickly) is a major issue for relational presenters. Fast access to content enables fluid, conversational delivery. In a perfect world, content flies into view with the ease of words rolling off the tongue. Superior Visual Clues aid this process.

Shapes: The type of AutoShapes you select for navigation might serve as Visual Clues. Rectangular buttons might indicate primary shows and rounded rectangle buttons indicate collections (categories). You might include a subtle shape on a slide that tells you when you've reached the last slide in a show or indirectly points out a hidden link.

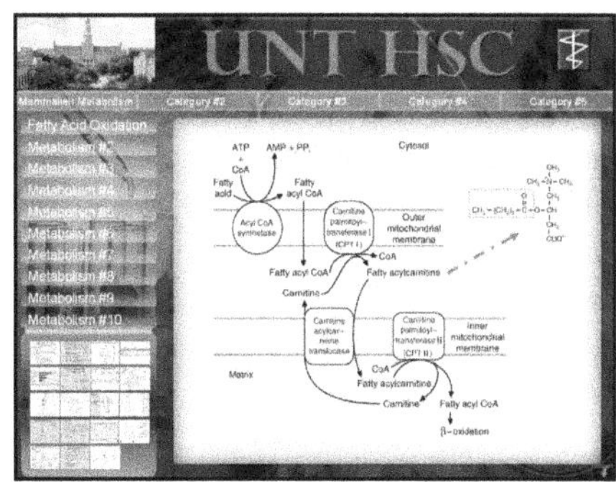

Figure 13.13

Highlight: It would be very difficult, if not impossible, for an audience member to notice the highlighted Visual Clues on the slide featured in Figure 13.13. And even if they did notice them, the clues would mean nothing. To the presenter, however, these clues are important. While delivering a demonstration to the University of North Texas, we knew that only six of the professor's original 19 sides had been changed. How did we remember which six? All 19 of the thumbnails in the bottom portion of the Nested Navigation (the slide links) had dark red borders—EXCEPT the six thumbnails representing the changed slides, which had magenta borders instead.

Subtle Difference: The highlighted Visual Clue example we just showed was very subtle. Sometimes highlights are subtle and sometimes they are more obvious. A subtle difference Visual Clue is ALWAYS intended to be very discreet, so that normally only the presenter notices it or understands its significance. Think back to the example of our Cover Show and Main Switchboard. They look identical except for one tiny difference that probably no one in the audience ever notices—the thumbnail link in the bottom right corner of the Main Switchboard. This thumbnail is the only indication we have for determining whether the Cover Show or the Main Switchboard is active. The audience doesn't care and doesn't need to know there is a difference. The distinction for us is absolutely necessary. A subtle clue is enough.

Subtle differences from one slide to another might cue a speaker about network operational details that are meaningless to viewers. A case in point might be knowing which links on a switchboard lead to real content and which lead only to placeholder slides. Small variations between link design or positioning can indicate which are truly valid.

Subtle difference Visual Clues are ideal for accessing multiple tracks or revealing hidden information on demand. In either case, you don't necessarily want the audience to know there are more options available. Only the presenter needs to know.

Symbolism: This last Visual Clue is the most esoteric of them all, yet nonetheless practical for relational presenters. It involves having shapes or images on a slide that mean one thing to an audience (or perhaps nothing at all) and something totally different to the presenter. A section of the network may be labeled *Case Studies, Examples,* or *Solutions* and indeed contain such presentation material. Known secretly only to the presenter, though, is that this section also doubles as a visually interactive way of handling objections in a sales situation. She, of course, would never reveal that fact, but the truth remains that the slide show material in this case has a symbolic, dual purpose to her. The labels imply different meanings, depending upon viewer perspective. Or, any given picture on a slide might appear innocent enough as content to the audience. The presenter also knows the picture has a dual meaning, serving as a link to supporting content—which may or may not ever be revealed.

Considering the number of bullet points seen in traditional presentations, it's no surprise people are curious about possible alternatives. In fact, there are numerous options for approaching bullet points in more flexible, interactive, and even visually stimulating ways. We highlight eight strategies here but this list is not inclusive. After becoming comfortable with Visually Interactive design and delivery techniques, you probably will think of others.

Alternative 1 (Figure 13.14): If you must continue using traditional bullet lists, at the very least make sure these slides contain Primary Navigation so that the presenter can spontaneously access other parts of the network in the middle of the list. You especially want a link that points to the Main Switchboard and a link that opens the Resources Switchboard. Also make sure all the slides in your network contain the magic back button. We described these elements previously but here is a reminder: Pretend you are in the middle of a bullet list and someone asks a question. Instead of merely giving a verbal answer and continuing with the list, use the Primary Navigation to find relevant content, and then use the magic back button to return to the list.

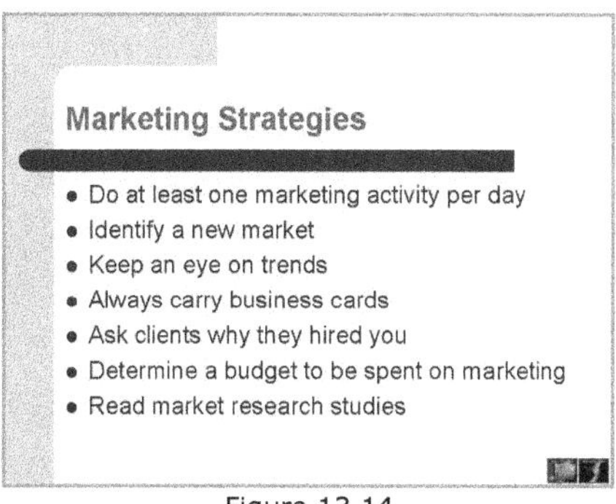

Figure 13.14

Alternative 2 (Figure 13.15): You can easily add a nice twist to traditional lists by animating a thumbnail along with each point. This book does not cover animation, but the process basically involves adding a **Fade** animation to the thumbnail and setting it to enter **With Previous**, along with its respective bullet point. This thumbnail, not surprisingly, links to supporting material, providing detail that

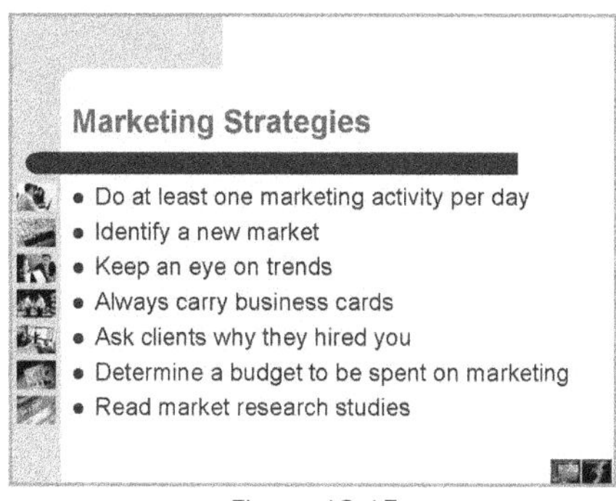

Figure 13.15

expands upon the bullet point topic. It can link to a slide later in the show or to a separate show entirely. It might even open a switchboard full of numerous additional links. The beauty of this design is that the presenter can choose to either access the supporting material or not, for any bullet point. The supporting material often is a visual example of the textual topic.

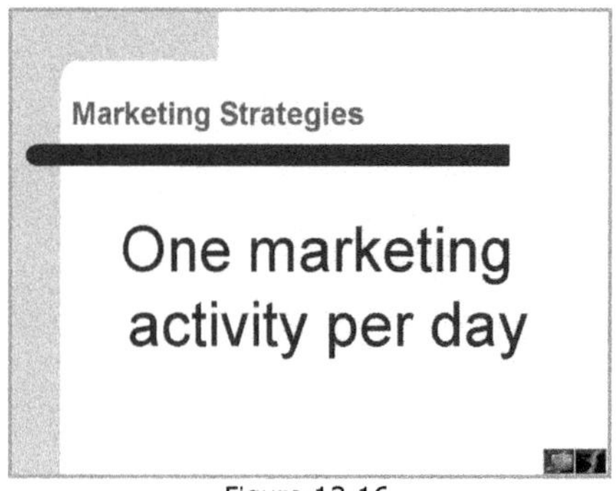

Figure 13.16

Alternative 3 (Figure 13.16): Consider separating each bullet point onto its own slide and making the text very large. Doing so allows participants to quickly digest the point, and then return focus to the speaker. If possible, simplify such points until they contain only a few words, ideally three or less. Separating points onto individual slides does not necessarily increase your delivery flexibility but aids audience comprehension nonetheless and is, therefore, superior to traditional bullet point structures. It also sets up the next alternative.

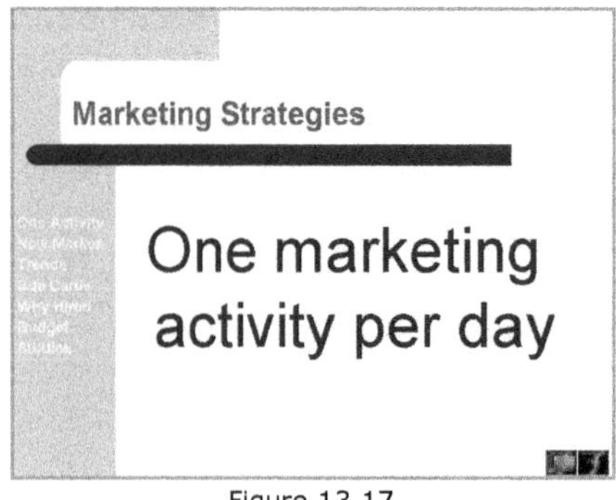

Figure 13.17

Alternative 4 (Figure 13.17): Once bullet points have been separated onto their own slides, add a simple panel or bar menu. This elegant strategy offers several advantages:

- Any point can be presented in any order.
- The presenter sees a preview of available points and then chooses to display ONLY needed items.
- Intentionally not displaying all the points gives the audience a sense you are customizing the message to their needs and not forcing them through irrelevant content.

- In some cases, especially when not displaying all the items, the menu might work to the presenter's advantage in another way. It potentially creates curiosity about what other information is available, yet is not being shown. This curiosity can lead to additional interactivity and engagement.

Figure 13.18

Alternative 5 (Figure 13.18): Separating points onto separate slides and then also adding a meaningful picture can accentuate the message in that bullet point. Viewers' eyes will be drawn to the picture first and then the text. This approach is even more effective if you also hyperlink the picture to supporting material, such as a picture story, research detail, reference sources, and so forth. When the extra detail is hidden, but available on demand by hyperlink, it does not clutter the current slide view.

Figure 13.19

Alternative 6 (Figure 13.19): When the pictures being used are especially descriptive, and are the main focus (content), make them large and de-emphasize the text. Such a design is far more visually appealing than a bullet list, yet accomplishes the same goal of disseminating information points. You probably can see where this trend is heading and predict Alternative 7. We are moving toward graphical—rather than text-based—bullet points.

Alternative 7 (Figure 13.20): By tradition, bullet points are always text-based. But why can't they be photos, graphics, or screenshots? The image itself would speak and the presenter could fill in extra details verbally. In the example shown here, the bullets are pictures and thumbnail bar navigation at the bottom of the slides provides access to the different

Figure 13.20

points. Likewise, one might have a showcase switchboard full of pictures, research results, training components, or other items.

Obviously, the lines now begin to blur between the definition of a bullet point and regular content. In a Relational Presentation context, the lines become very blurry indeed. If you follow the guideline of having only one idea per slide, your entire network acts like one gigantic alternative to bullet points. Each time you access a slide to talk about a specific topic, you are in effect advancing to the next point—yet in a much more effective way.

Using alternatives to traditional lists has other interesting advantages as well. Think about this concept: With normal bullets, the presenter is really nothing more that a lecturer. Each point comes up and is given to the audience, whether they like it or not. In other words, the communication is one-way.

When bullet lists are set up to be interactive with menus, they don't have to be given at all. The presenter can actually turn a bullet list into an interactive forum. She might say something to the effect of, "So, you guys give me some ideas for effective marketing," and then lets the audience contribute ideas. She can display the ideas in her list as they are mentioned and perhaps go into more detail with supporting materials available in her network. Inevitably, some of the answers will not be in her list. So what then? It's not a problem. She simply responds, "That's a good suggestion. I don't have that in my list, but let me write that down and include it later." In either case, she is fostering interactivity and engagement, which is the whole idea.

While mentioning this idea once in a seminar, somebody made a comment, "Well, yeah, but if the audience can see your menu items on the screen and those menu items are descriptive, aren't you giving away the answers?" The response was, "Of course." Isn't that the purpose of going through bullet points in the first place—to give them away? One could deliver the items by lecture, but why not let the audience volunteer responses, even though to some extent they are being spoon fed?

Alternative 8 (Figure 13.21): A final variation is to have small graphical bullets instead of text-based bullets—or some combination of text and graphics. As a case in point, when discussing the topic of rich media, we randomly display the items shown in Figure 13.21 and visually describe what we mean by rich media. For example, the animation graphic animates, piece by piece. The graphics are our bullet points.

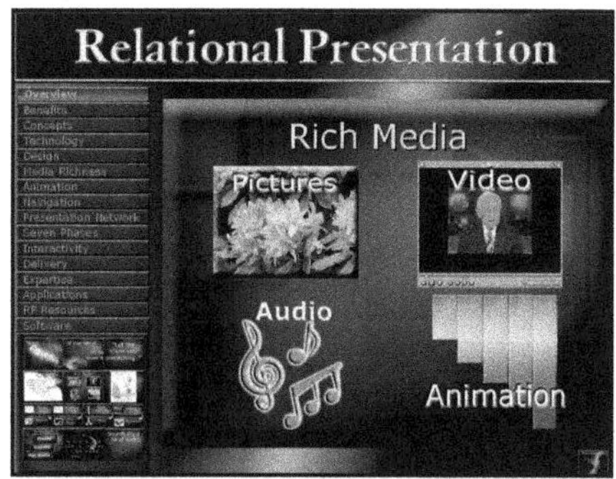

Figure 13.21

One gentleman once made a comment, "Gosh, those kinds of bullet points sound like more work? Slapping text on a slide is a lot faster." Yes, this is true. Think back, though, to our former discussions on quality and reusability. Our trainers and presenters use this slide over and over again. Frequently used bullet points deserve quality development. They should be treated with respect and designed to be audience-friendly. In other words, build your reusable bullet points right to begin with, and then you will have something valuable to show again and again.

"Yesterday I used my network for the first time! I absolutely love the flexibility. For the first time ever I had the ability to skip slides at will and to go where I wanted to go. I am a long, long way from having it where I want it but am moving in the right direction. I'm attacking development from several fronts simultaneously—keeping the network current with my classes and working on my resources switchboard, my music switchboard, and my video switchboard. It is a lot of work but I can't think of anything I have done recently that has been more fun or rewarding."

Fred Barbee, Professor of Accounting
University of Alaska

Chapter 14

The Four Types of Interactivity

Interactive
Navigation

Accesses
Content

Up to this point, we have focused mostly on mechanics—getting a presentation structure in place that a speaker can use in spontaneous, conversational ways. Now it's time to turn from mechanics to delivery. What does this spontaneous, conversational process look like? How does relational delivery work in practice? The answers to these questions are multifaceted and, in fact, are as intricate as human communication patterns. Some good, old-fashioned practical advice is needed to help you conveniently harness the power of the interactive platform being created. In this chapter and the next, we examine relational delivery from many different angles to understand its challenges and rewards.

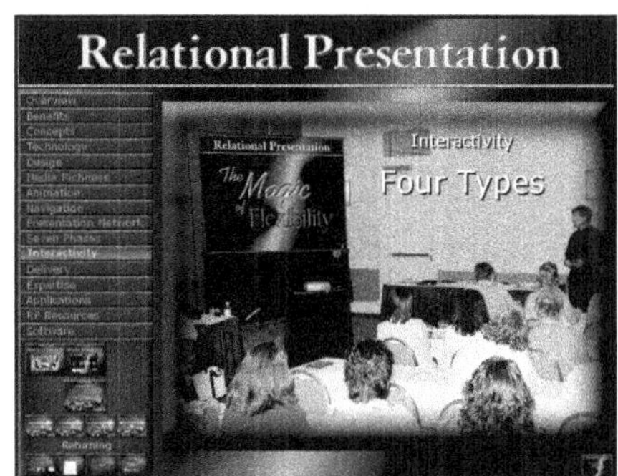

Figure 14.1

Visually interactive presentation, as the name implies, is intended to be dynamic and visually responsive to viewers' interests. As such, one of its overriding goals is to promote a back and forth exchange of information between speaker and audience. We refer to this process broadly as *interactivity*, but in reality there are at least four different types of interactivity possible with Relational Presentation. Distinguishing between, and understanding, these types will improve your performances and offer delivery options that are not possible with standard presentation alone. The four types are:

- Passive Interactivity
- Active Interactivity
- Full-Visual Interactivity
- Multipresenter Interactivity

All of the interactivity types presume you have the ability and desire to dynamically adjust your message focus at any time. Harkening back to our earlier mention of systems dynamics, you and your audience are a living system, what is known technically as a *feedback loop*. In this system, the speaker gives information, which causes the audience to react, which in turn causes the speaker to react, which causes the audience to respond, and so on. From now on, the final outcomes of your performances will be determined by the interactions that occur throughout.

If you are exploring dynamic presentation for the first time, this idea might seem scary at first. The thought of *not having full control* sends chills up the spine. What you will find, actually, is that interactive delivery has an opposite effect. It enables stunningly MORE control in the long run.

14.2 Passive Interactivity

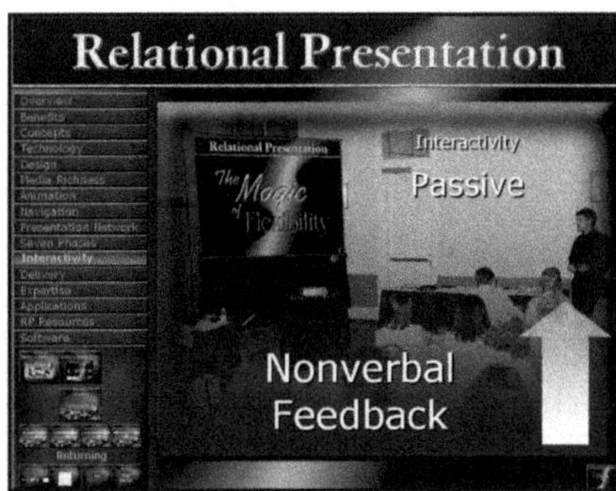

Figure 14.2

The expression *Passive Interactivity* may seem initially like a contradiction in terms. Here's what it means: Let's say you are addressing a group of people. Your network is in pretty good shape, and there is potential for navigating to all content on demand. However, with this particular audience, you are doing all the talking. As of yet, they have not said a word (a common occurrence considering we, as viewers, are conditioned to be passive). Most people analyzing this situation would say there is no interaction occurring at the moment. After all, how could there be interactivity if only one side of the loop is active? You are working through your content and participants are receiving.

An important lesson to learn right from the start, when experimenting with your network, is that the VAST MAJORITY of feedback you receive as a presenter will be nonverbal. Just because audience members are not talking does not mean they are not communicating information to you. That information, in nonverbal form, can be essential for helping you spontaneously craft a message to perceived needs and interests.

Nonverbal (passive) communication is surprisingly rich. Laughter and yawns can help you gauge impact. Looks of amusement, confusion, impatience, or boredom tell about engagement. Restlessness, eye contact (or lack thereof), drooping eyelids, side conversations, and a host of other expressions are extremely valuable clues an agile teacher, salesperson, or executive can tap into. These little pieces of knowledge can say as much or more as someone raising their hand and saying, "I don't understand."

Frowns or looks of uncertainty while discussing a complex subject might indicate you need to show available examples, or perhaps review prerequisite facts you thought they already knew. When a speaker has complete control over content, there is freedom to watch for signals along the way. Part of your brain is talking and another part is simultaneously analyzing the audience in a quest for feedback. These signals help you provide the best possible customer service.

In some cases, your analysis might prompt soliciting direct verbal feedback. "I'm getting the sense you guys are pretty familiar with this material already. Should I do a quick summary or skip it all together?" Audiences usually are so unaccustomed to that kind of individualized attention that they heartily welcome the change.

14.3 Active Interactivity

The exchanges most of us might readily label interactivity are referred to as *Active Interactivity*. With active interaction, there is both nonverbal and direct verbal feedback. Someone may ask a question, answer a question, offer a perspective, challenge a point, or desire a clarification. As you become more comfortable moving around within your presentation materials, this kind of interaction increases and performances take on a more conversational flair.

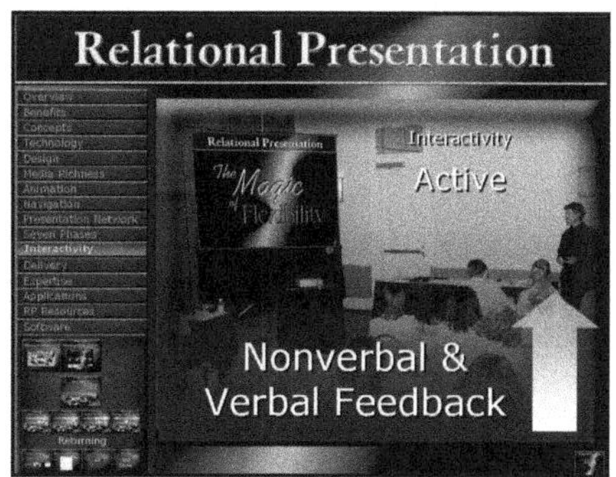

Figure 14.3

Active interaction opens bountiful possibilities for relational speakers. Once listeners are engaged enough to directly respond, the feedback loop builds upon itself. Now you don't have to guess as much about potential adjustments based on analysis—direction is obvious.

Active participation is also more interesting for the presenter. Differences in people's personalities and moods, as well as audience interactions, spice up otherwise uniform topics. Of course, one must be diligent to take advantage of this interaction by using it for further visual customization. Verbal interaction is great but any presenter can verbally respond. You represent far more potential. Be sure to back up your words with visual content and media as often as possible.

Active Interactivity does not always happen spontaneously. Sometimes viewers sit there like tree stumps, waiting for you to be their television. Realize you need to create an environment that encourages active participation. Design content and navigation in a way that says, "I want you to interact with me." Actively invite direct participation. By doing so, you are much more likely to have an engaged, interested group of people in the seats.

Earlier we mentioned the importance of educating the audience about the availability of interaction. They may never have seen a presentation like this before. We'll talk more about this component later, but be resolved to the fact that sometimes you need to prepare viewers by initially simulating interaction or at least demonstrating your capabilities. This doesn't have to be a big deal. We might say something like, "If someone were to ask a question such as ... here's the way we might answer it." Then we demonstrate by navigating to the content.

14.4 Full-Visual Interactivity

Interactivity reaches a higher plane when it moves beyond Active Interactivity into *Full-Visual Interactivity*. This type of interaction, admittedly, is somewhat sporadic, even for experienced relational presenters. So don't count on it happening every time. It is, nevertheless, a highly desirable state that should be *sought after* every time.

Full-Visual Interactivity means the presenter flexibly delivers verbal and visual information to the audience as usual, AND audience members begin incorporating the presenter's visual materials into their own messages back to him. The loop becomes visual in both directions, and people tend to be far more engaged in your performance. Such interaction might take various forms, similar to the following examples:

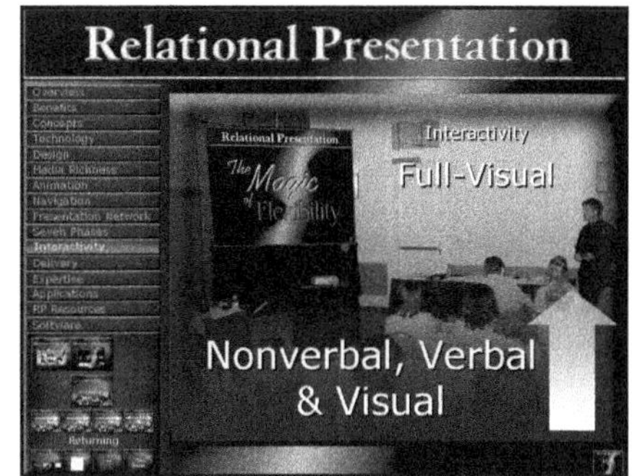

Figure 14.4

Maybe you are training people how to wire an alarm system in a car. Your network contains numerous visual illustrations of wiring configurations and options. Someone raises her hand and says, "Wait a minute. I thought you said earlier to put the red wire on terminal B. Can you go back to the slide that showed the terminals?" You navigate to the requested slide. Then she says, "Now which of those is terminal B?" In this case, the *viewer* rather than the presenter is directing the presentation, as a basis for asking questions, improving understanding, and making points.

Or someone might say, "Can you show me an example of that?" Here again, you as presenter are being directed to show visual information that may not have been shown otherwise. The audience is actively using your materials for their benefit, as if requesting information on the Web.

On occasion, people will incorporate your slides into their interactions as a way of launching their own comments. They might say, "That kind of looks like what we are working on but our situation is a little different. We are operating under different parameters." Your slide provides context that makes the comment relevant to ongoing discussions.

In a perfect world, participants become so actively involved that they literally want to grab the mouse out of your hand and begin making their points by directly navigating themselves. We've seen this happen in small group collaborations around a conference table. You will find most people have a natural desire to be visually expressive. When you give them that opportunity, they might do it without even being consciously aware of the fact.

14.5 Multipresenter Interactivity

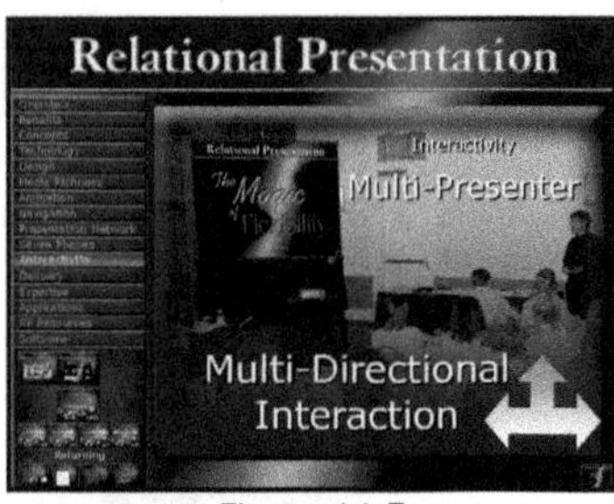

Figure 14.5

The final interaction type, *Multipresenter Interactivity*, probably should be reserved for later in your development cycle, when you (and others in your company or institution) have gained a reasonable depth of experience with single-presenter interactivity. The approach entails having two or more presenters simultaneously control a network, resulting in what amounts to a visual panel discussion. Interaction potentially occurs in two directions: between audience and presenters, and between the presenters themselves as they play off of each other's comments.

The inspiration for this approach came by watching a pharmaceutical sales rally that took place in a hotel ballroom. The company was introducing a new drug on the market. On this occasion, they brought together their sales staff of about 75 people for pep talks and to receive training on how to represent the new product in the market. Overall, the event was highly interactive and hands-on, with a great deal of participation by all parties. However, one component was glaringly missing.

During large group sessions, when everyone was together, they had a primary speaker who addressed the group, along with two additional experts who stood on either side of the room. Participants had many questions about expectations and procedures. Any of the three experts, consequently, might answer questions or make comments at any time. Needless to say, the primary presenter had a standard clicker that merely advanced through a linear presentation. Most of the questions were answered verbally for two reasons: either the required slide was not in view at the right moment or the experts on the side were answering the questions, without slide control.

We wondered, wouldn't it be interesting if all three experts had full control of an interactive network? Then one might say, "Yeah, that's a good point Joe. And don't forget about that other study completed just last month. Let's look at that." A multipresenter approach represents perhaps the highest possible form of Visual Interactivity. It also implies coordination between speakers and mutual familiarity with network contents.

Another interesting dynamic is the personality interactions between the presenters. It's a good idea, in general, to have a lead presenter and subordinates. Even then, be sure to respect speaking intervals and have a coordinated overall message plan.

14.6 Presenter Mobility

Although we don't go out of our way to specifically endorse products, there is one piece of equipment that is absolutely essential for facilitating all the interactivity types mentioned. It allows a speaker to be utterly untethered from the computer. The Gyromouse shown in Figure 14.6 is as important to a relational presenter as a surfboard is to a surfer. Your performances will be significantly hindered without it.

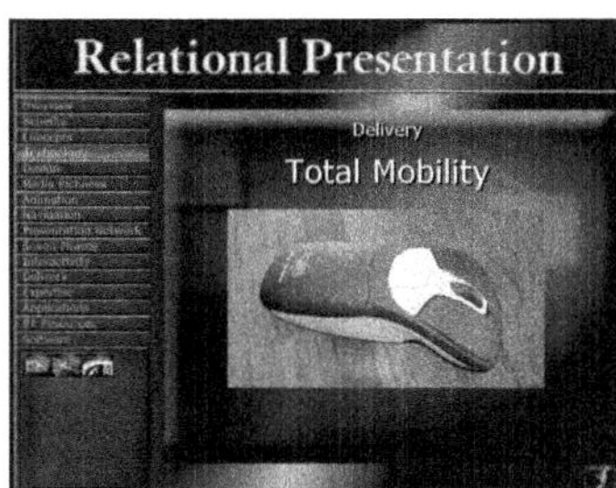

Figure 14.6

The Gyromouse is a regular wireless mouse in all respects, with all the buttons and optical tracking, except for one major difference: It houses a gyroscope that is able to sense the motion of your wrist as you move it in the air. On the bottom side of the device is a trigger. Pulling this trigger, while moving the mouse in the air, engages control of the computer cursor.

What this means is that you can be anywhere in a room, facing any direction, and totally control all aspects of your computer with flicks of the wrist and mouse clicks. What it also means is that you do not have to be near your computer to click links in the network.

We literally sit with the audience sometimes during parts of performances or trainings, and all the while have instant control of thousands of slides. In fact, there rarely is a reason to be near the computer.

One of the most detrimental practices a speaker can engage in is hiding behind the podium or computer. Doing so places a barrier, a wedge, between you and viewers. The Gyromouse provides a welcome freedom from that confinement. It is clearly important in a multipresenter environment, where all speakers need the availability of instant control.

This mouse does take some getting used to. So don't assume you will be an expert overnight. The effort is well worth it, however.

"I am inspired by your vision of Relational Presentation concepts to enhance the level of our communication. Having spent all of my adult life in sales or sales leadership I have a first hand appreciation for the work that you're doing at Aspire. After visiting your Web site and viewing your presentation, I found myself as excited as a kid in a candy store."

John Edmondson
Business Consultant,
Edmondson Consulting, USA

Chapter 15

Delivery: Strategies and Techniques

One Idea
Per Slide

15.1 This Delivery Is Different

In addition to offering heightened interactivity opportunities, relational delivery enables a host of other intriguing strategies. The options available are really quite fascinating. Such techniques simply are not possible with linear delivery alone. At the same time, recognize that dynamic selection of content has a very different feel and requires new perspectives, practice, and skill. Becoming polished at Relational Presentation does not happen accidentally. You need to take it seriously and develop necessary talents.

This chapter focuses on how to deliver nonlinear presentations in a professional and powerful way, taking full advantage of all the flexibility and optical illusions available. The two best tips we can give you as an introduction to visually interactive delivery are these: Typically, there is an adjustment period at first, where the process feels a little awkward—so be patient with yourself; and be flexible in your own thinking as you try most of the methods featured in this book—don't be content to *do it the way it's always been done.*

There will be a thousand *what ifs* and many are legitimate issues that require forethought and practice. The reason so much of this book focuses on the mechanical aspects of building the underlying network's structure is because this structure, when well done, significantly impacts your delivery options. Superior network design makes interactive delivery so much easier and more fun. Take the time to build the network well—and if something isn't working in a delivery sense, be willing to acknowledge that fact and fix the problem, even if doing so requires reorganization. Don't try to impose smooth delivery on poor network design.

15.2 Visual Fluency

Visual Fluency refers to feeling so comfortable with relational delivery—with the spontaneous selection of visuals—that you don't even think about the process most of the time. It just happens as a natural and expected part of your communication activities. This will be your ultimate goal from here on, to reach this level of comfort. Just as you might randomly banter with friends in a café and form syntax with words, you will be able to randomly navigate and form syntax with visuals, while using presentation materials. Having a well-organized Presentation

Network that is loaded with Visual Clues (assuming you know your content) allows you to converse visually. In a visually fluent state, navigation to supporting material becomes effortless and automated. Public speaking is REALLY fun.

Keep in mind that as you approach fluency, an interesting phenomenon occurs. People begin to notice PowerPoint less and less. Technically, they do pay attention to the slides, but the focus shifts more to you as the presenter. The slide shows merely offer visual support, and the computer no longer forms a barrier between you and the viewers. It's difficult to describe this effect until you experience it in action, but it is the best possible use of PowerPoint.

Becoming visually fluent takes time and practice. You are ultimately learning a new language. Consistently develop your skills and fluency will come.

15.3 Preparing the Audience

As mentioned earlier, an important routine when interactively addressing audiences is to let them know your delivery style is different. Listeners undoubtedly assume your performance will be like all the other PowerPoint presentations they have seen. The potential for spontaneous visual interaction probably won't even cross their minds. Even if they are familiar with your capabilities, they may not know how to interact with you.

Figure 15.1

A regular part of our opening remarks is to give people a *heads up* on what to expect—and what we expect (or ask) of them. If you don't invite viewers to interact with your message, they probably won't. Following are the basic components we say in advance, in different ways. Your situation may vary and require different approaches. That's fine. Remember, the idea is to get them involved, whatever that might look like.

- If using a Seed Presentation, inform attendees you will give a short (5 to 10 minutes) introductory overview, and then the rest of the session will be visual dialogue, where they can actively participate in helping direct the show.
- Give them permission to NOT interact. Because interaction during a presentation is a novel concept for many, they may need a warm-up period—and some will never participate, no matter what you do. The way we approach this permission component is to let people know we have certain core topics to cover along the way, but we've also built in flexibility to customize the topic to the needs and interests of the audience. They are encouraged to help us tailor the message as we deliver by asking questions or by requesting clarification or more detail. Some will not join in and they need to know that is acceptable. In the absence of participation, we proceed with the prepared message as is. In other words, we let them know that either way is fine with us.
- Somewhere, in the early stages of your performance, it's vitally important to show participants the flexibility you have with menus. Seeing a presenter navigate within PowerPoint is unusual. They might not know what you mean by saying a message can be customized. A demonstration early on is a good idea. In fact, the ideal scenario is to visually converse with a few participants even before the session begins.
- Finally, once you are done with the Seed Presentation, or other introductory remarks, remind them again that the interactive section has begun and they are encouraged to participate. Sometimes we even tell them the question-and-answer period starts NOW, at the beginning.

15.4 Audience-Directed Presentation

Audience-directed presentation DOES NOT imply that an audience is allowed to control a presentation. No matter how visually interactive your sessions eventually become, you must always be 100 percent in control of the message. What it does mean is that you allow participants to tweak the agenda along the way. They might be permitted to pick topics of interest or request more detail. At all times, the speaker continues to call the shots and make decisions on how long the audience participation will continue, and to what depth. Do not allow interaction to get out of control or unduly divert you from the overall message plan. The only exceptions occur when interactions reveal your original message clearly was way off track to begin with.

Allowing an audience to help you customize the agenda may appear like a freeform event to them, but behind the scenes you maintain a fairly tight grip on the process. It is your responsibility to bring order to whatever interesting and consuming tangents may arise. In some cases, your role takes on the flavor of a traffic cop, subtly or overtly directing message traffic.

Here is an interesting characteristic of audience-directed presentation for you to ponder: Almost invariably people will ask questions, or make comments, about issues you intend to cover anyway. It's just human nature. If there are 10 issues you plan to discuss during the talk, probably people are thinking about three or four of them before you even finish your introduction. So, why not let them ask? That way they are more engaged in the process and you are able to make a point that would have been covered soon anyway. As a presenter, we often know what questions people are thinking. They may ask those questions out of order, but so what? You might even try having large, easily readable navigation buttons that give viewers ideas.

If someone asks a good question that wasn't anticipated, that's OK, too. Try to think of something in your network that allows you to respond visually. This time around, perhaps the response will be verbal, but make a note to add that visual before the next performance. We've actually noticed some presenters are afraid of this situation, as though not having EVERYTHING needed will be perceived as a sign of being unprepared. On the contrary, take advantage of the opportunity by saying, "That is an excellent question, and I'm going to make a note to add it to my presentation." Such acknowledgment gives the questioner a sense of satisfaction that they stumped the expert, so to speak.

15.5 Staying on Track

The issue of *staying on track* is at the forefront of most people's minds when thinking about interactive delivery. How is it possible to be spontaneous and responsive while maintaining clear purposes, direction, and outcomes? We don't take this question lightly and neither should you. Staying oriented within the planned communication goals is a basic skill you should master early on. Recall our previous discussion of the *Content Ladder*, where a speaker approaches the larger message as a collection of modular, sequential pieces. By using this strategy, anyone can stay on track with relative ease; high-priority topics are covered, even as individual points are rearranged as needed. The broader performance constantly moves toward the end goal, with allowances for variations and additions that occur along the way.

Figure 15.2

Staying on track does not mean we have a rigid path that must be followed, no matter what. We are constantly amazed at the number of people who believe it should be this way, even after starting down the Relational Presentation path. On the contrary, staying on track is more like planning a trip from Chicago to Dallas and knowing there are many paths and methods to accomplish the task. One path may be chosen over another, but they all lead to the same place in the end.

We realize some of you reading this text are thinking, "Well, but we really do our homework and we know exactly what needs to be said, how it should be said, and when it should be said. We don't want to risk such uncertainty in the delivery process." You will find that relational strategies forfeit none of this meticulous planning. It's a good idea to know exactly what you want to say and when. That being stated, however, we can almost guarantee you don't know as much as you think you know. None of us do. Staying on track in a visually interactive context means being always keenly aware of your position along the timeline at any moment, yet remaining sensitive to the interactions you experience. This process involves three critical behaviors:

- Having a very clear understanding of what needs to be covered and a preferred order for these topics

- Proceeding through the topics in roughly the preferred order but maintaining the agility to address issues out of order and likewise dynamically add or subtract topics when appropriate
- Occasionally pulling the agenda back on track without attracting undue attention to the act of doing so (covered next)

15.6 Redirecting Messages

Interaction, by definition, is somewhat unpredictable. There are times when you need to pull the message back on track. Although there is no single technique for magically doing so in all cases, various phrases we collectively classify as *redirecting messages* can help.

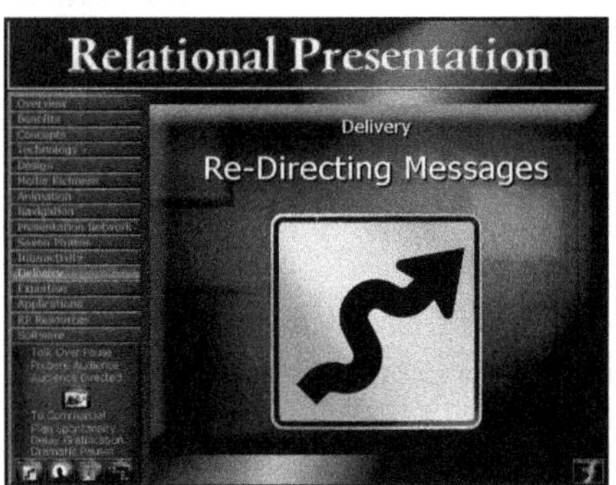

Figure 15.3

Redirection amounts to nudging messages in desired directions, as opposed to radically changing course. Most viewers are respectful and know you have an agenda to cover. Excessive questions, objections, or blatantly disruptive behaviors are not the norm (unless you are in a hostile situation). Try to make transitions as subtle and smooth as possible.

Pulling an agenda back on course involves listening to viewers' comments and noticing *key words* and *transition points*. A key word is something they say that allows you to make a logical segue to the next topic. A transition point is a vocal break or an apparent completion of thought, either of which gives you a chance to interject change. Your transitions might sound like:

- "That's a great point, Bill, and let me show you something else that comes into play here."
- "Oh! That reminds me of something. Take a look at this."
- "Here's something else to think about."

Notice how all of the above phrases are quite generic. They acknowledge the participant, softly cut him or her off from further input, and then give you permission, quite literally, to go ANYWHERE with the next comment or display.

Be prepared, occasionally, to pull up on the reigns and reassert control. We sometimes hold Aspire training workshops at a dude ranch outside Tucson and, not surprisingly, we ride horses in between sessions. We learned early that horses read your confidence level and test your authority. If you don't assert control, they will take it instead. Audiences have the same tendency sometimes. It is your responsibility to make sure individuals do not dominate discussions and to close down unproductive tangents. You must, in all cases, vigilantly respect time limits and never use interaction as an excuse for exceeding those limits.

15.7 Skipping or Adding Content

Skipping or adding content is an aspect of interactive delivery many people struggle with mentally, especially at first. We so carefully prepare our messages that the thought of actually leaving some of those slides out seems like heresy. And how could we possibly add more slides if the hour we have is already too short to cover everything we want to say?

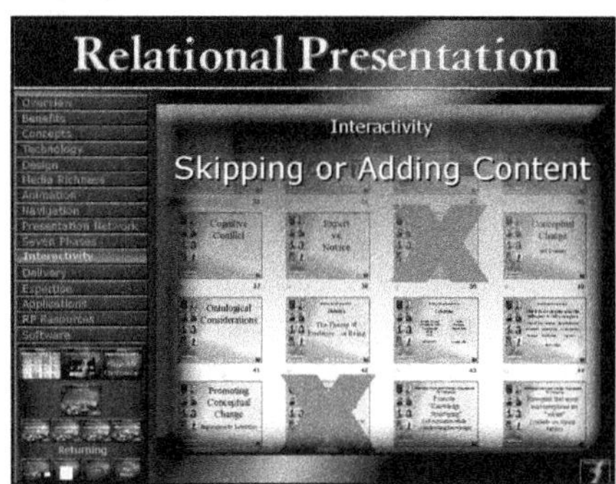

Figure 15.4

Sound familiar? A very important mindset to adopt right away is realizing that flexible presentation requires flexible thinking. You probably will not be able to show every slide; additional unplanned slides likely will be needed. That's just the way it is. Adjusting messages to the needs of the moment necessitates a willingness to make decisions on the spot.

Be careful not to box yourself in with too much content per session. We mentioned that our strategy is to schedule content for about three fourths of the amount of allotted time and leave the remaining quarter available for interaction. That extra time frees you to display additional content. Spontaneously adding this material throughout the performance is vital to customized display. You should be able to find anything quickly and display it naturally, as part of ongoing interactions. If you ever find yourself in the position of thinking, "Hmmm. Now where did I put that slide?" something is wrong with your organizational logic and you may need to rethink slide placement.

To help yourself develop a willingness to skip content when necessary, approach messages as collections of small informational packets, the modules we spoke of earlier. Then prioritize these packets. Usually topics contain a certain amount of critical detail, along with supplementary information that potentially can be dropped if necessary. Perhaps you are a researcher describing the ongoing development of a new scientific process. There's a good chance some of the detail can be left out or briefly summarized, if necessary, with a reference to handout materials. Or maybe you are in sales and halfway through the sales pitch, buying signs become obvious. At that point, skip to critical closing details.

Plan messages in a way that allows you to drop less critical slides THROUGHOUT the performance, gradually. This is very important. Don't wait until the last 10 minutes and be forced to drop an entire segment in a panic. Gauge progress along the way and prune where necessary.

15.8 Talking Over the Pause

Talking over the pause is a concept somewhat unique to Relational Presentation. It means that the verbal components of your message should continue flowing smoothly, even when there is a delay with the visual components.

Here's the issue: You may have noticed that when PowerPoint opens another slide show via hyperlink, there is a delay between the click and when the new show opens. The delay normally is accompanied by a momentary black display. We call this time period the *pause*.

The delay is short if you have a reasonably modern computer and the slide show being opened has a relatively small file size. If your computer is old and/or the file size is large, the delay might extend for many seconds. Our network contains an example presentation from a client that, even on the fastest laptop, takes about 12 seconds to open and display when using hyperlinks.

The pause, if unaddressed, is a problem for relational speakers. Our natural tendency is to stop talking, wait for the new slide show to open, and then pick up with a new sentence. Get in the habit right from the start of NOT doing this. Waiting for a computer to display information is always unacceptable. It breaks the continuity of message flow and distracts viewers.

The idea of *talking over the pause* is very simple and minimizes this disruption. Rather than waiting until the end of a sentence to click a link, form the habit of always clicking links in mid-sentence, particularly if you know a long pause is coming. This allows you to be fully facing the audience with continued eye-contact—and talking—while the computer is performing its task. The audience barely notices the delay because they are still engaged with you. By the time you finish your current sentence, the new display is in place and you can continue into the next sentence without a disruption.

Ideally, you should try to keep PowerPoint-caused delays as short as possible, by using a modern computer and dividing long slide shows into short segments (another reason for using modular strategy, by the way). But if doing so is not possible or practical, adjust your speaking style instead. By no means should you ever turn and face the screen and then wait. That is like putting a wall between you and the audience. Similarly, don't look down at the clicker and pause between slide transitions. Allow the slides to come up naturally while you maintain eye contact.

15.9 Simplicity to Complexity

A wide-ranging strategy we recommend regularly is *moving from simplicity to complexity*. This idea guides both network design and delivery. What it means is that your content should exist, in effect, as layers of detail. That way a typical discussion might begin by looking at a topic from a simplistic perspective. Then additional complexity and detail can be readily added if needed.

A healthcare worker might have a network that educates expectant mothers on the various stages of pregnancy, prenatal care, birth preparation, and postbirth development. During a short overview session, she might need only simplistic summary slides that show information at a general level. If, on the other hand, she is using the same network to conduct week-long classes on the topics, obviously she will need more detail.

In this case, the general slides serve as an introduction to the additional content that may be very detailed indeed. Perhaps you are learning calculus for the first time and have little experience with math. A good instructor won't force you directly into the calculation of complex, abstract equations. He will try to relate abstract mathematics to experiences in your everyday life, so that your new knowledge is connected to existing understandings. In other words, he will start simple and work toward more complicated lessons. Abstract ideas make more sense later if first grounded in simple analogies and examples you already know.

Use this approach often in your presentation activities. Remember that we as speakers frequently are *experts* in our fields, delivering information to novices. By *novices* we don't mean to imply audience members are unintelligent or even unacquainted with your overall topics. They merely are unfamiliar with the particular knowledge you embody and, therefore, are inexperienced learners in your subject matter. This fact dictates you are better off approaching topics from an easy-to-understand summary level first, before moving into complexity.

A network arranged and presented from this multidimensional perspective gives you options for adjusting meaning to viewers' perceived experience levels or knowledge. The *simple slides* link to other slides, slide shows, or entire categories of more information. The Resources Section is a special application of this principle. Any given slide in the network has access to a mountain of supporting material that can provide more depth if appropriate.

15.10 Multiple Tracks

The strategy of using *multiple tracks* was mentioned previously in a design context, but let's look at the concept now from a delivery perspective. Recall that this idea describes a situation where a presenter has two or more parallel slides or slide shows available to display the same topic from more than one perspective (perhaps secretly). That is, he can choose which of the tracks is most appropriate for a given set of circumstances.

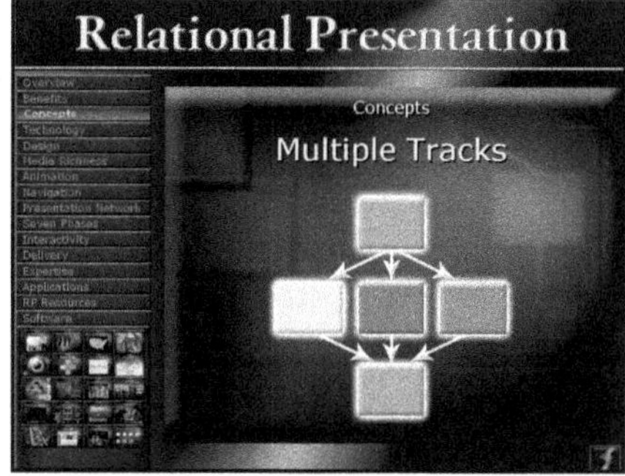

Figure 15.5

We have many examples of this functionality in our presentation materials. For instance, our affiliate company is working on software that integrates with PowerPoint 2007 and turns it into a network development environment (see last chapter, *Where Can I Find More Help and Resources?*, for details). During the development phases, various people need to see functionality at different levels of detail and confidentiality. Therefore, we have more than one track set up, allowing us to address the same topics in alternative ways with different groups. Any particular group doesn't even know the other tracks exist—and they don't need to know because that information is not relevant to them.

The reasons for using multiple tracks are diverse. Usually you are focusing on processes, data displays, or examples where presentation materials need alternative looks or functions, depending upon who will see them. In some cases, parallel tracks are set up for situations where the speaker does not necessarily know whom he will face in his audience. Maybe you are a vender manning a booth at a trade show and your products can be used equally well to dispense either beer or soda. In this situation, all product displays, demonstrations, and specs might be arranged in two separate yet functionally equivalent tracks, so that a visual discussion can be properly tailored to the interests and perspectives of a customer. Once you determine the needs of the viewer, the track (and all supporting materials) is set.

Depending upon the level of control and secrecy needed, the Navigation Elements accessing the tracks may or may not be invisible. Multiple tracks certainly do not have to be hidden. In the former example, having a switchboard containing two buttons, one for beer and the other for soda, might be entirely appropriate. Each of these links effectively represents a mini-network, and you really don't care if a given customer knows about both usages. Such an arrangement might even have positive psychological impact as the customer realizes you are tailoring the display to his or her specific needs. It also creates an impression you are *bigger* than one particular viewpoint.

15.11 Breaking Up the Action

A reality of our modern world—because of television viewing, video games, instant communication, and perhaps a host of other reasons—is that attention spans seem to be shorter and shorter as years go by. Researchers are finding additionally that the fast-paced, visual connectivity enabled by technology is changing the way we learn. We are being steadily pushed into a world where rapid shifts of attention are needed in an attempt to keep up with all the information bombarding our senses. Short attention spans are the result.

Figure 15.6

PowerPoint users need to heed this reality. We need to come to grips with the fact that long-winded, monotonous slide shows simply do not work when people's brains are being trained to bounce quickly from one stimulation to another. Either we will adapt to this new learning style and be able to flexibly and quickly change our focus as well, or we risk becoming digital dinosaurs. What is the point of presenting if few are paying attention?

One technique we use to enliven a performance is called *breaking up the action*. Basically, it means we jump around a lot between different slide shows, using navigation of course, so that no one really knows where we are going next. We may show a couple of slides from this show and a couple from that show, and then navigate somewhere else. All this jumping around may be well planned and coordinated in advance (unless we are spontaneously interacting) but nevertheless gives us attention-getting energy.

On occasion during trainings, we spontaneously jump to our video section and play a couple of videos, just to break up the concentration for a few minutes and simulate going to a commercial. Onsite workshops, after all, are intense. Imagine learning the entire contents of this book in two days. To keep productivity high during that much concentration, we find it helpful to continually shift people's attention, and have some fun and games along the way.

15.12 The Imagination Effect

We wish we could claim that becoming a skilled relational presenter just somehow magically happens one day after you have been kissed by a digital prince or princess. In reality, it requires rehearsal and real-world experience, as with any other skill. You need to be very familiar with your network's subject matter and organizational logic, and you need to feel comfortable finding information on the spot. It's really that simple.

Some preparation, as might be expected, entails sitting at your computer and literally navigating through content. You will be making sure needed slides are available, and that you know where to find them. At the same time, consider using another option called the *imagination effect.*

Researchers have found imagination techniques helpful for improving learning and the remembrance of information. We suggest you incorporate this imagination effect into delivery preparation. Yes, it sounds bizarre but it does make a difference.

Rather than actually staring at your computer screen and physically navigating through slides, imagine yourself doing so instead. Go for a walk, stretch out on a couch, or whatever you prefer. See yourself in the conference hall, the boardroom, or the classroom, and envision the interactions that will take place and the message modules that will be needed. In your mind, picture what slides you will use when, and how you will find them as needed. Imagine people asking questions based upon queries you've received before. Do you have slides for those questions? Can you find them quickly in you mind? If not, build them if they don't exist (and time allows). Rearrange slide positioning to better suit fast retrieval. Picture the navigation process as it occurs, the steps along the way. There is something about doing this process mentally that will improve your performance more than just navigating through slides directly. We don't understand how or why it works but then again, who cares?

And while on the subject of mental exercises, recall that becoming comfortable using the Gyromouse takes awhile. Try learning to use it in either hand. If you are right-handed, use it in your left hand. Because the hemispheres of our brains control opposite sides of our bodies, this exercise perhaps has an effect similar to the dual-coding process described earlier. You are teaching your brain twice, basically. Coordination improves markedly.

15.13 Handouts and Interactivity

We wrap up the delivery section with an issue near and dear to the hearts of most PowerPoint users, especially those of you who present in professional settings where paper documentation is expected. Let's address the issue of handouts. Why talk about handouts in a delivery context? Simple, because PowerPoint's ability to turn slide shows into handouts has done more to destroy (in our humble opinion) effective live communication than anything else we know.

The fact that slides can be printed as handouts means presenters tend to design slides to be printed. That is, they pack slides full of textual detail so that the slide show can be turned into a handout, as opposed to taking the time to create a separate document. Thus, we in the audience end up watching what amounts to notes, as if reading a book. This habit of printing slide shows as handouts is probably a major reason why interactive, modular-style presentation has been slow to catch on in many circles. People find it more convenient to keep all 60 slides in a single presentation and print the handout in a single operation.

You may be wondering, "So, if I adopt Relational Presentation methods and my delivery activities bounce all over the place, how will I print my slides as handouts?" Our response is "Hopefully you won't." If you want to give people a handout, give them a HANDOUT, containing just the salient facts and perhaps a few accompanying visuals—a one- or two-page summary that captures the essence of your performance. Yes, we have been taken to task for daring to challenge this sacred tradition. But the sad reality is, PowerPoint's ability to make handouts, coupled with lazy presenters, have thrust us into an ocean of boring, text-based slide shows that now drown us.

An alternative you might try is to place important information in the notes section of slides, and then print the *notes* for the audience. This way, your viewers have the visual content on slides, plus supporting textual detail below (see Figure 15.7). "What about the fact that I don't know in advance exactly which slides will be shown?" Just print the 20 slides you plan to give for sure. If supporting slides are also shown, that's a bonus. Other options are to create a separate document using screenshots, or to record the session using software such as Camtasia and turn it into streaming video.

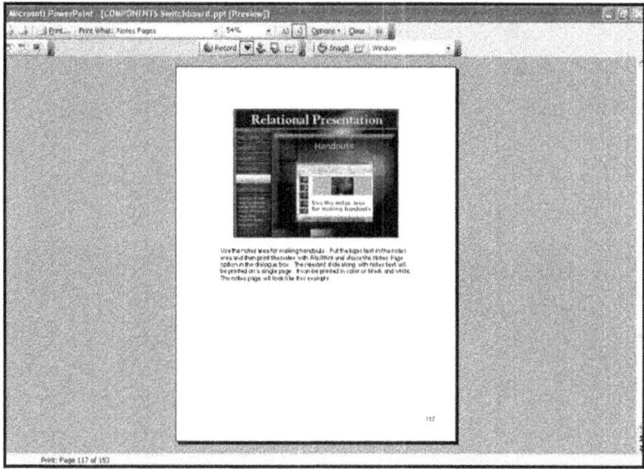

Figure 15.7

"I've noticed an interesting trend in my thinking about these ideas over time. At first I was just looking for new ways to spice up my presentations to our donors and doctors—you know, eliminate bullet points and incorporate images that would appeal to my audiences. Now I'm realizing that flexible visual messaging increases my ability to communicate ideas, and my presentations now engage people as never before. It's like I've learned a new language!"

Darci Slaten, Director of Communications
Steele Children's Research Center
University of Arizona

Chapter 16

Succeeding with Relational Presentation

Overview

Benefits

Navigation

Applications

16.1 Success Strategies

Your success in mastering the techniques featured in this book is of utmost importance to us. We hope that six months from now your presentation activities will look radically different than today, and that you will be on your way to Visual Fluency. To increase the odds of this happening, consider the strategies identified in this chapter. Over time, we have observed and tracked behaviors of successful relational presenters—people who attended workshops and those who learned the concepts on their own. Here's what we found, in summary:

You need to take development seriously *right away* and begin integrating aspects of visual communication into your regular presentation habits immediately. A lackadaisical attitude that you'll *get to it one of these days* almost certainly will produce poor and inefficient results. Prioritizing core development and gaining some initial interactive experience will boost your confidence level enormously.

As we explore nine critical strategies in detail, notice they pertain to those you should start now (short term), and those that take place gradually over time or that become more relevant later as part of your ongoing development and maintenance activities (long term). Our reference to *right away* indicates a period of time covering approximately the first two or three months after learning Relational Presentation techniques.

16.2 Strategy 1: Intense Initial Focus

Progressing beyond the experimental stage and entering active development of the network is a major milestone. It's the test of whether or not you really believe these ideas are usable and valuable. Assuming a desire to continue, one of the best determinants of success is the strength of your initial focus. Quite frankly, those who dive in immediately and put newly learned skills to use are far more likely to progress through all learning stages. Even a short delay decreases your chances of adopting this approach.

Figure 16.1

During the first three months, four goals are essential:

- Complete the initial planning activities.
- Build high-priority sections of the network.
- Use your network in live presentation activities as frequently as possible.
- Collect feedback and analyze your effectiveness.

16.3 Strategy 2: Plan the Ideal Network

Figure 16.2

Planning should take place on two different levels—short term and long term. Most people readily grasp the need for a short-term plan but are not always enthusiastic about taking extra time to map out the *big picture*. That time, nonetheless, is most beneficial. Planning what the network might ideally look like someday has several benefits that contribute to successful implementation, both now and later. The most important of these benefits is that you come to better understand the scope and interconnectedness of you message components. That is, you get a better look what you're trying to say and how to best say it.

16.4 Strategy 3: Decide Priorities

Once you have a sense of the network's grand scope, make a second pass through the organization and classify sections according to priority. Although the big picture can be inspiring, it might also prove intimidating unless practical steps are taken to narrow initial focus. Remember that the ideal network structure represents everything you could possibly want or need while presenting. It may take years, under normal conditions, to realize those ideals.

To maintain your sanity and avoid becoming overwhelmed, decide what is doable this week and this month. What must you have ready for performances approaching in the immediate future? Be sure your priorities are realistic. Allow at least a week between main construction activities and when the network will see action in a live setting. In other words, don't wait until the last minute. You need time to practice with the material and add additional content, or make adjustments if necessary.

Figure 16.3

16.5 Strategy 4: Stay Linear at First

Transitioning away from standard, linear, bullet-point slide shows into full-visual interactivity can be a shock. Making the switch cold turkey works for a few but is not the best strategy in general. A better tactic is to keep your current delivery style mostly intact and gradually add more flexibility and visual quality over time. Ease yourself into the change. Perhaps for a performance next week your show will be linear as usual but will include a few links to supporting slides. Navigation will become more sophisticated later, with experience.

Figure 16.4

Eventually, expand functionality by adding full internal navigation to these shows. Try skipping a slide during a performance. Experiment with occasionally pulling up optional supporting slides. Eventually, navigate using external links. Jump to the Resources Section and back. Visit a Web site. Over time, take small steps that include more and more navigation styles and strategies.

16.6 Strategy 5: Build Gradually

Once the initial period of intense focus is over and primary network components are in place, continually add small sections of content a little at a time. Every day or every week, add a slide here and there or perhaps build an entire small branch, all in one shot. Consistent building activities, at a relaxed pace, are better than waiting until the last minute and throwing everything together in a panic. Review priorities continually, and methodically increase the network's size with materials that contribute to the overall message. Take note of all times you are presenting and say to yourself, "Darn, I wish I had *that*."

Figure 16.5

Think in terms of reusability. Maybe a topic is needed for a speech next week but can be built in such a way that allows display within multiple future contexts. If possible, build slides generically enough to encourage multiple future applications as well. Naturally, this approach might mean taking more time to build high-quality visual appearance.

16.7 Strategy 6: Be Systematic

Being rigidly systematic and meticulous while placing or modifying navigation prevents frustration. It also greatly increases the efficiency of building activities. The same rule applies to all other editing procedures, along with the creation of graphics and media. Being organized, efficient, and methodical improves accuracy and consistency. In the long run it boosts confidence (when both presenting and designing) because of the certainty everything will work as expected.

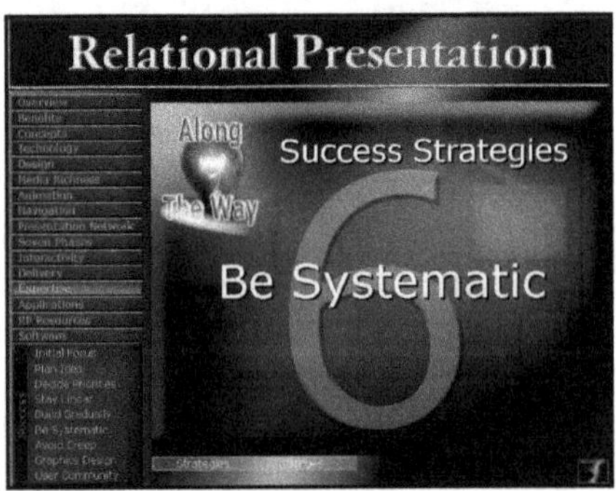

Figure 16.6

16.8 Strategy 7: Avoid Scope Creep

Scope creep is a term familiar to multimedia designers and project managers. It will become familiar to you as well. Scope creep refers to the tendency of a project to go beyond its originally planned parameters or get off track and onto side developments that are not the highest priorities.

Figure 16.7

What happens is that we plan the ideal network, set priorities, and begin building. It doesn't take long before some *really cool* or fun idea comes along that wasn't in the original plan, followed by another idea and another. Perhaps complex, showy (and nonessential) animations are added to slides, even though content required for next week's event is not yet in place.

If new ideas truly represent essential development not thought of earlier, they may be legitimate priorities and should jump to the top of the pile. Realize, though, that something else may need to be cut as a result. Don't fritter away valuable time and resources on nonessential components.

16.9 Strategy 8: Learn Graphic Design

Learn graphic design. "Oh sure," you say. "All I need is another learning curve, as though grasping Relational Presentation is not enough." Well, it is true that learning graphic design skills requires effort, and there certainly is a learning curve. Hopefully by now, though, you have a growing sense of how important the manipulation of visuals can be.

Figure 16.8

It is possible to put together a wonderfully effective relational network without knowing any graphic design skills. Marvelous design and messaging are possible using pictures and AutoShapes alone. Simply using PowerPoint in a more visually rich way is a vast improvement over purely text-based shows.

Nevertheless, learning how to work with, and form, graphics is a strategy that both boosts your enjoyment of using visually interactive presentation and increases its effectiveness. Without at least some basic knowledge in this area, your creativity and expressiveness are limited. The same can be said of other media creation skills. Once you know how to create rich media in all forms, that knowledge stays with you for the rest of your life and greatly expands your capabilities. Learning how to speak your new language fluently, in all respects, is worth the investment of time and resources.

16.10 Strategy 9: Join the User Community

Our final success strategy may seem obvious at first glance but is often neglected. Find other people who are using this style of presentation and take advantage of the opportunity to share ideas and resources. Collaborate on development, if appropriate. Tap into the larger community of Relational Presentation experts and contribute perspectives and experience. Just knowing other people are out there, working on the same issues, is an indispensable part of moving forward. One way to find such people is to take part in training workshops or participate in formal user groups.

Figure 16.9

Tell us your success stories and lessons learned, so that we can share them with others in the next edition of this book. Send us examples of your presentation strategies. We'll be happy to consider all contributions. Feel free to contact us with questions or ideas on how Relational Presentation models can be improved and expanded. We continually learn new ideas and perspectives from people just like you. We probably also have suggestions and resources you can explore in the broader Relational Presentation community.

The next chapter outlines additional resources available beyond the main contents of this book. Sometimes live, guided instruction on these techniques is a more efficient way of learning. Such instruction is available in both on-site and Internet-based formats.

We wish you great success in your journey toward visually interactive expression. Press forward and become an expert relational presenter. The rewards are well worth the effort!

"I teach sociology, psychology, and mental health counseling at a small university. I specialize in the more theoretical aspects of the social sciences, and my goal is always to bring abstract material down to earth. I am convinced that your work will go a long way in helping me do this.

I thank you—my students will thank you and their parents will thank you—and the whole world will be a better place because of what you and your colleagues are doing!"

Michael A. Brees
PhD, MA - LPC, CP NLP, PsyD in progress
Associate Professor, Social Sciences

Where Can I Find More Help and Resources?

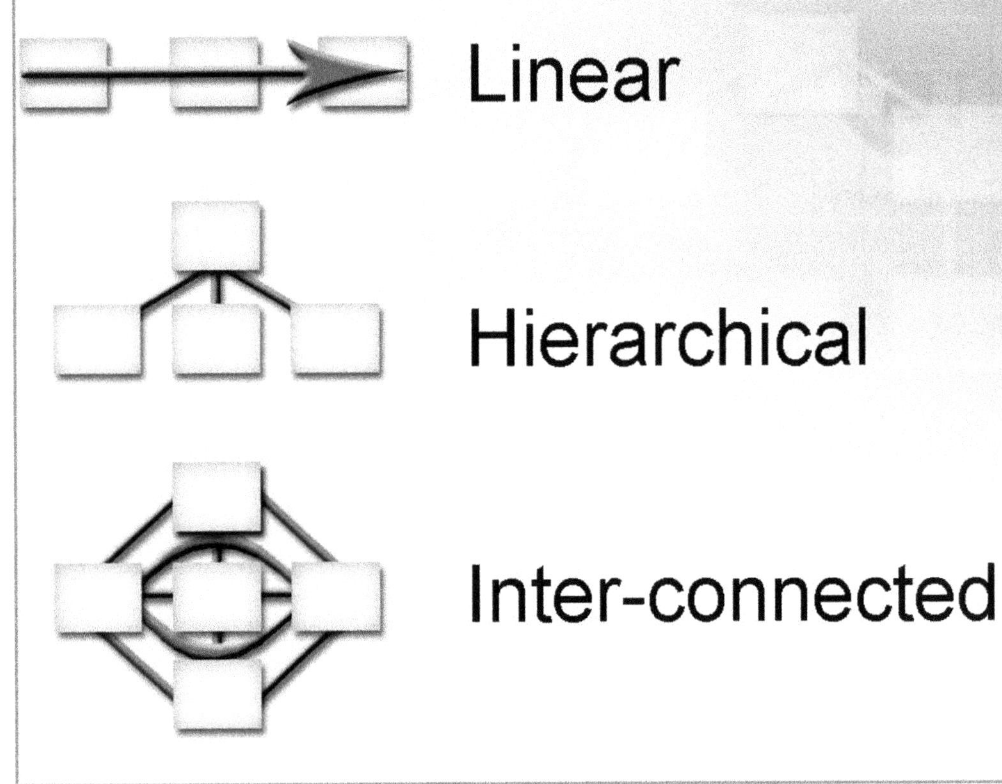
Linear
Hierarchical
Inter-connected

17.1 Support Options and Resources

This chapter is intended as a comprehensive resource guide to help you on your way while exploring all aspects of the Relational Presentation concept. If you still have questions that are not answered here or want to further expand your skills, other options and resources are available. Suggestions appear below or you can receive updated information from the Aspire Web site at:

www.aspirecommunications.com

Or e-mail us directly at:

support@aspirecommunications.com

17.2 Live Online Workshops

A fast and economical way of receiving direct, hands-on instruction if you are not already enrolled in some form of guided instruction is to attend Aspire's online workshops. These live, interactive teaching sessions occur in the convenience of your office or living room and are as active and effective as an onsite training—even more so in many respects. Each session is approximately 75 to 90 minutes long, and sessions are available at all levels of PowerPoint and Relational Presentation experience. Sessions cover basic PowerPoint skills, all the topics of this book, and media creation skills that will be featured in the forthcoming companion book (see 17.4 on the next page).

Workshops are a combination of instructor presentation and guided exercises. During the guided exercises, the instructor demonstrates on the top half of the screen as you work on the bottom half, directly in PowerPoint. You can enroll in as many or as few sessions as desired. Certification is available at different levels.

17.3 Self-guided Online Study

If live online workshop times don't match your scheduling or you simply prefer self-guided, Internet-based learning, that option is available as well. We are producing workshop sessions as progressive download

Web video. Some components are already available and more are on the way. These sessions are viewable at your convenience, 24 hours a day. Watch demonstrations of all concepts, procedures, and techniques discussed in this book, along with narration. Participating in these self-study courses allows you to review material at will and start or stop instruction at any time.

Recorded sessions mirror the learning format used in live trainings. Both training formats, recorded and live, employ the full-course version of this book as textbook, with exercises.

17.4 Companion Book on Media Creation Skills

After mastering the Relational Presentation skills covered in this book, you will be ready for the next challenge: learning how to create various forms of rich media and advanced PowerPoint animations. These skills take your visually expressive potential even higher.

A follow-up book covering media creation skills is in the works and should in early 2008. Again, check the Aspire Web site for up-to-date information. The book will unique instruction on everything you need to know for augmenting a Presentation Network with a full range of rich media. There will be four primary subject areas:

- **Graphics:** The first section showcases using *Adobe Photoshop*, specifically in a graphics-for-presentation context. In other words, we cut through the fluff and focus on Photoshop operations that are most helpful to presenters wanting to create stunning presentation graphics. We can't possibly cover everything this marvelous software does, but instead simplify the graphic arts learning curve enough so that even novice designers are able to build their own backgrounds, collages, decorative text, and many other useful examples of presentation imagery. All of the imagery you have seen in this book was designed using these same methods.

- **Audio:** Contrary to popular expectations, recording and editing digital audio is surprisingly easy. In the book's second section we explore recording, splicing, cross-fading, increasing volume, and many other topics. We also demonstrate how to create an Audio Switchboard in PowerPoint, where potentially hundreds of clips are instantly available on demand—to be played and paused in any order, at any time. The software featured is *Audacity*.

- **Video:** Basic digital video recording and editing is just about as easy as working with audio. The book's third section describes the use of *Camtasia* software and its numerous benefits to relational presenters. Video can be spliced together or split into pieces. Alternative soundtracks can be added and overlapped. Here we cover how to use Camtasia for recording live speaking events, so that a presentation can be made available for playback on the Web. We also look at turning video frames into thumbnail images for relational navigation buttons and demonstrate how to create a Video Switchboard in PowerPoint.

- **Animation:** Finally, the fourth section examines the bountiful ways animations might be applied to accentuate Relational Presentation methods—promoting better learning, assisting with navigation, and providing on-demand content display. A major subject of this section is learning how to build animation-based navigation.

17.5 E-mail Support Program

Sometimes all you need to solve a problem is a simple, direct answer that addresses your specific situation. Aspire's e-mail support program can provide these answers with a short turnaround time. A very low-cost monthly subscription gives you access to enormous expertise via e-mail. Readers of this book and workshop attendees are eligible to apply. No question is too basic or complex. We may be able to shorten your development activities—perhaps by hours—by quickly working you through perplexing Relational Presentation-related issues. See the Aspire Web site for more information on sign-up.

17.6 Upgrading Soon to PowerPoint 2007?

In the near future, an updated version of this book for PowerPoint 2007 will be available, showing how to use that software's expanded presentation features for even more robust Visual Interactivity. You will see a full range of user-interface screenshots along with explanations of what's new in PowerPoint 2007 and how to take advantage of these features. Because the overall concept of Relational Presentation supersedes the particular presentation software being used, most of the concepts in the current book will stay the same in the 2007 version. However, there are quite a few important modifications you need to be aware of. PowerPoint 2007 is VERY different from PowerPoint 2003. Its entirely new operating structure opens up new possibilities and poses a few challenges. Note that Aspire workshop sessions for 2007 will be available in the near future as well, if not already so.

17.7 Relational Presentation Software

One reason to strongly consider upgrading to PowerPoint 2007 before long is to take advantage of the Relational Presentation software, which is under development as a collaborative effort between Aspire, several Microsoft PowerPoint MVPs, and the Computer Science Department at Arizona State University. This software's purpose is to turn PowerPoint into a network development environment, similar to the way Web authoring software simplifies the process of creating Web sites.

The need for this new application software cannot be overstated. Many of the Relational Presentation methods you now must build manually in PowerPoint will be done for you in the future, saving countless hours of development time. The visual tricks and illusions you now must force upon PowerPoint will be part of the software's regular features, along with additional possibilities. The complexity of creating a Presentation Network will be cut to a fraction of its current level. Navigation methods not possible with PowerPoint alone will accentuate the network user's experience, turning PowerPoint into a true relational platform in all respects. This software is not designed to be backward compatible with PowerPoint 2003, so an upgrade to PowerPoint 2007 will be necessary.

We will keep you posted via the Aspire Web site about opportunities for tapping into the greater Relational Presentation community. From time to time we coordinate get-togethers at conferences. A blog or listserve is in the works as well. Stay tuned.

For general information or to find out about additional support, contact Aspire directly:

Aspire Communications
902 N. 4th Avenue
Tucson, Arizona 85705 USA
Main: (520) 629-0282
Fax: (520) 629-9573
info@aspirecommunications.com
www.aspirecommunications.com

Index

www.ingramcontent.com/pod-product-compliance
Lightning Source LLC
Chambersburg PA
CBHW060327200326
41519CB00011BA/1857

9780979415616